"You've heard about the books where, once you pick them up you can't put them back down? Well, this is one of those books! I even hesitate to call this "Ted's" story, because you'll discover very quickly that Someone Else has always been at work. And just as in Ted's life, God is very much at work in yours too. May this book help you see that."

-Pat Murphy, host of "Joyful Country" (FM 98.5 CKWR) and "Murphy In The Morning" (94.3 Faith FM)

"Ted, your dad brought one of your chapters to us to read...thank you! I was very interested in your experiences and letting the reader "feel" a part of what is going on inside your "head and emotions" while you were in jail.

I went through the experience with your mother when she called the police and turned you in. She told me that it was the hardest thing she ever had to do. On the phone a few months ago, you said, "that phone call saved your life."

We can't wait to read the WHOLE book. Bravo!!"

-Betty Mottin, best and closest friend of Patti Nellis, Ted's mother, for forty years

"Ted is a gifted writer with a truly honest evaluation of his own life. His life has been _____ ·hes the lives of everyone around him.

D1283485

-Phil and Sharon Dubois

"Ted opens the door to understand the life of a hustler, leading to outright criminal activity, resulting with the hopelessness and frustrating emptiness of life in prison.

Journey To Redemption is a truly inspiring story of a hopeless, empty, fearful life experience, being given hope through the powerful, yet invisible transformation of simple trust and belief in Jesus Christ's forgiveness and life changing principles."

-Jon Hill, Program Director, Ray of Hope Community Centre

"My father's life reads like something out of a movie. I'm very excited about his book."

-Cole Nellis

"Ted is a trophy of God's grace"

-Pastor Ken Miles

"I have been so very inspired by the story of Ted's life. It is a testament of God's grace, goodness and unfailing love. The Lord has shown me time and time again that He can capture the hearts of any individual whom people of the world would view as an outcast without any hope of a productive future.

But, God's word says, and I'm paraphrasing, that "the glory of The Lord is everywhere. It flows to the lowest valley and to the highest mountain. It breaks chains and sets captives free."

Ted was one of those captives who has been set free and he has a powerful, life changing word to share. I encourage everyone, whether you have been a christian all your life, whether you struggle with staying on the straight and narrow path or if you are wanting to be set free of addictions of any kind, read this book!

It will give you hope and change your life. We serve a powerful Savior and He is mighty to save. He has done great things in Ted's life. Bless you as you read."

-Florence Kreutzer, friend and sister in The Lord

Journey to
REDEMPTION

Small-Time pool hustler · convicted bank robber · born again Christian

Ted Nellis

JOURNEY TO REDEMPTION
Copyright © 2013 by Ted Nellis

Printed in Canada

ISBN: 978-1-77069-760-7

Word Alive Press
131 Cordite Road, Winnipeg, MB R3W 1S1
www.wordalivepress.ca

WORD ALIVE PRESS
Just Write!

MIX
Paper from
responsible sources
FSC
www.fsc.org   FSC® C016245

Library and Archives Canada Cataloguing in Publication

Nellis, Ted, 1960-
    Journey to redemption : small time pool hustler, convicted bank robber, born again Christian / Ted Nellis.

ISBN 978-1-77069-760-7

    1. Nellis, Ted, 1960-. 2. Pool players--Canada, Western--Biography. 3. Prisoners--Ontario--Kingston--Biography. 4. Christian biography. 5. Redemption--Christianity. I. Title.

BR1725.N45A3 2012   270.092   C2012-907271-0

DEDICATION

This very modest work is dedicated to the following individuals:

First and foremost, to my Lord and Saviour Jesus Christ. The words "thank you," though woefully inadequate, are—I know—acceptable to you.

To my mother, who loved me enough to inform the police of my whereabouts.

My father, for not only supporting this effort and helping in such a big way to turn a dream in to a reality, but for having the courage to read the manuscript as it was written. In the reading of it, Dad also had to re-live many of the most painful days of his life. Thanks, Dad.

For my best friend and number one fan, my dear wife Janet. What she ever saw in this crusty old street kid I'll never know, but I'm glad she saw something. Had I met Janet in my youth I might have saved myself and many others from a world of hurt. Had Janet known me in my youth, however, I'm sure she would have run as far away from me as possible. All is well. I love you, Janet.

Redemption: (theology) 1. the act of delivering from sin or saving from evil
2. salvation

TABLE OF CONTENTS

ACKNOWLEDGEMENTS

My sincere gratitude goes out to the following people for their valuable input towards this project.

Russ Nellis, Betty and Jim Mottin, Ken Miles, John Zivku, Phil and Sharon Dubois, Randy Roach, Bruce Nickolson, Tony, Pat Murphy, Jon Hill, Jeff McCrea, Janet Nellis, Julie and Steve Mundle, Glen Piovison, Tiffany Trithardt, Tom Buller and Janine Leclerc

FOREWORD

On a beautiful Saturday afternoon in the summer of 1996, I was enjoying a cold one with an old friend when our conversation was interrupted by a ringing at my door. We were comfortable out on the back patio, and I didn't really feel like getting up to address the disturbance. The majority of my friends knew simply to walk in, so I figured it was most likely a sales call of some sort. Regardless, something led me to get up to see just who was at my door.

The gentleman standing on my front porch introduced himself and said he was referred to me by a local fitness store that knew I had resources to build a piece of equipment he was looking for. His name was Ted Nellis, and just by coincidence, the very man who could build what he wanted was sitting in my back yard.

I found this stranger a little perplexing. He was a big guy, pushing at least six-foot-three with tattoos down both arms, but that body did not, for some reason, seem to belong to the gentle demeanor radiating from it. I felt an immediate natural chemistry between Ted and me, even though there was not much personal background disclosed from either of us, especially regarding Ted. The equipment he was looking for was not going to be a problem, and I felt good about being able to fill that need for him. My welder was sitting right there and assured us both that he had the time to do the job, and he did in fact hold to his promise.

Later that year over a Saturday night phone call, Ted and I discovered further just how much we had in common in terms of sharing sporting interests outside that of strictly strength training. Nonetheless, over the next several years, as our friendship grew it became evident that there was more to this fascinating man than he cared to reveal. Ted did eventually share with me that he was once the youngest inmate in Kingston Penitentiary but never would expand on the particulars surrounding that part of his life. He possessed a street savvy amplified by a natural intellect that allowed him to successfully manage the environments in which he interacted. His psyche, I would learn, was forged decades back and was still at work keeping recent friends at an arm's length, basically on a need-to-know basis. This would change.

I never burned with curiosity over Ted's past simply because it didn't really matter all that much to me, for good reason. Over the past sixteen years, I watched him traverse many of life's toughest hurdles with a level of integrity and dignity rarely seen in those difficult circumstances. Whatever lay buried in the secrecy of Ted's past certainly appeared to have been conquered, so it couldn't really have been all that bad. Could it? That question would be answered for me through the manuscript of this book.

"Surprised" would certainly be an understatement for what came to mind after reading just a draft of the first chapter. I don't know what startled me more, the shocking details of Ted's teenage years or the fact that I, too, am a writer with a college education, years of mentoring, and two large book publications yet this man, possessing no more than a grade eight level of schooling, was authoring a story in such a style that I could not duplicate. Ted has never ceased to amaze me in his accomplishments, so my astonishment quickly changed to marveling at what he was doing. His manner of penmanship only served to magnify the allure of his fascinating story, a complete revelation of those early days about which he previously chose not to share.

I was totally captivated right from the first chapter, not just with Ted's early experiences, but in the education I was receiving in Pool Hustling 101. In the early 2000s I had a billiards table, and Ted at that time did mention he had hustled a bit of pool long ago. Although he hadn't played in years and his skills showed some corrosion, it didn't take too much time before the rust was gone and those balls were snapping into the pockets with authority, making it quite clear that the man definitely had played the game before. Nonetheless, I had no idea as to the depth in which pool hustling commanded his early years until reading his manuscript a full decade later. It wasn't simply a passion expressed by most teenagers towards their chosen endeavors, pool was a life venue for Ted often mitigated with a trichotomous mindset that bounced between good, bad, and at times sociopathic.

In telling his story, Ted freely shared his fascination with specific fiction and non-fiction characters, many of a dubious nature, who influenced him in his growing years. Throughout the book, he draws some comparisons and relationships with some of Canada's most historically notorious criminals. It is also quite interesting to see how the burgeoning media and social outlets of the more liberal western culture of the 1970s were at work in shaping the malleable young minds of that era, yet the electronic technology of today…

Whatever the influences that set the life course of the teenage Ted Nellis, by the time he was nineteen, he was viewing the world strictly as his antagonist: "I had long been an anti-establishment figure. I had turned my back, completely, wholly and without compromise, on everything and anything even remotely connected with 'normal life,' including everyone and anyone in it."

Obviously this pent-up, skewed view of society would put Ted on a collision course with the law in a manner that over thirty years after his actions he found it very difficult to express his deeds: "I simply stared at the keyboard for two weeks without typing a single word, not knowing what to articulate, in words, the horrendously hurtful, almost diabolical decision I made all those years ago. How do I rationalize, adequately, the decision I made to…"

I earnestly invite you to join Ted in his incredible *Journey to Redemption*. Most amazingly, dear reader, this is but only one aspect of this man's life worthy of publication.

–Randy Roach, author of *Muscle, Smoke & Mirrors* book series

INTRODUCTION

I have been invited to speak many times over the years, in churches, at men's breakfasts, on radio shows, and more recently, to youth in church and in high school. That I am invited to speak at all seems remarkable to me. Perhaps even more remarkable is the response of the listening audience. Without fail, there are always a few present who seem to react very emotionally to what I've shared. God seems to use me in some way to connect with my audience, and to do so at a personal level.

This is something of a mystery to me, as I feel ill-equipped to speak or to share in any capacity, under any circumstances, to anyone. God, however, seems to feel rather differently. To be used by God in any way, for any reason, just once, is no small thing. For someone with my background, my education—or rather, lack of it—to not only speak publicly on occasion, but to also write a book is nothing short of absolutely miraculous.

What in the world would I ever write about, and even if I could write a book, how in a million years would it ever be published? Who am I kidding? I'm Mister Nobody! And yet, here I am with pen in hand, or rather, fingers on keyboard, staring at a blank monitor (a gift from a gentleman who heard me speak), unable to quiet the small, relentless whisperings of what can only be the Holy Spirit who seems to be saying, "Do it for Me, for My glory!"

I have been encouraged to write a book about my life, or at least parts of it, many times over the years, by my wife, friends, and family, but I've never given the idea much thought. I've always dismissed the notion as flattering words from well-meaning friends and family. Of course they're encouraging and flattering me. That's what friends and family do...*sometimes.*

However, when God makes His presence known and felt deep down in one's very soul, and whispers, "I have work for you," well, that is another matter altogether. With God, I could no more talk, reason, or beg my way out of writing this book than Moses could talk, reason, or beg his way out of leading the Israelites out of Egypt and into the Promised Land.

What is impossible for us is absolutely possible for almighty God. Using unassuming, everyday, ordinary people with no particular skills or training, with no particular background in any one given area of expertise, to accomplish His will is not only doable with God's help. It's God's specialty.

Let me be very clear that this effort, modest as it is, could not—in fact would not—be possible were it not for the personal relationship I have today with Jesus Christ. The verse, *"I can do all things through Christ who strengthens me"* (Philippians 4:13, NKJV) has never had more practical meaning to me than right now, in the writing of this book. Though I am the central figure in this autobiography, for obvious reasons, it's really God's story. Through God's interaction or dealings with me, through His son Jesus Christ, I found forgiveness, love, peace, and purpose.

I am aware of the concern some readers may have regarding the content of an autobiography in general. Does the author only highlight the pleasant or more flattering areas of his or her life and character, while failing to draw attention to the more questionable, darker, or perhaps more disturbing areas of his lesser known or private self? I believe this concern is legitimate. I have attempted, to the best of my ability, to display myself, warts and all, with honesty and complete transparency. To serve up less than this in any way would be a disservice to you, the reader, and to the purpose of this work. After all, what would be the point of painting only a sunny, all-is-well after picture? The after picture is of no consequence or value without first gazing, at length and in depth, at the before picture. My before picture is not pretty and has many times been difficult for me to reflect upon, much less write about.

More than once during the writing of this book, I simply had to walk away from it for a week or two in order to clear my head and to remind myself that the person described on many of the pages of this book no longer exists. I assure you, dear reader, I was more than a little uncomfortable taking myself down memory lane—a place I would just as soon forget, were it not for God choosing to use such a life as mine to in some small measure add value, inspiration, motivation, and/or hope to others' lives.

I also think it important to mention that my decision to write this autobiography myself, rather than use a ghostwriter, was intentional. I was concerned that something of myself, my personality or my character, could be lost in a more polished or professional style of writing. I'm an uneducated street kid. That's who I am, period. I did not want the "flavor," if you will, of my personality, my character, or my lack of formal education or career training to be lost or hidden from you in any way. I am neither embarrassed nor ashamed of who or what I was or of what I may or may not be now.

My clearest intention for you, the reader, is that this work you are now holding in your hands be a source of encouragement to you, from me, in some way, at some level. I sincerely believe this could only be possible if you, the reader, are able to get to know me intimately through my writing—my words, not someone else's—regardless of how talented or gifted another writer may be.

Though I've made every effort to articulate, through the written word, a clear and concise journey of an individual, this is by no means a literary masterpiece, nor was it ever intended to be. While I have been diligent in my attempt to write this book in a grammatically and politically correct fashion, it is and will remain a little rough around the edges—because so am I. You see, you are getting to know me already.

With these thoughts in mind, I invite you to join me in the following pages. Perhaps you will find bits and pieces of yourself, your own highs and lows, your own moments of despair or desperation, your own challenges, as well as your moments of triumph or victory found in life's many privately fought battles written within the pages of this book.

Perhaps I will connect with you in some way neither of us really understands yet neither of us could ever deny. Perhaps we will one day meet, but even if we don't, we have, through the pages of this book, already touched each other's lives, spiritually as well as eternally, and that is really what is important here, isn't it?

Oh, by the way, if you're reading this but do not presently have a relationship with Jesus Christ and all of this writing about God and Jesus is making you a little nervous or uncomfortable, don't worry about it. Set aside your personal feelings about God or spiritual or eternal matters as you peruse the pages of this book. Jesus Christ is a part of my story but may not be a part of yours at this time in your life. This book is about the journey of a human being and every one of us can relate to each other on that level because we are all humans on journeys.

I *do* want you in heaven one day. I *do* believe it is only through Jesus Christ that we can find forgiveness, be in a right relationship with God, and spend eternity in heaven. However, this is not a sermon and if you are anything like me, you have fallen asleep during far too many sermons already.

It is my hope and prayer that within this book lie nuggets of truth, reflection, and thought which may impart to you a little "soul comfort" and, with a little luck, some wisdom or insightful reflection into your own life.

May you be as richly blessed in reading this book as I was in writing it.

Your friend, Ted.

POOL ROOMS/BAR ROOMS

"I moved into a cheap hotel. I can remember waking up there
one afternoon with a terrific hangover. I stared at the ceiling
for a long time, and then I said to myself, 'McGoorty, what
you have turned out to be is a two-bit, drunken pool hustler.'
That didn't depress me at all.
Listen, I was glad to have a profession."
–McGoorty, A Pool Room Hustler

"I would rather be a pool hall bum than anything else
in the world."
–Ted Nellis, 1978

I remember standing in front of the Colonial Hotel in Calgary, where
I'd been living for several months, and watching a small group of
people across the street as they waited for the bus. I lit a cigarette and
leaned against the hotel wall, considering the men and women waiting
for the bus while I pondered breakfast possibilities. I didn't know who
the people were, where they were going, or how long they'd been waiting
for the bus.

I just remember being so thankful I wasn't one of them. I wasn't on
my way to a job I disliked intensely, nor was I about to spend the next
eight hours of my day working for a boss I disliked even more than my

job. Of course, this was assuming these folks disliked their jobs and bosses in the first place. I was only nineteen at the time, but I just didn't get the whole nine-to-five thing people in our culture seemed to resign themselves to without the slightest thought of what might be waiting out there for folks who dared to step out of their comfort zone.

That was a long time ago, thirty-three years or so. Yet, in many ways I still carry many of the same thoughts and concerns today, I suppose, about living, and life in general. I'm not as arrogant today as I was in my teens and twenties, or as sharply judgmental. God, in His grace, has brought me a long way. Yet, when I consider my youthful insights and observations regarding the human psyche, lifestyle choices, and habits, and thought patterns about people's lives in general, at least in this part of the world, I sometimes wonder if I wasn't too far off the mark.

I never, *ever* wanted to be a nine-to-five guy. To settle in to such a lifestyle was, in my opinion back then, the kiss of death. As far as I was concerned, the nine-to-five lifestyle lured people into a rut by offering a steady pay cheque and, if one were lucky, benefits. Get up, go to work, come home, watch TV, go to bed, and then do it all over again the next day. Week after week, month after month, year after year, until…one day we're sixty-five and wondering what happened. What did I do with my life? Where did the time go? If only I'd…what? The "if only I'd" syndrome is a silent killer plaguing millions of people every day. Regret walks hand in hand with "if only I had…" and parks itself on Pity Party Avenue. "What ifs" will haunt a person all the days of their life. It seems like a lot of profound and heavy philosophizing to be floating around in a nineteen-year-old's head, and yet it was all very real to me back then. I just could not get the notion out of my head. To settle for the nine-to-five lifestyle was to settle for mediocrity at best; one gigantic, perpetual rut, and it has been well said that the only difference between a rut and a grave is the depth. No thanks.

Looking back, I cringe at my brash assumptions. Who was I to judge anyone? Yet, considering the divorce rate today, both in and out of the church, substance abuse, alcohol abuse, suicide, bullying, teen pregnancy, bankruptcies, clinical depression, pornography addiction, and so on, one wonders whether something is drastically wrong or at the very least missing in today's psychological makeup. It can be so easy as a Christian to say Jesus is the answer to all that ails us. Jesus is, in fact, *the* answer, but many, if not all of the above-mentioned maladies, addictions, and hang-ups are every bit as prevalent in the church as they are in the world. What a mess.

Perhaps one of the contributing factors in today's issue-laden, somewhat manic, ultra fast-paced world is the tendency many people have of resigning themselves to a life or lifestyle far below their potential. Do we settle for less? Do we have a tendency to settle for what comes our way without much thought or concern for what may have been? The Bible says in Proverbs 29:18, *"Where there is no vision, the people perish"* (NKJV).

I have always had a vision. I have always carried deep within me a yearning to be more, in some way, at some level, than what my current situation offered. I've always possessed a keen sense of adventure. I've used visualization, a very real and powerful tool, as far back as I can remember. I have always allowed my imagination to take me to places in my life I had not yet been to or attained. In days gone by, this was not always a constructive or productive process for me. Harnessing my thoughts, energies, ambitions, and abilities in a way in which I'm able to use them productively, constructively—for God's glory—has come with time and maturity. (Some would argue about how mature I am today.)

In my mid to late teens, the nine-to-five life spelled slow and painful death—as did school, homework, parental advice, curfews, religion, family outings, nosy neighbors, organized sports, respecting one's elders, steady girlfriends (cramped my lifestyle), living at home, working full-time (also cramped my lifestyle), and hanging out with the guys I grew up with ('cause they were all nine-to-fivers). But most of all, *absolutely* the very worst thing imaginable was to do whatever the rest of the crowd was doing: going with the flow.

In 1979, at the age of nineteen, standing in front of the Colonial Hotel in downtown Calgary, Alberta, about 2,300 miles from home, smoking my first cigarette of the day, earning a part-time living playing pool (I only worked a real job two days a week), well, I was just about as far out of the normal flow of life as one could get.

This particular morning began as so many others. Once my cigarette was finished and I felt I'd solved, in my mind at least, most of life's problems and challenges for the greater majority of the world's population, I was ready to get down to the business at hand for the day. I walked across the street and down a couple of blocks to Billiard Square, the local pool room. It was time to make some money.

***

The pool hall back in the mid to late seventies was my sanctuary, literally. When one thinks of or hears the word sanctuary, one immediately thinks of a church-like, tranquil, meditative setting. There's a broader meaning of the word as well, which can include, and I quote from Webster's dictionary: "a place where one can find safety or shelter; also, the safety found there."

To say that the pool room was my shelter would indeed be the understatement of the year. For that matter, to say it merely offered safety would tie for understatement of the year. The pool room offered me both, as well as much, much more—but safety and shelter from what?

Safety and shelter from a world I felt I simply did not fit into, nor did I particularly want to fit into. This worldview of mine did not depress me or cause anxiety in any way. I simply could not figure out life or my part in it. This is not an altogether uncommon frame of mind for a young teenager, or for that matter, many adults as well. The question, *Where do I fit in?* echoes across this nation from the minds of millions of teenagers and adults every day. There are the fortunate few who seem to find their way in life at a very early age. Many others simply lose themselves in such pursuits as sports, hobbies, school, or just hanging out with friends, and find tremendous joy and satisfaction in these endeavors.

For me, however, there just had to be more of…something. I seemed to possess a spirit of restlessness deep within my soul that could simply not be satisfied for any length of time. What was it I was looking for? Excitement? Absolutely. Day-to-day variety? You bet. A little danger, perhaps? Sounds good. Questionable company? Now you're talking! Oh yeah, one more thing. I was looking for a place, a location, a part of the world, any part where I could find people, young or old, male or female, who had at least some of the same characteristics and interests in life as I did. Not an easy order to fill, and yet by about the age of fourteen or fifteen I did find it.

Given the frame of mind I was in as a young teenager, it is little wonder to me that learning how to play pool—in fact, just being in a pool room—was the answer to many of life's big questions for me at that time. From the get-go, from the very beginning, from the moment I walked into a pool room for the first time, I was "all in," hook, line, and sinker. I simply could not get enough of the "action." I was a pool hall junkie and had to have my fix every day.

At fifteen, seeing grown men gathered around the pool table, money changing hands, some in three-piece suits, some dressed casually in jeans and t-shirt, all seeming to know each other regardless of their differences in background, dress, vocation, education or social standing, some laughing, others cursing, shaking out little peas with numbers on them from a plastic bottle to determine the order of players for the next game, well, I was head over heels, madly in love with the players, the camaraderie, the action, and the possibilities of making a little cash in a way that intrigued me tremendously.

Snooker was all the rage in pool halls back in the seventies and eighties in Canada. Sometimes referred to as "chess on a pool table," the game required much thought, strong defensive play, as well as accurate potting ability (the ability to sink balls in the pockets). Snooker is played on a six-foot by twelve-foot table, and utilizes fifteen red balls and six other balls of various colors: yellow, green, brown, blue, pink, black, and a white cue ball. While I learned and played many different pool games on a variety of pool-table sizes over the years, snooker always stood out as the game I played and enjoyed the most.

The game of snooker occupied my thoughts entirely. Learning the game consumed me, every waking moment of every day. I was still in school at that time, but whatever enthusiasm I had for education, which had always been sadly lacking even on a good day, was very quickly falling away. Replacing it was no-holds-barred, unbridled enthusiasm for snooker and all that went with it. It was the "all that went with it" that would tempt me in all the wrong ways in years to come, but for now life was all about those colored balls, chalking the cue, and making magic happen on that beautiful green cloth covering the slate on those gorgeous pool tables.

Every evening after school, and every weekend from nine in the morning until midnight, I was in the pool hall. Shot after shot, practiced hundreds, if not thousands of times, executed from different angles and varied distances day in, day out, as much as time and money would allow. I would practice until my shoulders, neck, and back ached. Whatever I lacked in focus and desire in the classroom, I more than made up for on the green felt in the pool room.

Even more important than the game itself, in some ways, was the sense of belonging I was beginning to feel in the pool room. There was camaraderie, a brotherhood among the players that was very appealing to me. I desperately wanted to be a part of it, to fit in. I wanted to be one of the guys. A large group of regulars all seemed to know and respect one another. I wanted that respect from them. I wanted to be known as a "stand-up guy" in the regular group of patrons and I wanted to be regarded as a solid pool player as well.

Saturday was *the* day of the week for me, at least where snooker was concerned, and I looked forward to it all week long. Every Saturday, starting at nine or ten in the morning, four or five of the best players in town would get together for an all-day game of Follow for twenty-five cents a point. This was *the* game in snooker in those days. The same game was played in western Canada but was called, perhaps more suitably, Cutthroat.

The game played best with four players and the strategy was simple enough. Everyone took their turn at the table, in an order determined before the start of the game by tossing out little peas with numbers on them. The lowest number played first, and so on. The only player you had to be concerned about was the player who shot after you. If that person ran, say, twenty points, at twenty-five cents a point, you would owe him five bucks. Everyone kept score of their own points on a blackboard and at the end of every game the differences were totaled up, the money paid accordingly, and then it was on to the next game.

I often played very little on Saturday while the "Big Game" was going on. Logic dictated to me that there was a time to play the game and then there was a time to study the game. Saturday, at least during the day, was study time. School was in and I was a very attentive, focused student with perfect attendance, sitting at my desk, paying close attention to everything my teachers were demonstrating at the green-felted slate blackboard.

I would grab a chair and sit as close to the action as I could, and then spend the next several hours or so just observing, absorbing. I made mental notes and retained as much as I could concerning the players' respective styles of play. The players I was studying were much older than I, far more experienced and skilled in every aspect of the game. I had much to learn and couldn't wait to get on a table and practice what I'd seen the big boys do. I noted carefully their shot selection, their safety play, their use of angles, and the various spins or siding they put on the cue ball. It seemed as though they could make the cue ball do anything, go anywhere on the table they desired, effortlessly, at will.

At fifteen or sixteen years old, at least for me, these players represented the big time. I had no idea of the calibre of talent playing the game in western Canada. As good as the guys were in my neck of the woods, I seldom saw a run of any decent size. A run or break in snooker is the total amount of points made by a player while at the table. Runs of thirty, forty, and sometimes fifty points were common, but I seldom witnessed much break-building beyond that. When I moved to Calgary at seventeen, I saw century runs made all the time (a century break in snooker is a run of one hundred points or more).

The more time I spent in the pool room, the more remote or distant "ordinary" life became. The snooker scene was my world. The more I embraced it, the less I embraced the world outside the pool hall, including my own family. The vast array of characters I was getting to know in the pool room—some pool players, some card players, and some involved in various aspects of criminal activity—were slowly becoming my new adopted family.

I was accepted by most of the regulars in the pool hall without question. No one seemed to care where I was from or why I wasn't in school or how old I was. Just being a regular in the pool room was common ground enough. There was such a diversity of people playing pool on any given day that I had little trouble blending in.

***

The potential to make money in pool halls is very real. Always has been, and always will be. Not only does money change hands among pool players at the tables, but also over games of crib, backgammon, euchre, and just about any other card or dice game one can imagine. Many pool halls around the country have it all going on. If an individual is looking for a little "action," it can often be found in any one or all of these various games of chance.

This is to say nothing of the betting taking place among the spectators viewing their preferred sporting, gentleman-only games, nor the side betting that often occurs during matches with big-name players. It's not uncommon at all for an individual to make more money or just as much money on the side as the players are making in the game itself. I knew a fellow in Calgary who regularly did quite well financially, side-betting at the major snooker tournaments in and around town.

Gambling has always been associated with playing pool and pool halls in general. In a very broad sense, I suppose, anyone who plays pool for money could be considered something of a hustler, or at the very least, a gambler. One individual attempting to relieve the other of his money, in great or small amounts, does indeed constitute the proper use of the word gambling, or in the case of pool, hustling.

When one thinks of the pool hustler or pool "shark," images of the old western gunfighter come to mind. The lone drifter riding into town on his horse, his tied-down holster in full view for all to see. The townspeople cautiously chancing glances at the stranger, who gives away nothing in his steady, indifferent gaze. This somewhat romantic comparison to the pool hustler is not altogether inaccurate, minus the gun and horse. In place of the gun is the pool hustler's two-piece pool cue, carried in a case which could be made of a variety of materials.

The cue and case are the pool hustler's most important and prized, if not at times only, possession. I can attest to that, personally. I gave my two-piece cue to my youngest son a few years ago. It was custom-made to my specifications thirty-two years ago, and would have cost me about one hundred and fifty dollars back then. I say "would have" because I did not pay for it. It was a birthday gift from a "lady of the evening" I knew in Calgary. It finally dawned on me during one of my "deeper" moments of thought and reflection that it did not really have a place in my present home, given its history. But I digress.

The pool hustler may arrive in a new town or city by automobile, train, plane, bus, or, in my time, by hitchhiking. On one mini road trip in 1979, I hitchhiked from Calgary to Vancouver and then returned to Calgary by Greyhound bus a month later. I had more cash in my pocket returning to Calgary than when I left, thanks to some snooker, some bar pool, and working the welfare system.

I was gambling for money almost immediately upon learning to play snooker. One was synonymous with the other, a least in the pool room where I learned to play. Two dollars a game, five dollars a game, or simply the loser having to pay for the table time—it was all money and it conditioned me mentally to play with focus and concentration. A group of us would get a game of Follow going, playing for ten cents a point. After several hours of play, I was often up twenty or thirty dollars, which went a long way thirty-five years ago.

In 1976, a pack of cigarettes, large, was only about one dollar and a case of beer was just five bucks (I was a pack-a-day smoker and enjoyed a beer at every opportunity). In those days, Mr. Submarine was the only sub place in town, and an assorted was just a dollar or two. I also frequented the local tavern and strip club in the downtown core (I was only sixteen, but looked much older), and would typically order a couple of glasses of draft beer for the whopping price of twenty-five cents a glass. The draft beer would wash down my two-dollar order of cabbage rolls, roast beef and potatoes, or chicken strips and taters.

Walking away from a session at the pool hall with an extra twenty dollars in my pocket was a good day's work for me in those days. My needs were simple and twenty bucks easily sustained me, in terms of spending money for the day. I could have a meal, a couple of beers, buy a pack of smokes, and still have ten bucks in my pocket, which was enough to get me going in another two- or five-dollar game, provided my opponent was selected carefully.

On occasion, I would stay in the tavern after I had eaten and get into a game of bar pool. Pool tables in pubs are much smaller than the six-by-twelve-foot snooker tables I was used to. Most bar tables are about half the size and have huge pockets, which made potting balls relatively easy compared to the much smaller or "tight" pockets on most snooker tables.

The pool game played in most bars was usually eight ball and would cost fifty cents to play, with each player putting up a quarter. The normal bet among the players was a dollar a game, although five- and ten-dollar games did occur, which meant the winner would make seventy-five cents per game. The winner would keep the table until he (or she, on occasion) lost, and would then have to wait his or her turn to play again.

Weekday afternoons from four o'clock on and Saturday afternoons were always busy at the downtown tavern and the pool tables were typically full of activity. It was not unusual for me to win five to ten games in a row before finally losing one, at times on purpose. I would put a quarter back up on the table and wait my turn to play again.

It wasn't big money, but it was easy money and a pleasant, relaxing way to spend a day. Sipping beer, watching strippers, and getting paid to do what I loved: play pool. Those small tables with big pockets offered me little challenge, and making fast, easy money was almost guaranteed. This was my "ace in the hole," as far as making quick cash was concerned, and it served me well many times over the years when I was hungry and just wanted a quick bite to eat.

Needless to say, with all of my time being spent downtown playing pool or just hanging out with the other players, not to mention a variety of other characters of very questionable reputation, quitting school was inevitable. My heart had not been in my studies for some time. I'm not sure it had ever been. Had I finished out my grade ten year, I would have missed most of my credits, and I hadn't completed all of my credits in grade nine. My last full year of school was grade eight, and remains so to this day. At sixteen, however, a lack of formal education was the least of my concerns as I was well on my way to earning a B.A. in hustling pool, a Masters degree in the art of survival on the streets, and a PHD (piled high and deep) in rebellion and bad attitude.

As I've said, pool and gambling more often than not go hand in hand. While I was indeed shooting pool for money very soon after learning to play, I wasn't always winning. If memory serves me correctly, I was in fact losing money quite often during my first year or so of serious snooker play.

I was working part-time at a convenience store when I was fifteen and sixteen years old, and investing every dime of every paycheck towards my career of choice: hustling pool. Like so many other pursuits in life, it was first necessary for me to learn the ropes, or in this case lose some cash, in order to learn how to make a little cash in the future. I considered every penny lost in those early days money very well spent. It was merely an investment that would, I was certain, pay me back one-hundred-fold down the road. Losing money did not necessarily mean I had lost to another player, although that definitely happened. Often, I was just broke because I spent all of my money practicing hour after hour. Playing pool cost money, even when it was by myself, which was the case often enough.

It wasn't just the game of snooker I was learning to play, however. I was also learning the fine art of reading my opponent. Every professional poker player will readily attest to the fact that it's the player sitting across the table that he or she is reading, not the cards. Playing pool for money, or more specifically hustling for money, is much the same. Knowing or reading my opponent, his strengths and weaknesses at the table, as well as off the table at times, was just as important to me as sharpening my own skills on the pool table.

When I talk about knowing my opponent off the table, I'm referring to such things as his general temperament, his moods, what upsets him, where he works, and what kind of job he has. Knowing when he got paid, as well, was especially helpful on more than one occasion. Profiling a potential mark was just as exciting for me as playing the game itself. I loved playing snooker and watching the game played by top-calibre players. However, what I really loved, perhaps even more than the game itself at times, was hustling someone. I mean truly, without apology, picking someone's pocket clean on the pool table. The art of the hustle, the perfect hustle, was what I thought about, dreamt about, imagined and pursued with tireless zeal bordering on obsession.

ON THE ROAD

"Best cure for a hangover? Have another drink."
–Ted Nellis, 1978

About a month before my eighteenth birthday, a friend of mine, Don, was back in my home town visiting his family at Christmas. He had been living in Calgary, Alberta, for the past year or so and was going back out sometime in January. He loved life out west and invited me to go back out with him. He thought the change would do me good and assured me I could live at his place until I got settled. He also assured me there was plenty of work out west and that the snooker scene in Calgary was incredible.

Don had my undivided attention. The idea of change, not just geographically, but in lifestyle, new friends, and a new pool of guys to draw from playing snooker held great appeal for me, to say nothing of the overall adventure of moving some 2,300 miles away from my home town. I was excited as well at the thought of perhaps traveling around western Canada for a couple of years.

As I said, I was only seventeen at the time, but I was beginning to feel very restless, perhaps a little cooped up. I longed for a little more… of something. What? I wasn't sure at the time. Adventure is a rather broad word and could imply any number of things. For me, at that time,

I think it meant travel, new places, new faces, all of course within the world of the pool player.

October 4, 1983

Mr. Ted Nellis
c/o University Centre
3rd Floor, Games Room
University of Guelph
Guelph, Ontario
N1G 2W1

Dear Ted:

On behalf of Valhalla Inn, I would like to thank you for helping to make last evening's opening of our new Recreation and Fitness Centre such a success.

By all accounts, our guests enjoyed the evening tremendously, due in part to your snooker exhibition. I thank you for refraining from "hustling" our guests!!!! - and also for all the "nitty gritty" details on the life of a snooker player - I found these facts amazing!

I wish you good luck in your future tournaments, and University championship - I'll remember to check the "News" section. Again, thank you for your assistance last night.

Sincerely yours,

Wendy Gilchrist

Wendy Gilchrist
Public Relations Co-ordinator

/wg

The Vallhalla Inn in Kitchener, On. had just opened a new recreation room for it's guests and I was invited, with another gentleman, to put on a snooker exhibition. It was something of a gala evening. The mayor was in attendance, along with the Miss Octoberfest beauty contestants and best of all, there was an open bar. They did not have a snooker table as advertised. It was a smaller, 4ft. by 8ft. eight ball table. No matter. The place was full of beauty queens and free booze.

From time to time, out-of-town pool players would arrive in my home town looking for some action. I immediately identified with them and longed for their lifestyle. Although I did not get to know them very well on a personal level, I did pick their brains enough to learn a thing or two about where they were from, how long they'd been playing, how long they'd been on the road, etc. I saw in these drifting pool players (and con men, at times) everything I desired to be in life: to be my own boss, living where I wanted, coming and going as it suited me, answering to no one, working or not working depending on my own personal needs, and most of all, having complete freedom to choose the how, when, where, and why in life apart from anything and anybody.

Without question I romanticized this lifestyle somewhat, but what did I care? It was, or could absolutely be, a reality for me if I chose to make it so. The prosperity potential or general financial well-being of the traveling pool hustler was insignificant to me. Money, or a lack of money as was the case with me more often than not, was not a true measure of success as far as I was concerned. Success for me meant being who I wanted to be, regardless of the opinions of others. This remains very true for me today.

I believe that my romantic views of the traveling pool hustler's life were fueled, at least in part, by two movies I'd watched at a relatively young age. One was *The Hustler*, starring Paul Newman and Jackie Gleason as professional pool hustlers. Jackie Gleason's character in the movie is nicknamed Minnesota Fats (I saw the real Minnesota Fats play in Calgary in 1981–82). I believe I was about thirteen the first time I saw it on TV. The other movie I saw at the drive-in when I was perhaps ten years old. It was called *The Flim-Flam Man*, starring George C. Scott as a traveling con man.

Even at such a young age, pre-teens basically, I was drawn to the characters on TV or the movie screen who portrayed the traveling, easy-come easy-go, slightly less than honest figure. Such is the influence of media, at times. This influence, of course, is not limited to the movie screen, but is every bit as powerful in books, music, and TV as well. (Parents, what are your children watching, reading, and listening to?) Years later, when the pool room became my home away from home, those characters—seen only in the movies as fictional to most people— were not only a part of my life but were in some cases good friends of mine as well.

TED NELLIS

With all of that in mind, Don's offer for me to go with him when he returned to Calgary was more than just a little tempting. It was indeed an opportunity I simply could not refuse for a variety of reasons. Besides, what was I giving up in my little home town? Absolutely nothing. At the time of the invitation to move out west, I was living in a hotel room above the local strip club in the heart of the downtown core. Also, my friends—or rather, acquaintances—at the time were not limited to pool players. Several of the guys I hung around with were well-known to the police for a variety of reasons and I had had a few very close calls with the law. A change of scenery afforded me more than just a change in climate; it was, I felt, a necessary move in order to avoid the possibility of ending up in jail.

With those thoughts, or perhaps concerns in some ways, floating around on the back-burner of my brain, I boarded a train with Don in the second week of January 1978, just two weeks shy of turning eighteen, with a one-way ticket to Calgary. I had a small duffel bag of clothes, and one hundred bucks in my pocket after paying for the train ticket. My needs were simple: a roof over my head, which would be the train for the next three days, a few bucks in my pocket, and a pool hall that offered a bit of action.

Before boarding the train, Don had assured me of three things: a place to stay when we arrived in Calgary, lots of work, and pool rooms larger than I had ever seen. Well, two out of three isn't bad. Calgary did indeed offer ample employment opportunities. Finding work would be the least of my problems. And the pool room Don brought me to shortly after arriving in town was indeed the largest I had ever seen. The room held, I believe, twenty-eight pool tables, most of them six-by-twelve-foot snooker tables. There was also a full kitchen with a great menu and a more than adequate seating area in the lounge. It was pool room heaven for me. As far as having a place for me to stay, however, well, that turned out to be a bit of a problem.

Don's roommate had no idea where he had been the past couple of weeks. This made the situation a little tense when we showed up. Not only did Don's roommate not know where Don had been, he had absolutely no idea that when Don did return, he would be bringing a

16

friend along with him. To add to this, the apartment was only a one bedroom. The dining room had been converted into a bedroom, which was where Don had been sleeping. As for me, it was the couch in the living room, if in fact Don's roommate agreed to it.

I couldn't blame the roommate for being less than pleased with either of us. Both the roommate and I were a little upset with Don. Don had not been clear with his intentions with me or his roommate. If I remember correctly, Don was also late with his January rent, broke, and out of work, which pretty much described my position in the scenario as well. What little I had when I'd left my hometown, about one hundred dollars, had long since been spent on the train on food and in the bar car.

The living situation did not move forward in a positive way for any of us. Don's roommate moved out at the end of January. I believe he moved in with his girlfriend. When he moved out, he took most of the furniture with him, including the living room couch I'd been sleeping on. My friendship with Don became a bit strained under the circumstances, and we decided to go our separate ways mid-way through February. Don moved in with a couple of guys he knew, which left me in an empty apartment I couldn't afford, with nowhere to live.

I packed up my duffel bag and walked into the heart of downtown Calgary, which took just under half an hour. I stopped at the unemployment office and enquired about places to stay. They directed me to the Single Men's Hostel, about a fifteen-minute walk from the Calgary Tower. I had no idea what a hostel even was at that time. I only knew I needed a place to get out of the cold, and if I could score a meal or two until I got on my feet, then the hostel worked just fine for me.

The Single Men's Hostel was an eye-opener for me in many ways. I learned a great deal about myself during the times I stayed there. It was in that environment where I realized just how simple my needs really were. I also realized, with glaring clarity, just how differently I was wired up from most of the people I had known and grown up with back home in Ontario. I was now living in an environment that offered only the barest of bare essentials: a cot with a blanket in a dorm with a dozen other guys, most of whom snored and smelled; a simple breakfast and supper and a bagged lunch consisting of a baloney sandwich if desired; and an overall lack of privacy, which in itself would have driven most people crazy.

I didn't go crazy. In fact, I felt right at home with both my surroundings and the other individuals I got to know in the hostel. I met a group of men of all ages, from eighteen to eighty, of such diversity in nature, temperament, and background as well as race that I could probably write a book on just the characters themselves with little trouble, and I fit in like a hand in a glove. I had just turned eighteen, was some 2,300 miles from home, was flat broke, and living with an assortment of guys most people would not have gone within one hundred feet of, and not only was I okay, I was actually quite content.

I quickly came to the realization that being broke and/or destitute was not something to fear. I'm not certain it ever had literally frightened me, but I definitely had had moments of concern about my overall well-being while on the train to Calgary. I did not second-guess myself for a moment regarding my decision to move out west, but I did consider the challenges of being broke and not knowing anyone in a big city so far away from home.

Any concerns I had about my ability to survive in less than ideal circumstances disappeared almost immediately during my initial stay at the hostel. I use the word "initial" because I would stay in the hostel on and off many times over the next couple of years. When I was flat broke, which I typically was after going on a bender for a week or so, I would stay at the Single Men's Hostel until I was back on my feet.

Almost directly across the street from the Single Men's Hostel was the Calgary Youth Hostel. This fine establishment was a cut above the seedier—desperate, if you will—atmosphere generally found in the Men's Hostel. The rooms were much cleaner and brighter in the Youth Hostel and the beds were actually quite comfortable, with relatively soft sheets and pillows. The Youth Hostel was also co-ed, with females sleeping in their own rooms but sharing the common areas such as the laundry room, dining room, and kitchen.

The Youth Hostel cost, I believe, two dollars a night for a bed. I stayed there often when I was almost broke. When I was completely broke, it was the Single Men's Hostel, and when I was "sort of" on my way to broke, I stayed in the Youth Hostel. I got to know the staff in both places quite well and whether I was drunk or sober, I never caused any trouble. I was always grateful to have a place to lay my head at night and didn't want to ruin a good thing.

The Colonial Hotel, long since torn down, was located a dozen or so blocks away from the hostels and was just five minutes away from one of the city's larger pool rooms. I lived in the Colonial Hotel when I was a hundred or so dollars above being broke. Like the hostels down the street, the Colonial Hotel would be my on-again, off-again home over the next couple of years depending on how much money I had in my pocket. A room at the Colonial was just twenty-seven fifty a week. The rooms were comfortable enough, with maid service once a week and a bathroom and shower down the hall. The second-floor lobby had a coin-operated TV set, the first one I'd ever seen.

The longest I ever stayed in the Colonial at one time was six months. I believe that was the longest I ever stayed anywhere at one time in those days. Although it carried the unfortunate nickname "hooker's haven" among some of the local street people and downtown crowd, I was always quite comfortable there. It suited my needs perfectly, which were very simple, and the staff, and ladies, were very friendly.

Across the street from the Colonial Hotel was the Regent Hotel, which was another notch up in both comfort and cost. A decent room was about thirty-five a night, and I did stay there as well, several times over the span of two or three years, when I was doing particularly well financially. The rooms had the huge old claw-foot bathtubs that allowed me to stretch out almost entirely and were deeper than a standard tub. Casinos were legal back then in Calgary. A decent night of blackjack or a particularly good streak of pool playing would allow me the option of getting a room at the Regent for a night or two.

It was while staying in the Single Men's Hostel for the first time, however, that I realized, with certainty, that I had nothing—absolutely, completely, entirely nothing—to lose or fear in my chosen lifestyle. The worst thing that could happen to me was to run out of money and have nowhere to live. The hostel, however, was my ace in the hole every time I busted out financially. It was my safety net in case of a fall. Knowing the hostel was there for me provided a sense of security and confidence in the very uncertain world of gambling, hustling, and street life in general.

While many or most other individuals living in that type of lifestyle may vow to never return to an environment like the Single Men's Hostel once they were on their feet, and for obvious reasons, I couldn't have cared less how often I stayed there or for how long. I was eighteen years old and didn't have a care in the world. I was a long, long way from home and the peer pressure that went with it. Out there, in Calgary, I could be anyone I wanted to be, live the way I wanted to live, where I wanted to live, and most importantly, I had to answer to no one.

The least of my concerns was measuring up to anyone else's standard. "Fitting in" was not something I'd ever had a strong sense of, at any time in my life. A friend of mine once drew a circle on a piece of paper and explained to me that the circle represented the world, in general. He drew a much smaller circle an inch or so away from the first and informed me that the smaller circle was me. He went on to explain that the circles illustrated how I lived my life in relation to the rest of the world, which was to say that I was not really a part of the rest of the world at all.

My decision—and it was an intentional one—to become a pool player, a pool hustler, and more often than not, a pool hall bum, set me apart, far apart, from the world in general. I had no desire for most of what the world or society had to offer. I had little, owned nothing, and wanted nothing except a good game of snooker, a meal, and a place to lay my head at night. Any place—it simply did not matter.

WIN SOME, LOSE SOME

"Every person I hustled was trying to hustle me."
–Ted Nellis, 1978

I recall vividly one gentleman I got to know while I was in Calgary. I'll call him Tom for the sake of the story. Tom was a nice guy, and I enjoyed playing pool with him. We would typically play snooker for five dollars a game, with the loser paying for the table time as well. Tom was a regular in the pool room I was working in at the time, and over a period of several weeks, perhaps a month or two, we had gotten to know each other quite well. We played once or twice a week without either of us really making or losing any money to speak of.

I knew I was a much more experienced player than Tom. In order to win a game against him, I needed to use perhaps seventy-five to eighty percent of my game. That extra twenty or twenty-five percent advantage may not sound like much of a margin, but it was plenty enough for me to rely on at the end of every close game, to make the shot or shots necessary to win on a consistent basis, if I so desired.

After going back and forth in money on the pool table with me for a while, Tom felt we were reasonably close in skill level and never hesitated to play me whenever I asked him for a game. The atmosphere was loose and friendly between us, which afforded easy conversation while we played. It was during one of those conversations that I found out where Tom worked and when he got paid, which was every other Thursday.

On one particular Thursday, a payday Thursday for Tom, he came into the pool room to play a little snooker. We played for a couple of hours and finished with me ahead perhaps one or two games at the usual five bucks a game. I knew he had just been paid and mentioned to him, casually, that I'd be around the pool hall on Saturday and invited him to join me for a relaxing day of snooker if he wasn't doing anything.

Tom showed up on Saturday around noon and there I was, practicing on a table by myself. Our time together at the snooker table began as it had on so many other occasions. We were shooting pool, chatting, buying each other coffees, and just having a good time, except for one thing. There was a subtle, almost unnoticeable difference in my style of play. I wasn't leaving as many easy shots for Tom to make, and I was making one or two more difficult shots than usual, at just the right times to ensure a win.

Tom had known me for a couple of months at this point and chalked it up to me just having an "on" day, nothing for him to really worry about. We had begun playing for the standard five dollars a game with me winning most of the games but Tom winning a few as well. With me playing "a little better" than usual and Tom still winning a few, he felt that he too was playing a little better than usual and was more than happy to play for ten bucks a game.

Ten dollars a game turned into twenty dollars a game when I was ahead about sixty bucks. Twenty dollars a game turned into fifty dollars when I was ahead almost one hundred and fifty dollars. At fifty a game, we went back and forth a bit, with me playing at about eighty percent. The conversation was still very relaxed, with both of us commenting on the various good shots or solid runs of balls we each made.

The match ended in the early evening with me ahead about three hundred bucks, cash, in my pocket. I was more than happy to pick up the table tab and offer Tom a bite to eat or drink, which he accepted without any ill feeling towards me at all. We talked about the long session we'd had and how Tom just could not seem to make the right ball at the right time. I remarked on how many of the games I felt I hadn't really "won," but rather that Tom had thrown away because of a bad shot, or because maybe the balls just hadn't seemed to roll his way at certain times.

Tom and I played many more times together after that match, although not for near as much money. We were back to the five- and ten-dollar games, with me usually coming out ahead ten or twenty bucks and Tom feeling that with the games so often being so close, he was just bound to win and get the better of me sooner or later. I agreed with him and often consented that I was very "lucky" to win on so many occasions.

Knowing and understanding Tom, how he thought, when he was feeling confident or rattled, when he had money or when he was broke, was every bit as important to my making money as the actual skill involved in making the right shots on the table at the right time. All of the ability in the world amounts to nothing if a player can't get into a game. Every pool hustler or poker player in the country would quickly agree on that point.

When playing for money, which was most of the time, I tried to choose my games carefully. Getting into the right game, with the right opponent, at the right time, was at least half the battle for me. Keeping my emotions in check from the beginning of a match to the very end was also a crucial element of the game. My friendship with Tom and the subsequent pool games we engaged in as a result of our rapport was a pool hustler's dream. Such was not always the case. Some scenarios with dream-like potential turned into nightmares I would just as soon forget.

On one of my return trips to my home town in Southern Ontario, I got into a snooker game with a guy named Lou. I was about nineteen at the time and had been out west for a couple of years. In that time I'd seen a lot of incredible snooker played. Snooker in Canada was in its prime in the seventies and eighties and there was a lot of talent in western Canada. My game and my knowledge of the game of snooker had improved substantially just from watching semi-pro and professional players in Calgary, Edmonton, and Vancouver.

Lou was a pretty fair player, although not nearly of the calibre I was used to out west. He had been the local small-town snooker champion at least once. His potting and safety play were consistent, though I seldom saw him put together a run of more than fifty points. At the time, I was running fifty and sixty points every day, with many runs over seventy.

On this particular evening in the pool room, I had been practicing by myself when in came Lou asking me in a loud voice in front of a dozen or more regulars if there were any decent pool players out west. The sarcasm in his question could have been heard and felt by a deaf person. Lou was, by all accounts, very arrogant. He was a legend in his own mind. He was a big player in a very small pond and an ungracious one at that.

Lou was the type of player who would do anything to get an edge over his opponent. He would regularly stand behind the guy shooting at the table and crinkle up candy wrappers in his hand—a very distracting noise for his opponent, who was trying to focus. Another of his favorites was to stop the play in the middle of the game and "double check" the score just to make sure that it was right. This would disrupt the flow of the game and shake his opponent's concentration. Or he would cough at just the right time when the poor guy he was playing was about to make a crucial shot.

These were all deliberate attempts to psyche out his opponent or simply to throw his opponent off his game. I could go on with more examples, but I think I've painted a pretty clear picture of Lou's character and style of play. I had no respect for the cheap tactics he enjoyed using. It was unnecessary and beneath him and resulted in me admonishing him to grow up on more than one occasion, although I was still in my teens and he would have been about fifty years old at the time.

My blood began to boil the second I heard the words come out of his mouth regarding the skill level of the players in western Canada. The tone of his question implied that there were not, in fact, any decent players out west and that I was, in fact, not much of a player myself. In my mind (what there was of it in those days), I sensed he was suggesting that I was just a kid who should just keep on practicing and maybe one day I would be ready for the big boys.

Pride is indeed the root of all kinds of evil, including selfishness, disillusionment, discontentment, and angry, negative-driven, emotional thinking. I think that at that particular moment, at that particular time, I was demonstrating a level of pride fueled by anger that had the better of me before my match with Lou even started. My emotions were out of control, and Lou was well aware of that, I'm sure. With that, it stands to reason that thinking clearly and quickly, developing a solid strategy to relieve Lou of some of his money went out the window as well.

In response to Lou's question regarding snooker talent out west, I suggested he have a word with my secretary and continued with my practicing. My response was sarcastic, to say the least, and was intended to be a full-throttle insult aimed at Lou's ego. Whether it had the desired effect or not, I cannot be sure, but Lou did respond by asking me if I'd like to play a game or two, for perhaps five bucks a game.

Had I been in control of my faculties, I would have sensed a great opportunity to just play it cool and walk away with a little of Lou's money, much the way I had handled myself with Tom in Calgary. What did I care what Lou thought or felt about anything or anybody? He was just another guy in a pool room looking for a game, right? *Wrong.* In my mind he was an arrogant degenerate who needed a lesson in humility, and I was just the person to teach it to him. (I think I was the one who needed the lesson in humility.)

Without looking at Lou, I continued practicing and answered loud enough for everyone within twenty feet to hear that if we were going to play, it had to be worth my while: fifty a game to start, cash in the pocket every game, before the break. I then stopped hitting the balls around and looked Lou in the eye, waiting for a response.

My challenge had the desired effect. There was doubt in Lou's eyes and perhaps a little confusion. He could not have been prepared for my response or the dead seriousness of my gaze as I regarded him, waiting for a reply. You could hear a pin drop in the old pool room that night. Lou was the one with the reputation on the line, not me. I had nothing to lose and everything to gain and I was moving in for the kill. I was in no mood for a long, drawn-out session, slowly raising the amount we were playing for, hoping to eventually come out ahead a few bucks, leading to another match for more money down the road. It was now or never, no messing around. Tonight was the night the young upstart was going to put the big man in his place.

I had been gone for most of the past couple of years. Lou really had no idea how I played. He would not have hesitated for a moment to spot me some points had I asked for a bit of leverage. With an advantage in points, a win would have been in the bag for me before the game even started. All I would have had to do was make the easy shots as they presented themselves and then play safe—nothing fancy, no pressure, just slow and easy, candy from a baby. That was not, however, how my mind was processing the situation. I didn't care about the money. I wanted to destroy the man, his confidence, his reputation, and his ego once and for all.

Lou gathered his thoughts and replied in the affirmative. I enjoyed watching him borrow the fifty dollars to begin our first game. My no-nonsense assertiveness in naming the stakes had succeeded in rattling Lou. He was playing well below his ability at the start of the first game but, unfortunately, so was I. My obvious contempt for Lou and his antics had not only thrown him off, but I had thrown myself off as well due to my intense dislike for the man. I could barely make a shot.

The first game was crucial. If I won, whatever was left of Lou's confidence would be shattered, along with his ego. He would never recover from being manhandled by a teenage kid. The momentum of the game would sway entirely my way, which is how it should have been anyway, had I played my cards right before the first game began. Such, however, was not the case.

The first game was very close, with neither of us making any decent runs or, for that matter, any decent shots. In the end, Lou just managed to win, just, but it was all he needed to regain his composure and begin to play some pretty solid snooker. I never did get my emotions under control, and it was all downhill for me for the rest of the evening.

My negative feelings towards the man eclipsed the entirety of my game, from my mental approach to the physical act of putting the balls in the pockets. I lost my head and with it, about two hundred dollars in cash. I didn't win one game. With every loss, Lou's ego, to say nothing of his confidence, just got bigger. Not only did I not knock him down a peg or two, I only succeeded in proving him right: I was just a young upstart of a kid who had a long way to go before I was ready for the big boys.

Losing some cash didn't bother me much, but losing my head did. I behaved and played recklessly, and in the process made a fool of myself in front of the people I wanted to impress most—the guys I had learned to play from years earlier. I did, however, learn something valuable that night: humility. I'm not sure if in my mind I saw or heard that word, humility, but it was certainly what I felt. I was not who I thought I was. (Coincidentally, a few years later a full-time pro told me that it was my ability to be humble that would enable me to make a living playing pool. Perhaps I did learn something from that embarrassing confrontation with Lou.)

I knew instinctively and through experience that in order to play pool for a living, one needed much more going for him than a bit of skill at knocking balls into pockets. The match with Lou drove home the absolute necessity for focus, concentration, and—above all—keeping a cool head, whether playing for five or five hundred dollars a game. It was a lesson learned the hard way but learned well. Many times in years to come, I saw lesser-skilled players beat superior players simply because the lesser had a better grip on his emotions.

Stan Holden ran 123 of a possible 147 points on his way to a 5-2 victory over Rob Munn in Thursday's sixteens of the Southern Alberta snooker championships at Towne Billiards.

The winner of the Southerns meets the Northern champ in the first half of the provincial championships in Edmonton Feb. 8. The second half of the final will be played in Calgary Feb. 15.

Thursday's other results are as follows:

Ted Nellis 4, Dennis Dombroski 3; Joe Big Plume 5, Dan Scullion 1; John Jorgensen 5, Doug Petrie 1; Paul LaFontaine 5, Bob Kennedy 2; Del Ziegler 5, Ron Posehn 3; Jim Grant 5, Ellis Adams 0.

An old memento from one of the few tournaments that I played in. The line-up of players was very tough but I managed to make it through the first three rounds before being beaten by Joe Big Plume, which would have placed me in the quarter finals. Joe was a top amateur, a century player and had won the Calgary and Alberta snooker championships many times. I made more money side-betting than I ever would have in tournament prize money.

SNOOKER, WHISKEY, AND A TIDY SUM OF MONEY

"Look, you want to hustle pool, don't ya?
This game isn't like football.
Nobody pays you for yardage. When you hustle,
you keep score real simple.
At the end of the game you count up your money.
That's how you find out who's best."
— The Hustler

Most, if not all gamblers, whether full-time or part-time, experience both the highs and lows of their chosen lifestyle on a fairly regular basis. By highs and lows, I'm referring to the emotional as well as the financial roller-coaster existence that simply comes with the territory. No two days are alike and the inconsistency of the big paydays, which in my case were never very big anyway, can wear out, psychologically and mentally, the most resilient gamblers in the business.

I was, for the most part, strictly smalltime, nickel-and-diming my way around town and across the country at times, making a living—if one could call it that—in various pool rooms simply because living like a bum did not deter me from doing what I loved to do. Not only was I more than content to win a few dollars here and there scuffling around from pool room to pool room, I was actually quite proud of myself.

I had a skill, a trade if you will, that few other people possessed (very few would want to possess it). I was my own boss. I "worked" if and when I felt like it and my days were as long or short as I wanted them to be. The price I had to pay for the life I had chosen was being sandwiched between two snoring, stinking drunks down at the hostel from time to time, but what of it? Nothing's perfect, right? In fact, very little of it was perfect but as a teenager living a long, long way from home, I just didn't look past the next bend in the road. As for sleeping between a pair of snoring, stinking drunks from time to time, well, what's a little inconvenience every now and then?

More often than not, I had very little to lose and everything to gain in most of my forays into the world of the professional gambler, or pool hustler in my case. My indifference to my surroundings when I hit skid row alleviated most, if not all of the pressure I may have otherwise felt were I chancing the loss of big cash or valued property or assets of another kind.

My confidence was not in my ability to play a great game of pool, but in my ability to adapt to my present circumstances regardless of how bleak they may have been or appeared at the time. My confidence came from knowing I could survive—in fact, be quite content—even if I was flat broke and had nowhere to live. I knew I could arrive in any city in Canada, hungry, without two nickels to rub together, and in a matter of just a few hours have a bed to sleep in, a roof of some kind over my head, and a meal in my stomach, and could find a pool room around the corner to make a little cash, somehow, in some way.

At times, it was an honest day's work that put a little money in my pocket. Other times, it was a long hard day at the pool table, sweating for every dollar but at the end of the day feeling terrific due to winning some tax-free cash doing what I loved to do more than anything else in the world: hustling pool. Still, at other times, money came from neither an honest day's work or from playing pool, but from crossing the line into the seedier side of life, which, for me, just came with the territory. I'm referring to criminal activity, but more on that in the following chapters.

My pockets were lined with cash for once. It was, at least on this occasion, thanks to an honest day's work—several days of honest work, actually, as rare as that was. I had been picking up a day's work here and there from the labour corner in downtown Calgary. All one had to do was show up around 7:00 a.m., grab a number, a chair, or simply stand outside and wait for a car or truck to pull up offering a day's work, quite often for cash.

This situation was more than just a little convenient for me. It suited my needs perfectly. I could pick and choose the days I felt like working and the type of work I was in the mood for on any given day. It worked for me. A day's work was not always guaranteed at the labour corner, but I was rewarded for my effort in just showing up most of the time. If the pickings were slim on any particular day, no matter, I'd go back to the pool room where I really wanted to be anyway.

The type of work prospective temporary employers offered me was wide and varied. I did everything from moving people out of their homes to construction and handyman repair work in apartment buildings to landscaping and everything else in between. The jobs were often for just a day or two, but some did develop or at least had the potential to develop into more. On more than one occasion, I was offered a full-time or part-time position, usually because I had good rapport with the employer of the day.

Such was the case with the employer I had been working with for the past three days. On a Wednesday morning, a gentleman walked into the Day Labour office and asked me if I'd like to help him paint an apartment suite. The first day went well, and he offered me more of the same work. He had brought me lunch, paid me in cash at the end of the day, and even brought a radio into the apartment I was painting, which I gladly accepted, to keep me company while I worked.

I agreed to stay on a couple of more days with him, continuing in the same type of work. When I finished painting one apartment, I continued on painting another. The work was somewhat tedious, but I did enjoy working by myself. I found it very peaceful, particularly since I was staying in the Single Men's Hostel at the time which was never, and I mean ever, peaceful.

Friday had come, day three for me in the working world, and I was offered work the next day, Saturday, as well. I agreed, thinking I may have come across something good here. My boss had paid me in cash at the end of every day and supplied me with those free lunches as well. I was staying in the hostel, which meant supper was also free. Actually, my entire lifestyle was free except for two expenses: cigarettes and beer.

After three days' work and with little or no overhead, I had about one hundred dollars on me and the promise of more to come. Actually, I had a feeling that my employer was going to offer me a full-time job as a handyman in his apartment building. I could settle down a bit, live in a decent apartment in a nice neighborhood for a change, and make some decent cash working on my own. Not bad.

I spent Friday night just hanging out at the hostel, watching TV, reading, going out for a walk, and thinking about my current situation. I couldn't remember the last time I had laid low on a Friday night, but I wanted to get a decent night's sleep and be up in good time for work on Saturday. For that matter, I couldn't remember the last time I had worked on a Saturday.

What was happening to me? Thoughts of settling down into a normal life—whatever that was—were going through my mind for the first time in a long time, if ever. Me, working on a Saturday? Behaving myself on Friday night so I'd be well rested for another day's work? No bars, no pool rooms, no action, just relaxing for a change, exploring ideas of possibly leaving this on-again, off-again, in-and-out-of-the-hostel, homeless lifestyle I'd become accustomed to.

I did indeed go to bed, or should I say, to my cot, in the hostel at a decent time that Friday night, and got up early for breakfast before making my way to the apartment building. Today's workday would make four in a row for me, practically a record.

How would I respond if I was offered full-time work, especially if the offer included an apartment of my own? Could I really walk away from an opportunity which appeared, from every angle, to be at the very least worth considering? A hundred thoughts were going through my head as I walked slowly to my job site that morning.

It was about a half-hour walk to the apartment building from the Hostel. The first half of the walk was primarily through downtown Calgary. I was just taking my time walking to work on that particular morning, thinking about things, like my life, and how it could be different. I do remember feeling a little restless, uneasy perhaps, without knowing exactly why.

I stopped at a coffee shop along the way to grab a coffee for work and to have a smoke, and then it hit me. I mean it hit me with absolute eye-opening clarity. I knew I wasn't going to accept a job offer, if one actually came. In fact, I knew I wasn't even going to work that day. Who was I kidding? I had about a hundred bucks in my pocket, breakfast in my belly, a full pack of smokes in my shirt pocket, and a clear head from having an alcohol-free, decent night's sleep.

It was Saturday, the busiest day of the week in every pool room in the city. My decision in the coffee shop was as clear, determined, focused and logical, as any decision I had ever made. Enough of the painting, it was time to get back to the pool tables. If nothing else, it was time to spend an enjoyable day, all day, hitting the balls, hanging out with the guys, and just talking shop. I convinced myself, in a second flat, that I deserved a day off after working hard three days in a row.

The uneasy, restless feeling I'd been feeling for several hours, or perhaps days, was gone. In its place was a sense of absolute peace, an inner stillness and calm that came from knowing without a doubt that I had made the right decision. The inner struggle I had been marginally wrestling with regarding my lifestyle for the past several days had been clearly, completely, utterly dealt with in a moment. *Whew.* For a few days there, I had almost become an average working Joe. What a disaster!

For reasons I cannot explain even today, I knew I was going to score big on the pool tables that day. Perhaps it was just a gut instinct, a gambler's instinct maybe, but I knew my decision to not show up for work that day was the right one for me at that time. It would not be the only time I would make the decision to walk away from a potential solid employment opportunity in favor of the more uncertain up-and-down life of a pool hustler.

The feeling or intuition in my gut that I was going to enjoy a very solid day on the pool table was very real. There were times playing snooker when absolutely everything went my way. It didn't seem to matter what I did at the table, somehow it would work out in my favor.

No shot was too difficult, and even if I missed I'd end up leaving my opponent safe or with a very difficult shot, to say the least.

Athletes may refer to this heightened sense of things, this "can't do anything wrong" temporary state, as being "in the zone." When I was in the zone, in those moments, I knew before I hit the cue ball that I was going to make the shot. My concentration would be so peaked that it seemed, or felt, as though the pool table was moving for me. Rather than me walking around the pool table lining up and sizing up different shots, the pool table moved for me while I stood still, in one spot, making shot after shot until there were no balls left on the table to make.

Inevitably, I would find myself surprised, or perhaps a little stunned, as if I'd been in a trance, with the realization that I had just run the table or whatever was left on the table and had little or no memory of having done it. I had been away, in those moments, mentally, in a different place of such acute concentration that I was completely unaware of my surroundings, who had been coming and going, who was or was not watching the game, because my only focus had been on the green cloth in front of me and what shot I was shooting next.

I was in the zone that Saturday morning when I decided, in a heartbeat, that I was going to play a little pool rather than paint walls in an empty apartment. I had not yet walked into a pool room that morning and I already felt this day was going to offer up something special.

Again, for reasons I cannot to this day understand, I did not go to the pool room where I normally played. Instead, I walked down the stairs of an old office building in downtown Calgary to the basement floor, which opened up into one of the most classic old-time pool halls I have ever been in.

When I refer to the pool room as "old-time," I mean the place was right out of a movie—and I'm talking an old black and white movie. The room had absolutely nothing to offer other than pool tables. There were no pinball machines, no food counter, no TV sets, no lounge area to just sit and relax—nothing, just pool tables and some rickety old chairs for the players to sit on in between shots. There was not a couch, bar chair, or anything resembling a comfortable place to sit down anywhere, and as for decorating, forget it! Plain walls, just a clock behind the counter.

The old-timer who ran the place was every bit as nondescript as the pool room itself. He could not be described in any way, shape or form as colorful in the personality department. He maintained a deadpan, emotionless expression, continuously, even while he spoke, which was seldom. The man was either bored to death or had undergone far too many Botox treatments, leaving his sullen expression permanently frozen. He was friendly enough, he just didn't offer up a real big slice of enthusiasm regarding conversation or life in general. Perhaps he'd spent too many years living out his days in that sub-terrain, below sidewalk level, wonderfully plain, nothing fancy, it's pool and nothing else, little dungeon I embraced with all the wonder and intrigue of a small child making his way to the candy counter of a variety store for the first time.

That little den of iniquity did not even have a name. The sign outside the office building simply said "Billiards," with an arrow pointing downstairs. While it certainly did lack, well, anything really, which could be seen or viewed as welcoming or inviting to passersby, it did offer, at least as far as I was concerned, terrific ambiance for the serious pool player. With few, if any distractions, coupled with a low volume of players and onlookers, one had little trouble concentrating on one's game.

I had known of the place for some time, and had used the room to practice in occasionally because of the quiet and solitude it offered. I had even had a game or two, on occasion, with a couple of the regulars who were as old as the paint on the walls, when I was in the mood for something different. Sometimes I just wanted a quiet, friendly game, just for the enjoyment of playing, not for money, and when I felt that way, that old pool room was my first stop.

This day, however, was different. I was there looking for action. I had enough cash to get started in a game of any reasonable amount, from five up to a comfortable twenty dollars a game. Why I thought I would find such a game in that particular pool room on that particular day is beyond me. I just knew that I had come to play, wanted to put some money in the pocket, and that my apartment painting days were over. This day was all about pool, and I wasn't looking past the next several hours on the clock.

I was the only one in the place, besides smiley behind the counter, when I walked in. I took a snooker table around the corner from the counter and turned the light on over the table. From the moment I began practicing that morning I knew I was "in stroke." What I mean by this is that I was hitting the balls well. My stroke, the way I hit the cue ball, was very smooth. This was not always the case. Some days I was definitely "out of stroke" and couldn't make a shot if my life depended on it. Not today.

After a half-hour or so of hitting the balls around, a man, perhaps in his mid thirties, walked in and, after chatting with Mr. Personality behind the counter, approached my table. He asked me if I'd like to play a game or two of snooker. I began to rack up the balls while he selected a cue off the wall racks. After finding one that seemed to satisfy his needs, he introduced himself as Jim and asked me if five dollars a game would be okay with me. I nodded and followed with a "Sure, we can try it and see how it goes" response in a non-committed, casual kind of way.

Jim was a fairly big guy. He was as tall as I am—a couple of inches over six feet—and at least fifty pounds heavier. For the sake of this story, I'll refer to him as Big Jim, as that's how I was thinking of him at the time. Big Jim had an easygoing manner about him. He made light conversation in a very non-threatening, non-intrusive kind of way with both me and the proprietor behind the counter. He was quick to pay a compliment when I made a tough shot and to shake his head and mutter a "tough luck" comment if I missed or the balls didn't quite roll the way I needed them to.

Big Jim could not have known in a million years what was going through my mind while he was making polite conversation. I was focused on one thing and one thing only: emptying the guy of every dime he had in his pockets. I was scrutinizing his every move, his body language, his shot approach, and his reactions when he made a few shots, as well as when he missed. After perhaps thirty minutes of sizing Big Jim up, I concluded, to myself of course, that I could win consistently without coming even close to using my full potential.

This was a dream-come-true situation for me. Big Jim was just there to play a little snooker, have a few laughs, and maybe walk away a few bucks richer at the end of the day. Never, ever, could he have suspected for a moment that he was playing a seasoned hustler who, given half a chance, would take him for every cent he had in the blink of an eye. While I was only eighteen years old, I had been playing almost full-time for the past three years in dozens of pool rooms, against many dozens of players of all skill levels, and at a level of intensity that had made me much older than my years.

My age itself was an advantage. At just eighteen, I was either still in school or just recently finished high school, as far as those who didn't know me were concerned. How could anyone ever guess I'd quit school to play/hustle pool full time? The match I had going with Big Jim is what I had quit school to do! No one I ever played, so far away from home, whether in a pool room or bar room, could ever imagine that the young, "polite, nice" kid they were playing was a street-savvy, smalltime con man looking for a fast buck.

From the first break of our match, I was never really in any serious trouble. Big Jim had definitely played before but did not have the ability to make more than a few shots before either losing shape (not controlling the cue ball properly, thus leaving himself without a shot), or just missing the shot entirely. He could run maybe twenty or twenty-five points if he was hot, but overall his game was fairly inconsistent.

I actually hoped he would put together runs of twenty or twenty-five points because it would help to keep the games close. The better Big Jim played, the less I had to "play down," which made my job of marginally winning a lot easier. Regardless of how well Big Jim hit the balls, he was not going to win games, at least not consistently. While he did win some because that's how I wanted it, he was never going to walk away with the money at the end of the day.

We took two breaks from our play that day: once to have lunch and once for supper. On both occasions we went our separate ways to eat and agreed to meet back at the billiard room at a set time. I was up about thirty or so dollars when we stopped to get some lunch. We'd been playing for a few hours at this point, still at five dollars a game.

I was waiting for Big Jim to request a hike in the wager, which he did immediately after lunch.

For my part, I was feeling quite content. I was already ahead in cash what I would have earned up to that point had I gone to work that morning. Remember, this was 1978 and thirty dollars went a long way back then. Also, our match wasn't over and held the promise of more money to come. Big Jim was enjoying himself, and suspected nothing. Our games up to that point had been reasonably close, with both of us making some decent shots and missing some as well. I was simply coming out ahead more often than not, usually because of a bad miss on Big Jim's part, which only fueled his desire to play better and get me next time.

Resuming play after lunch, Big Jim asked if I'd like to shoot a couple for ten bucks a game. Nodding in agreement, we continued to play in a back-and-forth manner for the next couple of hours. I had very slowly pulled out ahead about sixty bucks when Big Jim said he wanted to play for twenty a game. This is what I'd been waiting for, hoping for—heck, who was I kidding, flat out longing for—since we started the session. We had paid each other off in cash after every game and when Big Jim paid, he pulled out a sizable roll of bills from his pocket.

At this point, Big Jim's demeanor had made a subtle shift. He was not as quick to make compliments on my play as he had been earlier, and he was taking himself far more seriously as well. He was, I thought, settling down to play some serious pool. This was absolutely alright with me. The more intentional he became in wanting his money back, the more I could play up my part as a decent but somewhat lucky young pool player trying to hold on to his winnings.

I made sure Big Jim won our twenty-dollar game. It didn't matter if he blew me off the table or if I just choked on some key shots. A win was a win for him and, as far as he was concerned, it was enough to tell him he could beat me and win his money back, if not even come out ahead if things really turned around. Winning the first twenty-dollar game was crucial for Big Jim, as it gave him all the confidence he needed to stay in the match.

Those twenty dollars were the best investment I could have made. His play relaxed and his confidence soared, and that is exactly what I wanted. I was still ahead about forty bucks, and felt sure I could get ahead at least a hundred before Big Jim might start to question his chances of either winning or getting his money back.

I did in fact get my winnings up to a hundred-plus dollars before Big Jim suggested that we take a break for some supper. It was late in the afternoon and we'd been playing for hours. Had the day ended at that point, I would have been more than happy with my day's work. I was up just over a hundred and having the time of my life. My decision to choose the pool hall over painting apartments had panned out beautifully.

We took about an hour for supper before meeting again at the snooker table and resuming play. I immediately noticed a change in Big Jim. I don't know if he had something to eat or not, but one thing I do know is that he'd had a few drinks. This couldn't be happening. He wasn't staggering or slurring his speech, but his style of play was far more reckless than it had been before supper.

I honestly did not know what to make of this. I had played many times against inebriated players in bars, but never in a snooker room. I wasn't sure if this was a good thing or not for our match together. In my mind I concluded that this was now the end of it for me and that he would pack it in after another game, if we even made it through one more game. Two things happened, however, that I could not have anticipated in a million years. First, Big Jim wanted to play for fifty a game and second, he pulled a bottle of booze out of his pocket when he suggested upping the wager. *Unbelievable.*

Never before and never again did anything like that ever happen to me in a pool room. I didn't have to move in for the kill. Big Jim was doing it all by himself. I could hardly believe my ears or eyes at what I was seeing and hearing. I did not reveal one iota of what I was feeling or sensing at the time. I remained as poker-faced as possible and answered his challenge with a sincere, "It's okay with me if you're sure," type of answer.

Big Jim responded in a friendly, why not, kind of way and we continued to play. The owner of the billiard room, Mr. Happy behind the counter, seemed unconcerned about the bottle of booze Big Jim had pulled out. He kept it in his coat pocket on a small side table and brought it out from time to time to pour some of its contents into an empty Styrofoam coffee cup he'd brought with him.

Play continued but with a noticeable difference in the manner in which we were both playing. Big Jim was both a little reckless in his shot selection and hurried in his approach. In a word, he was playing sloppy. I, for my part, was no longer concerned with keeping the games as close as they had been until now. I just capitalized on all of Big Jim's errors as often as possible without going too crazy.

Any hustling I had been doing up to this point was now over. At this stage of the game, I was simply taking advantage of Big Jim's sloppiness and could honestly defend my winning against him as just that: taking advantage of sloppy play. Big Jim, however, did not voice any concerns but simply played on and drank on for another couple of hours.

Winning was easy. Safety play, which is normally a consideration while pondering shot selection during a snooker game, had become irrelevant. Big Jim was in no condition to pose much of a threat regardless of how many easy shots I left him. In fact, it would have played in my favor had the big guy made one or two balls rather than playing so poorly.

I fully expected him to quit at any moment, whether in the middle of a game after missing an easy shot that he would have made were he sober, or simply deciding that he was bored of the whole thing and packing it in. My only real concern was Big Jim suddenly turning ugly and either wanting his money back or wanting a piece of me before we parted company.

The evening went on without incident, however, and with Big Jim losing all, or at the very least much, of his money. I was up over four hundred dollars, cash, in my pocket when he decided he'd had enough. A good chunk of his money was gone as well as most of the bottle he'd brought in. Big Jim could barely make a shot during our last few games. I suspect he was doing what so many gamblers seem to do, which is to play on until the money is all gone.

For many gamblers, it's not about winning; it's about how long they can keep the action going until they're broke. As sad or desperate as that seems, it is nonetheless true. I saw this scenario play itself out many times in various forms over the years with a variety of individuals. I suppose I was guilty of it myself a time or two, although I demonstrated this self-destructive, "pity-party" type of behavior in a marginally different way.

I would simply mismanage myself and my lifestyle every time I landed a solid win like the one against Big Jim. Rather than re-invest my winnings into another game and continue to build a solid bankroll as well as some financial security, I would typically hang it all up only to go on a booze run until the money was all gone. It was like I couldn't handle doing well or somehow thought I didn't deserve to do well, and would then punish myself with destructive habits until I was flat broke. It was an endless cycle. Man, I lived on the corner of Nowhere Street and Loser Avenue for a long time.

Our final game played itself out very much like the others had since reconvening after our last break for a little dinner (or in Big Jim's case, a few drinks). Big Jim played loose and sloppy with little regard for what he was leaving me to shoot. I won with little effort, trying to keep the game at least reasonably close. Big Jim paid me another fifty dollars and then called it a day.

The big guy suggested that I pick up the table tab, which I readily agreed to do. While I was paying for the table time, Big Jim said something like, "Well, you really got me this time," in a very casual, conversational kind of way. I nodded and remarked that the balls just weren't rolling his way. With that, Big Jim made his way up the stairs and out into the evening. I never saw him again.

I spoke with Mr. Happy behind the counter for a few moments and then returned to the table and racked the balls back up. I turned the light over the table off and then said goodnight. I felt as though I hadn't been outside in days, although it had only been a few hours. My mind was racing, processing the match that had taken up the better part of the day as well as my decision that morning to not return to work.

Had I gone to work that day painting an apartment, I would have made about forty dollars, cash, over a period of about eight hours. In about the same amount of time, I made just over four hundred dollars, cash, playing pool. It was 1978. I was eighteen years old. Not a bad day's work.

I walked slowly back to the hostel, smoking a cigarette, enjoying the feeling of having a thick wad of bills in my front pocket. The money I'd started with, plus the day's earnings on the pool table made for a tidy sum of cash. If I played my cards right I could coast on this amount of "doe-ray-me" for a long time. I lived rent-free at the hostel, and even my meals were free if I cared to eat there.

I could settle in and just play some easy bar pool for the next few days. Making enough to cover a bite to eat, plus cigarettes and a few glasses of draft playing a little eight ball was a piece of cake. Or I could easily afford to get into a good game of snooker, for any amount. I could also afford to get a decent hotel room for a couple of weeks if I felt like treating myself. All of those thoughts and many more were racing through my head as I made my way home to the hostel.

After a long hot shower, I laid awake for a long time, well into the night. I thought of Big Jim and wondered if such an opportunity in the billiard room would come my way again. I closed my eyes and replayed the match over and over again in my mind. If Big Jim had wanted to continue to play for more money, if he really did have much more cash to lose and had insisted on one more game, just one more to try to get his money back, would I have kept playing? Would I have continued taking his money, regardless of how inebriated he was? Maybe just one game, double or nothing, wiping him out for about eight hundred easy dollars? Oh yeah, I thought. I would have. In a heartbeat. I slept like a baby.

MEMORIES AND MUSINGS

"I had enemies, no question about that."
–Ted Nellis, 2012

I had absolutely no idea who they were, nor did I ever find out in the days, weeks, months, and years following the incident that evening. I may very well have been in their company several times afterwards and not known it since that night in 1977. I just knew I was scared. Blind luck had saved my life, or at the very least, saved me from a severe beating which would have certainly put me in the hospital for an undetermined length of time. I was sure I'd seen either tire irons or baseball bats, which make short work of the human frame, to say nothing of the dent they can put into the skull with very little effort.

Were they armed, or was my mind just racing, processing, calculating, measuring the situation, fighting hard to remain rational? So this was how it was going to end for me. Seventeen years old, squaring off against a group of thugs I didn't know from a hole in the ground, who were carrying out a vendetta for something I was completely in the dark about. Maybe I could fend them off with my laundry bag.

It had been a very close call. Too close. Just seconds earlier or later and I would have been lying on the side of the road, an unrecognizable heap of bloody pulp. At one o'clock in the morning, how long would I have lain on the ground on a quiet side street before being found?

I chanced a glimpse through the blinds of my living room window and saw the car drive slowly, painfully slowly, past my apartment. The automobile full of my would-be assailants circled the block and made its way down my street again, determined, it seemed, to locate me and finish the job.

How had my life gotten so crazy? The year was 1977, and I had just turned seventeen but felt, at times, like I was going on thirty. I had not yet made the move out to Calgary, and there was a lot more going on in my life than just playing pool. Who were those guys circling the block and why were they so intent on making me their "victim" of the week?

Maybe I needed to get out of town for a while. Maybe I should have given some serious thought to just moving back home and living quietly with my parents. Perhaps going back to school wouldn't have been such a bad idea after all. I could try to apply myself, try to make decent grades, quit the pool room, the bars, the night life, and weed the criminal element out of my life once and for all. I could try, at least make a reasonable attempt, one more time, at the straight life: school, hockey, dances, movies with the boring but "safe" friends I'd grown up with.

It wasn't too late. I was hardly "over the hill." I had only been out of school a year or so and could easily blend back in with the student population in any high school in my home town and just start over. Why not? Replace the pool players, poker players, drug dealers, criminals, mobsters and every other less desirable member of society with the more ordinary, unassuming, everyday kids my own age. Perhaps hang out with young adults who would certainly have a more positive influence on me than the crowd I had been hanging out with downtown.

I didn't have a clue what it was like to just go on a date with a high school girl, or any other girl my age, for that matter. Actually, I had never really been on a date, period. The only females I had ever kept company with were the dancers from the local strip club downtown. What on earth would I even talk about or do with a "regular" girl from school or from the neighborhood I'd grown up in? I had taken a young lady from my grade eight class to my grade eight graduation dance, but I'm not sure that really counted. We had hung out for the evening in the gym of my junior high school with everyone else from my class, had a few dances, talked a bit, and called it a night. I did walk her home and gave her a kiss on the cheek before parting company, so I suppose I could say I had been on a date.

I wasn't so sure, however, that I really wanted to go out on another one, with anyone. It just wasn't my style. The last thing I needed was some angry broad calling me up (if I had a phone) and giving me the third degree about where I had been for the past week, why I never called, and why I spent so much time with those "bums" from the pool room. (I recognize that the term "broad" is not the most flattering word for a female; however, it was a part of the language in use by yours truly at that time.)

I sat up most of that night, smoking one cigarette after another in the dark of my living room, being careful not to let the glow be seen by any passersby on the road who might just steal a glance at my living room window on the way by. I couldn't take the chance. Blinds down, lights off until daybreak. The car I had run from hadn't driven down my street in some time. I was too scared, to keyed-up, wound up, too *screwed up* to get any sleep.

One minute I was taking care of my laundry in the laundromat a block or so from my little bachelor apartment, and the next I was running for my life. It was just a little after midnight, I believe, when I was finishing up with my clothes. I typically did my laundry late at night when no one else was around. I'm sure that this particular evening was a Sunday, which made for an even quieter night than usual, suiting me fine. I didn't like dealing with crowds when I was washing my clothes. Having to wait for a machine was annoying and besides, the color of my underwear was nobody's business.

I threw my freshly washed and dried clothes into a garbage bag and, stepping out of the laundromat, began to make my way home. The parking lot of the laundromat was deserted, and so was the street. In fact, the whole block and surrounding area was quiet, given the time of night and the fact that it was a Sunday evening. Except for the occasional car driving by, there wasn't a sound. I was the only one walking down the street, just the way I liked it. Quiet. Peaceful. Still.

I don't know how many guys were in the car that night—three, four, five? Who knows? I do know that when they came around the corner and the headlights of their car fell on me, the car came to an abrupt halt and they immediately began to climb out, one by one. They were perhaps fifty feet away from me and I thought I could see weapons of some kind in a couple of the guys' hands. Whoever they were and whatever was or wasn't in their hands was not clear. What was clear was that I was outnumbered four, maybe five, to one.

I froze momentarily, my mind racing in a dozen directions at once. I thought, these guys are here to inflict some serious damage to my person. Maybe it was payback for something I'd said or done to someone at some point in the past. Perhaps I had offended, insulted, or hurt someone in some way and these guys were here to even the score. Maybe it was just a car full of goons and I just happened to be in the wrong place at the wrong time.

None of those thoughts mattered at that moment. Figuring out the whys and how-comes of the situation I'd found myself in was really not important. What was important was getting home in one piece, which did not seem likely. A betting man observing the scene would not have bet in favor of a good outcome for me. Even if I could outrun them and get to my place first, I couldn't be sure they wouldn't kick down my door and finish me off in my own living room if they saw which house I ran to.

It would have been no good, getting away from my assailants at the cost of them knowing where I lived. That, in some ways, was the worst possible scenario. If they found out where I lived it would only be a matter of time before my number came up. I would wonder every day if they would be waiting for me while I made my way home from the pool room, typically very late at night when most people were already at home and in bed. In some ways, it would have been better to just hold my ground and get it over with. Take the beating for whatever reason and move on. It just wasn't my night. *Okay*, I thought, *here we go, let's just do this.* Maybe I'd get in a solid shot or two before they went to work on me.

Whether it was blind luck, fate, divine intervention, chance intervention, none of the above or a combination of all of those fate-related variables, I couldn't be sure at the time. I have little doubt now, all these years later, just who exactly was responsible for the sudden turn of events that saved me from a vicious pummeling that evening, if not saved my life. It would not be the first time in those tumultuous years or the last that I was saved—incredibly, miraculously saved—just seconds before receiving a severe or harsh lesson dished out to me in one form or another.

Why God would choose to "show up" on a quiet street in my little town, outside a laundromat well into the evening to save an arrogant, seventeen-year-old kid with a bad attitude like me is beyond my comprehension. I should have been hurt, badly hurt, so many times in those days and yet was spared over and over again from almost certain physical harm, somehow, in some hard to believe way that would leave me shaken, grateful, and confused all at the same time.

The turn of events that evening was both completely unpredictable and unfathomable. That a cab would come around the corner onto the street I was standing on just as the goon squad was taking their first steps towards me is remarkable. Wildly coincidental. My heart was pounding, adrenaline was racing through my veins, my hands were clenched into fists so tight that my arms were cramping up all the way to my shoulders, and suddenly a taxicab—a beautiful, gorgeous taxicab, comes around the corner and stops directly beside the car belonging to the mystery men who were about to put my lights out.

The cab driver must have realized what was taking place or sensed what was about to happen and decided, in a heartbeat, to take action. Pulling up beside their car, he had the headlights from his taxi shine straight at the goons, making them clearly visible to both the cab driver and to me. The moment the headlights shone on them, they stopped coming towards me and began glancing back and forth from the cab driver to me. They were now just as busy processing the situation as I had been moments or seconds ago in planning my possible escape, which there now was—maybe.

The cab driver got halfway out of his car and, while shouting a word or two at all of us, began to talk into his radio mike, the old school kind from the seventies. He was speaking, I presumed, to either the cops or his dispatch office. This entire scene was playing out in front of me, and I hadn't moved a muscle in seconds, minutes, how long? I didn't know, didn't care. The cavalry was coming. (Not long ago, after a speaking engagement, an older gentleman approached me and, while shaking my hand, asked me if I remembered him. I did not. He told me that years ago when I was a teenager, he had picked me up many times in his cab, very late at night, from the downtown area. I would have him drop me off a block or two from my home and then walk the rest of the way. I didn't want him to know where I lived in case the police ever questioned him about it.)

The goon squad stood as still as I did. They knew the tables had been turned entirely against them and that they had to make a decision fast. I didn't stick around to see what that decision was. I found my legs and got out of there in as calm a fashion as possible. I didn't run or even power-walk my way out of there—just a nice steady gait without looking back. An empty parking lot divided the street I lived on from the street I was fast trying to put behind me. A minute, maybe a minute and a half, and I'd be home.

Once I was across the empty parking lot and had walked down my street past a few houses, I was just out of sight of the cab driver and the hoods who were after a pound of my flesh. As quickly and as calmly as possible, I walked up the few steps onto the front porch of my house and without chancing a glance to either side or behind me, I unlocked the front door and stepped inside. Locking the front door, I turned to my apartment door on the left and let myself inside, closing and locking the door as quickly as possible. I stood absolutely still, almost afraid to breathe.

I had no idea whether I had been followed or not by either the cab driver or my enemies out there, whoever they were. For all I knew, they may have been right behind me, on foot. I was half expecting my apartment door to come crashing in any moment. Standing motionless just inside my door, I strained my ears, trying to hear something, anything, but there was nothing at all. I placed the garbage bag filled with my laundry on the floor and quietly made my way to my living room window, which faced my street and the empty parking lot I had just crossed moments earlier.

Peering out between the blinds, I looked up and down my street for any signs of the car full of guys, the taxicab, or a cop car but saw nothing. I had no idea if a cop car had even showed up. To this day I do not know how it all played out between the hit squad and the cab driver. Was there an exchange of words? Did the cops show up? I'll never know. I do know that although I had made it home in one piece, I was not out of the woods entirely.

Moments after making it safely home, the carful of bad boys drove slowly down my street, guessing I suppose, where I might have gone. I had no idea if they had seen what house I had disappeared into, which bothered me. Maybe I really had been in just the wrong place at the wrong time. Or maybe those guys were in exactly the right place at the right time and had it not been for a fluke visitation from a taxi driver, their evening's entertainment—bashing my skull in—would have gone off perfectly.

I had told my parents over and over again that I just wanted to be a pool player. I had tried to reassure them that I was doing fine and that no, not all of my friends and/or acquaintances were of the criminal element. Who was I kidding? Only myself, I suppose. Part of me dreaded the life I was living. The other part, however, embraced my lifestyle with reckless abandon. One more look through the blinds and I saw what I was looking for: nothing. An empty, quiet, ordinary street with quiet, ordinary people sound asleep in their beds, oblivious to what had just taken place a stone's throw away.

And me? Not so quiet and nothing ordinary at all about my circumstances. Taking a deep breath and lighting another cigarette out of sight of the window, I slid down the wall inside my little bachelor apartment and sat on the floor, smoking my cigarette, thinking about my life, my choices, and the "too close for comfort" episode I had just escaped. Would I change anything if I could? No, probably not, at least not at that moment.

I thought of myself as a social misfit, someone who simply did not, could not function like everyone else. I was not interested in how the rest of the world was living their lives. This was how I lived my life. This was the way people like me lived and that was that. It mattered little what was right or wrong or if the day-to-day made sense to anyone else, or even to me for that matter. I saw little evidence that those who lived a "normal" life, whatever that was, were any happier, more or less, than I was.

That night, I told myself, was just one of those nights. It could happen to anyone and may very well never happen again. For all I knew those guys out there, whoever they were, had the wrong guy altogether. I was just a pool player. Sure, I knew some tough characters, even played pool with a few. Okay, so once in a while I had a beer with some well-known criminals from the downtown core, maybe even helped a little with a small score here and there, what of it?

I was in over my head, that's what of it. I was on a one-way trip to nowhereville. I would not change and would one day pay the price. It was not a question of if, but when. I told myself I was just a pool player, but that was simply not true. Perhaps I had started out as just a pool player when I was fifteen, but a lot had changed since then, like my attitude. I was turning bad. The light of my conscience was off.

***

John C. Maxwell, best-selling author, speaker, and expert in the field of leadership training, asserts that our attitude equals our altitude. How high we fly, or perhaps soar, in life is in direct proportion to our attitude towards life. Our perception, our outlook on life in general, on our family, on the people around us, as well as our own self-image can make or break us as growing, maturing, responsible human beings.

That I had a bad attitude in my teenage years is without question. That my bad attitude or bad behavior continued well into my adult years is also without question. The question is not whether I had a bad attitude, but *why?* Now we are getting somewhere, but the answer or answers that will help us or at the very least, me, to understand are not so easy to figure out.

I have logged in, if you will, countless hours in recent years mining for clues in the storehouse of my memory that would help me to understand my own destructive and self-destructive behavior patterns.

This journey has often been a painful one, as I have looked at my life with glaring honesty. Tough love to oneself is not an easy road, but can be a productive one if traveled with the right motivation and with a spirit of forgiveness and love. Forgiving ourselves can often be far harder than forgiving others.

I have learned, with God's help, the important—no, the imperative—art of self-forgiveness over the years. Perhaps even more importantly in some cases, I have learned to not take myself quite so seriously. Cultivating a sense of humor regarding our own shortcomings and mistakes, both past and present, can take an enormous load off one's conscience. Carrying guilt can be a real heavy. I speak, or in this case write, from much experience on this matter.

I have witnessed, up close, much of the darker side of human behavior. Violence was a part of the lifestyle I lived for many years. Beatings, for one reason or another, were an everyday occurrence in prison, as were stabbings, suicide, attempted suicide, attempted murder and occasionally murder, to say nothing of the psychological oppressiveness or just flat-out hopelessness one can feel in such an environment. These and other acts of violence or, at the very least, detrimental behavior to the extreme, were not limited to prison life but loomed near—very near—to this writer on the outside as well. Yes, a sense of humor and a little self-forgiveness can go a long, long way indeed.

My last name is Nellis. Growing up, I heard a half a dozen times or more from adults on my street, "Why don't you go play at the Nellis' house for a change?" This verbal reprimand would come from the parents of some of the kids I played with regularly when I was a child. Inevitably, the statement would come from seemingly nowhere, unprovoked, and was both hurtful and embarrassing to me. It was always spoken aloud, in front of everyone, leaving me feeling unwelcome.

I believe that at times the child of the parent making such an outrageous statement for all to hear was just as embarrassed and uncomfortable as I was. This remark, as far as I knew, was never directed at any of the other kids. I seemed to be the one singled out, repeatedly, never really knowing what I had done to warrant such a rebuke. I was perhaps seven or eight years old the first time I heard the words spoken.

A child of that age has a limited capacity to understand all or any of the dynamics of the emotional psyche. All I knew then was every time I heard that remark I felt bad, period.

The adults were saying, "Why don't you go play at the Nellis house?" What I was hearing and certainly feeling was, "We don't want you here." To say I felt a little dejected would be another contender for understatement of the year. What I felt was that some of the parents on the street did not particularly want me hanging around their kids, for reasons unbeknown to me. The result of this was that a "truth" was taking shape deep within my spirit: "I'm not good enough. There must be something wrong with me."

My hometown was largely Italian in the sixties and seventies. The street I grew up on was also largely Italian, with my family being more of a Canadian heritage. While my grandparents have some roots in England and perhaps Scandinavian ancestry, my mother and father are just good old Canadian folk. This may have set us apart somewhat from the rest of the families on the street. Maybe some of the folks on the street were a little closed to new people moving in or were just very cliquey or tight in some way. I'll never know, and at this stage of the game it really doesn't matter.

Not long ago, while visiting my mother in her care home, I found out that one of the adults of whom I speak was also there. After one visit with my mom, I decided to also visit with my old neighbor, if possible. I found her in a sitting room, very old and bent over at the waist. She didn't recognize me when I began to speak with her, but remembered me immediately when I introduced myself. We talked about the old days, old times growing up on the street, where everyone was today, who was still alive and who had passed away. We had a lot of laughs. I'm so thankful I had an opportunity to say hello, say goodbye, and to part company with a warm and sincere, "God bless you," spoken from the lips and heart of this author.

Where am I going with all this? Zig Ziglar, author, speaker, and Bible teacher, shares some terrific insight in the area of handling old hurts and offenses. Zig suggests that while it's reasonable to be angry or upset with someone for hurting us, in the moment, we are never to give them or the situation permission to ruin our future. I could not agree more. The past is indeed the past. The responsibility is ours to let go, forgive, and move on or we will be forever held hostage to the events and emotions of our past.

Understand that I am in no way laying the blame for the choices I've made in my life on the adults I knew and grew up with so many years ago. To do so would be both irresponsible and immature. I accept full responsibility for my actions and the decisions I've made along the way. I'm simply relating events as they happened and I am doing so as impartially as possible. I cannot begin to imagine why I seemed to be singled out in that fashion on more than one occasion. I also understand that we are all "wired" differently. While those comments were hurtful to me, they may very well have fallen on deaf ears on many other children. We all internalize things a little differently. For me, it became personal, for others, water off a duck's back, big deal, who cares?

I wish I hadn't cared, but I did. I cared a lot. As I grew older I resented those remarks and the adults responsible for speaking them. The feeling of "not fitting in" was birthed, in part, out of those early experiences—and with it, anger. The emotion of anger and a profound sense of not quite belonging walked hand in hand deep within my being for many, many years. Perhaps this was largely self-imposed, or perhaps I held a certain amount of contempt for a few of the adults on my hometown street. I do know with certainty that the contempt I felt towards my neighbors carried over into the classroom, towards my teachers when I started school, and again towards adults in the work world, and then towards the world in general as I grew older.

Way, way down in the farthest recess of my being a question burned continuously, begging for answer, yet remained unanswered for a long time. In fact, the question wasn't answered and dealt with until in my late thirties, but more on that later. The question was, "What's wrong with me?" I knew there must have been something. That thought, as negative, misguided, self-defeating, and self-condemning as it is, plagued me—haunted me, really—well into my adult years.

Non-productive, negative questions can only produce negative, non-productive answers. Out of all of this grew a jaded, somewhat warped perception of myself, the world, and the people in it. I rationalized my bad behavior and the inevitable consequences that resulted from it by falling back on my own self-imposed paradigm. I did this or did that or behaved this or that way because there was something wrong with me! I was being punished or I was in trouble again because something was wrong with me. My jaded outlook, which very early in life became the foundation on which I stood, gave me license to misbehave, act out and, as I grew older, break the law.

What a mess. It's so easy to look back now and see, feel, and understand some of what was happening inside of me from my pre-teens right through my thirties. I'm a lot older now, a little wiser (have a lot less hair), and have developed, I think, a reasonably mature, impartial take on most, if not all of the choices I've made, and why I made them. We cannot go back, but we can move forward with an awareness of our shortcomings, our "not quite there yet, but I'm working on it" faults which will only help us chart the waters of life in a sensible, productive, positive manner that will not only benefit ourselves but even more importantly, benefit those around us as well.

PETTY CRIMES AND POOR GRADES

"School house, out house, what's the difference?"
–Ted Nellis, 1976

Charley and I had known each other since the first grade. We grew up just a few blocks from each other until Charley's family moved to another part of town when I was about ten years old. We played baseball in the city league together for a number of years, and knew most of the same people. We were average students, didn't stand out one way or another, just a couple of kids doing what normal pre-teen kids do.

After he and his family moved, we bumped into each other from time to time, but for the most part we'd lost track of each other. We had never been super close, just had a few things in common and hung out in the same circle from time to time. When we did reconnect, it was under altogether different circumstances and we were no longer just doing what typical pre-teenage kids do.

The year was 1976. I was sixteen years old, as was Charley. We had both dropped out of high school, smoked, drank, got high now and then, and shared the same love for the game of snooker. Charlie went on to be a very good player, with several century runs under his belt and at least one city championship title to his name. He had a smooth stroke and became far more consistent in building good breaks around the black and pink than I ever did.

Our love for the game of snooker, however, was not the only thing we had in common. We also walked a fine line between good and bad, morally speaking—right and wrong, honest and dishonest behavior. There was a lot of temptation, forbidden fruit if you will, all around us on an almost daily basis. The local pool room was our home away from home and was located, at that time, in the heart of downtown, which in those days supported a wild, anything-goes type of atmosphere. Two young guys with far too much time on their hands hanging out in an atmosphere offering up everything and anything in the way of excitement, legal or illegal, and the inevitable brush with the law was a foregone conclusion. Always will be, for many individuals who find themselves hanging out in that kind of environment.

We had pulled off several small petty cash type jobs around town. Stealing was becoming almost second nature to both of us. It was never anything big, just rolls of quarters, dimes and nickels, and some bills at times that may be found in a small cash box behind the counter of any given store. These small thefts would keep us in a position to play snooker for money, should there be an opportunity to do so, and also bought us a meal, smokes, or whatever else we might be in the mood for. It beat working for a living.

The cycle was always the same: pull a small job, use it to make a little more in the pool hall, bust out eventually, and then pull another small job. Smalltime, going nowhere fast living. We hit one place three times before they finally moved their cash box to a different spot. The thought of getting caught never entered our minds. I think we had become de-sensitized, in a way, to what we were doing. It had just become normal, everyday life. We felt sorry for the poor chumps we grew up with who had to go to school every day. What were they thinking?

One day, we decided to return to a dry cleaning store we had hit once before. It was a fairly easy place to steal from because the checkout counter, cash register, and small cash box behind the counter were just a few feet inside the door off the street. Charlie and I would hang around outside until the employee was called away from the counter for one reason or another. Then, while I kept watch outside, Charlie would crouch down, get in behind the counter unseen and take whatever was in the cash box. He would be in and out in seconds.

On this particular day, the door we needed to get through was propped open because it was a warm, sunny day. As far as we were concerned, the place had "rob me" written all over it. We assumed our usual positions, with me watching the street while Charlie waited for his chance to grab the stash of cash behind the counter. When the opportunity presented itself, down went Charlie and in he went.

Across the street from me were a row of stores and restaurants, along with various small businesses. Some of the businesses were two-stories with windows on both levels facing out on the street. My eyes were scanning back and forth along the sidewalk opposite me, as well as up and down the street while Charlie ducked inside to raid the cash box. As my eyes were scanning the windows of the stores and businesses across the street, they froze on one second-story window. There, standing in the window, was a uniformed cop! I couldn't tell if he was facing us or was turned a little sideways, perhaps speaking to someone else in the room, but there he was and there we were directly across the street just seconds from committing a robbery.

I had no idea how long he had been standing there or if we had even been seen or not. Was he there for us or was it just a coincidence? Turning just slightly sideways and speaking loud enough for Charlie to hear, I said one word, "Cop." Charlie was out and back on the sidewalk, empty-handed, in a flash. I told him to just stand still, act cool, and have a smoke. Looking over the street quickly and not seeing any police, he looked at me questioningly.

I lit a cigarette and told him to take a look at the second-floor window across the street. There was the cop, doing who knew what, but one thing he was not going to do that day was pick us up. I told Charlie to just relax and walk slowly down the street, away from our job-gone-south, which is exactly what we did. We strolled down the street, stopping to look into store windows and waited, every second, to hear, "Hold it."

The words never came and in a few moments we were back in our office, the pool room, counting our lucky stars. A second earlier or later and we may have been pinched. Charlie was shaking his head, grinning from ear to ear wondering how I had spotted that cop while keeping six for him, a slang expression for keeping a look out. "Just luck, man," I said, "just luck." Yeah, just luck, over and over and over again, but not forever.

***

Will the real Ted Nellis please stand up? In my early teens, I was a living dichotomy. One moment it was all about Bruce Lee, the famous martial artist/movie star of the early 1970s, and the next I would be watching the latest episode of *The Waltons* on TV. I could be found in my backyard practicing martial arts, working up a sweat with my nunchaku (these were illegal, considered to be a dangerous weapon by the police. Mine were confiscated by the police when I was fifteen), or watching John Boy, the oldest son in the Walton family, on a hit TV series in the 1970s and early 1980s. Just as there are two sides of the same coin, so too were there two sides of this writer. I could be hitting the books with a sincere effort and desire (although not often) one day and the next be hanging out with friends for the sole purpose of getting into trouble.

I absolutely have many, many great memories growing up. Friday night hockey games downtown at the Gardens, cheering for our city's Junior A team. All day street hockey games on weekends in the winter and drive-in movies in the summer. Lots of sports, always lots of sports. Hockey, baseball, golf, and tennis. There was always something going on and always plenty of friends to have fun with.

Day-to-day life for the most part was fairly routine. My Achilles heel was, without question, school. On the rare occasion that I did apply myself in school, I actually did derive a certain sense of satisfaction from my studies. The problem was that the productive times were few and far between with the gaps being filled by a lot of clowning around, going through the motions, and generally developing a dislike for authoritative figures, which would include about ninety percent of the staff in any given school.

I viewed adults with a certain amount of suspicion. The root of this, at least in part, has already been noted in the previous chapter. My perception of the adult role, particularly those who were in a position of authority over me, was flawed somewhat because of other negative experiences elsewhere. I definitely felt at times that it was me against them and that I would come out on top as long as I played the game by my rules. This somewhat misguided and extremely detrimental mindset was not limited to just the adults in my life, but also gave way towards older kids as well.

I was involved in physical altercations from time to time, both at school and in and around my neighborhood as well. At times I was the antagonist, but on other occasions I was on the receiving end of flat-out, ongoing bullying, or at the very least intimidation by kids who were several years older. This on-again, off-again cycle of finding myself on both the giving and receiving end of a round or two of fisticuffs continued throughout my school years.

Without question, bullying today is much, much worse than when I was in school. I feel sick every time I read in the newspaper or hear on TV about another student taking their own life as a result of relentless bullying by other students. If you are reading this and have been bullied in the past or are being bullied presently, understand that you are not at fault. It is not you who has the issues, but the bully, who does not have the courage or the maturity to deal with their own issues. It is the bully, not you, who needs help.

Was I a tough guy? No. No way. I was, for the most part, a scared kid when it came to physical altercations, and I was in way over my head more often than not. I was afraid and angry, all packaged up into one big stick of emotional dynamite just waiting to blow. What came first, the chicken or the egg? Did I fight because I was a bully or did I begin fighting back because I had been bullied? Now there's the million dollar question. Solve that one and I'll have a handle on the first fourteen years or so of my life.

I mixed it up a bit with others as a pre-teen, but no more than anyone else in the neighborhood or at school. My biggest problem in those early years was my mouth. It would get me in trouble time and time again with both the kids and the adults living on and around my street, as well as at school. I was a verbal disaster area! I would regularly respond verbally to any and all taunts, challenges of any kind, insults, and teasing, real or imagined, from anyone and everyone regardless of their age.

It seemed I was always in hot water with someone, for something I had said and/or done, and in my mind I was always the victim. With every passing year I had less and less respect for both my peers and the adults I interacted with on a daily basis. My disrespectful behavior often resulted in much older kids picking on me as well, which only deepened my belief that older kids and adults could not be trusted. My lack of respect for individuals in general, their property, and the system, etc., was not just outward but was also directed inward, at myself. As the years rolled by I had less and less respect for myself as well.

During my junior high years, there was a group of guys who picked on me continuously. I was in grade seven while they were in grade eight and they were always together, perhaps three, four or five of them, always in a group, never alone. On the way to school and on the way home, they would push me around. I would take different routes to and from school occasionally to avoid any confrontations, but would soon tire of the extra effort it took to avoid them and would resume my usual, shorter route to school, which resulted in them resuming their bullying if they happened to see me.

The altercations were never very explosive physically, but were more of the jeering, taunting, shove-me-around-a-little type of behavior typical of kids just not being overly kind to one another. They could not have known, however, that I had been on the receiving end of insults, one way or another, from others over the years, including, uniquely I suppose, from some of the parents on my street, and that I was, by grade seven, very close to blowing a gasket in a big, out-of-control way.

One day while walking home at lunchtime I was suddenly hit very hard from behind. I went down face first into the ground, grass and stones and twigs in my mouth and hair, not knowing what had happened or what or who had hit me. Gathering myself up off the ground, and shaking myself off to get my bearings, I saw those guys, perhaps ten or fifteen feet away. The same group of guys who had been picking on me all year.

They were enjoying the moment tremendously: me scuffed up a bit, my pants a little dirty from the fall, watching me slowly getting back on my feet, a little disorientated from being hit and from going down so hard, and there they stood, arrogant, cocky, and gazing my way with expressions that simply oozed the challenge, "What do you think you're going to do about it?"

When I had regained my senses and realized what had happened and by whom, I felt a rage, a level of full-blown hatred towards them unlike anything I had ever felt or experienced previously. My only thought, my only focus at the time, in the moment, was to inflict as much punishment, pain, humiliation, and shame on them as possible, as quickly as possible, as ruthlessly as possible, as relentlessly as possible, for as long as possible.

I was not looking at a group of grade eight students who had gone a little too far in their bullying, teasing antics. I was looking, with uncompromising hatred, at a group of grade eight kids who represented to me everyone and anyone who had ever wronged me, one way or another, since I was perhaps seven or eight years old. This leering, smug, daring-me-to-try-something group of grade eight kids represented, stood for, championed if you will, all that I had come to despise, and they would pay. Them, and anyone who looked like them.

I can only imagine that in some way everything I was feeling in that awful moment somehow showed in my facial expression, my body language—the heaving of my chest, trying to get my breathing under control—or perhaps the almost maniacal look in my eyes. I'll never know exactly what it was that day that caused concern among my antagonists, but I do know that when I advanced towards them, they ran from me.

I had made up my mind that enough was enough and that whatever was going on between me and those guys would end that day, one way or another. The tables would be turned, permanently, on them and on anyone else who would dare to attempt to intimidate me either physically, psychologically, mentally, or emotionally from that day onward. No one was exempt. Not my friends, not my acquaintances, not classmates, or teachers, or neighbors, young or old, not even my own family. No one. Period. Ever. Anyone and everyone who crossed me in some way would feel, sense, or realize one way or another, my deep-seated hatred towards them. This would be accomplished not simply by fighting, which I didn't always engage in, but by my behavior as well. My contempt, my lack of respect for those in authority in general, would be clearly seen and felt by everyone.

When I had come around and realized who had knocked me to the ground that day when I was in grade seven, I saw red, plain and simple. I was too angry, too full of thoughts of revenge to be afraid. With a string of curse words and bloody murder in my eyes I ran towards them, and they turned and ran from me. Could they have handled me? Almost certainly, but whatever it was that they had seen in me when I got up off the ground convinced them that they did not want to find out.

The chase lasted only a few seconds. Running was not what I had in mind. I watched them run a fair distance from where I was and then they, too, stopped running. They continued on their way, looking back over their shoulders from time to time while I continued to make my way home for lunch. My mind was racing in a dozen different directions at once, processing what had just happened. I was as shocked, overwhelmed, and confused at the turn of events as I'm sure they were. I don't know that they ran from me because they were afraid necessarily, but perhaps because the situation had simply escalated to a place that was out of their comfort zone.

Over the years, the scene would play itself out many times in my mind. I had been willing to put it all on the line that day, and they had not. I was prepared to take it up another notch, physically, violently, and they were not. It wasn't that they could not or would not have walked away victorious had it come to blows. They absolutely would have. They outnumbered me four or five to one. They were simply not willing to become the kind of people necessary to hold their own in a violent, explosive situation, and I was. They ran from me because I had come to a place where I no longer cared, and they did, and it frightened them.

It was, in some ways, a bluff. I had been far too angry to be afraid. My level of rage had fueled my lack of concern for my own personal safety. I had hidden my fear and shown only courage—courage they had not known existed and didn't know what to do with when confronted by it. I was to discover in years to come that if people "believed" I was prepared to take a situation to a level far out of their own comfort zone, whether I really was or not, they would inevitably begin to lose heart and I would play on this to invoke fear or uncertainty.

At an age when most kids were going through their day-to-day routine without much thought of the why and how-comes of behavior, emotional or psychological triggers, I was spending considerable time reflecting on the human psyche and even more time observing and studying people's body language, actions, behavior patterns, etc. It was an education that would serve me well in years to come, whether I was hustling pool, avoiding potentially harmful altercations, sizing up a prospective "job" or simply avoiding trouble of a serious nature in prison.

SCAMS, FLIM-FLAMS AND THE BLACK...WHO?

"We men are wretched things."
– *Troy*

"To do evil is like sport to a fool."
–Proverbs 10:23 (NKJV)

Life in the pool room was what I most desired in my mid to late teens, in the mid to late seventies. No better day could be had as far as I was concerned than to get into a long session of follow or 101, poker pool, or just a solid match with someone interested in playing some serious pool. On other occasions, simply watching a decent session between players I could learn from was equally enjoyable, as was a game of pinball or just having a cup of coffee and hanging out with the guys. What I was doing, exactly, was at times not as important to me as where I was doing it.

It was never life in the pool room, however, which got me into trouble, but life outside the pool room that proved to be something of a challenge for me. I simply did not seem to have the discipline to focus exclusively on that which gave me so much pleasure: snooker. The individuals I looked forward to being around on a regular basis in the pool room were also the very individuals I would inevitably end up breaking the law with. For some this was never a problem, but for me it was a colossal problem. Like a moth to the flame, the very thing I was attracted to was also the very thing which would threaten my life.

I am in no way implying that everyone I played pool with was of a dubious nature or influenced me in a negative way. The pool room was filled with regulars who were mature, hard working, responsible family men. Unfortunately, it was also full of immature, out-of-work (some permanently it seemed), less responsible individuals as well (guys like me). It was the latter half with whom I got into trouble.

Although there was quite a selection of characters to "push the envelope" with on any given day, it was usually Charlie I'd partner with when it came to break-and-enters, thefts, and robberies. Others came and went—drug dealers, criminals of various backgrounds and ages, other high school drop-outs just looking for a little excitement—but Charlie was the one I would intentionally work with to make a little fast (dishonest) cash. Several times we even stole the rolls of quarters out of one of the drawers behind the counter of the pool room that we played in, before they wised up.

We had very little respect for anyone in those days, including ourselves. There were no boundaries, no "off limits" or "just don't go there, it's wrong" scenarios which would or could play on our conscience, stopping us from pulling a score. All and everyone was fair game with little or no regard of consequences for either the victim or us. We pulled off small scores randomly with no regard for tomorrow, ourselves, or our families. Whatever we did, whenever we did it, could be chalked up as a day's work, period.

One unfortunate young man, a stranger to both Charlie and me, found himself in the wrong place at the wrong time and with the wrong people—me. I had never seen him before the night he wandered into the pool room, and I knew nothing about him nor did I care to. He appeared to be a little out of place in an awkward kind of way. There was a certain naivety about him that's hard to describe but could be seen or sensed a mile away.

He had the word "target" written all over him. As far as I was concerned, Christmas had just come early. It wasn't every day that a "mark" like this guy walked into the pool room, and I wasn't about to let him slip through my fingers. I approached him in a casual, friendly fashion and asked if he would like to play a game or two of pool. He responded that he didn't play much, to which I answered, "No problem, neither do I."

He didn't know how to play snooker and asked if I minded playing a little eight-ball instead. I played very little eight-ball back then, or ever for that matter, at least in the pool room. There were four or five smaller tables in the pool room while the remaining tables, seven or so, were all the larger, six-by-twelve snooker tables. Though snooker was the dominant game played, the smaller, four-by-eight tables were busy as well. Nine-ball was almost virtually unknown in the 1970s, at least in Canada, though today it's *the* game to play and most certainly receives the most coverage on TV.

I couldn't have cared less what game we played that night, or on what table. Unless this stranger in town was a hustling me with an incredible act, I was sure this would be the easiest money I had made in a long time. Snooker, eight-ball, nine-ball, poker pool, bottle pool, golf, big table, small table, what did I care? Rack 'em up! We decided on a small table in the back, free from any distractions, where we could talk freely.

To my dismay, he wasn't interested in playing for any money; however, he was interested in scoring a little dope. I agreed to bang the balls around the table with him, just for fun, all the while sizing him up, trying to get a handle on him, which wasn't easy. Was he setting me up, playing me for an easy take, or was he just out to lunch? The entire time we played eight-ball, I was playing a little game of mental chess with this odd, didn't-blend-with-the atmosphere fellow who had, I thought, fallen into my lap for one reason or another.

Charlie was hanging around the front of the pool room. Excusing myself for a moment to check with a friend about the possibility of scoring a little weed, I left the stranger at the pool table and had a little chat with Charlie. Very quickly I told him that I had a live one but couldn't quite figure him out. We decided to play the scenario out together. I returned to the game of eight-ball, feeling slightly more confident about handling this guy with Charlie in the loop. Should he turn out to be something other than what he appeared to be, there were now two of us, so we could watch each other's back.

I introduced Charlie to the stranger and explained that he was looking for a little dope and that perhaps we could help him. Our demeanor was very casual, non-threatening, friendly all the way, as we made easy conversation with Charlie, who was now taking a shot or two of eight-ball himself. When we informed the guy that we could probably help him out, he responded enthusiastically and asked us if we'd like to smoke a little right then, in his hotel room, which was just a block away from the pool room.

Still not sure where this was all going but wanting to play it out, I insisted on paying for the table time, reassuring our new "friend" that he was in good company. As we walked to his hotel room, we asked him how much he wanted to spend, where he was from, why he had rented a room, if he knew anyone, etc. No, he didn't know anyone, had just gotten into town that day, and was glad to have made some new friends so quickly.

Once inside his room he began to roll a joint. Lighting it, he passed it around for us all to enjoy. Why not, I thought—if nothing else, I'll get a good buzz, on the house, and maybe even score a few joints for lining this guy up with a dealer Charlie and I both knew very well. He pulled some cash out of his pocket and counted out about a hundred dollars, anxious to get things going. In 1976, that was enough to score a decent-sized bag of pot or a good chunk of hash, oil, or whatever else floated your boat.

He asked us how we planned to set it all up. I told him that a certain dealer we knew often operated in the downtown area and that with any luck we would track him down. I insisted that this had to be done ourselves, that introducing the stranger to our dealer friend was out of the question. He had no problem with that, and asked if Charlie could stay with him in his room until I got back. I suggested it would be much easier to track the dealer down with two of us, and reassured him several times that both Charlie and I could be trusted. We reminded him that there was a little something in this for us as well, convincing him, in part at least, that there was no possibility of us ripping him off.

After some time and much persuasion, the poor guy reluctantly entrusted us with his money, which, even to this day, seems remarkable. We told him to give us a half-hour or so, plenty of time to make the buy and come back. We reminded him that everyone in the pool hall knew us and that we would not be hard to find should he have any concerns. We said this knowing full well that we held all of the cards. He couldn't go to the cops, he was trying to score weed.

The adage, "There's a sucker born every minute," could never have held more truth than in that moment with that guy. He was gullible to the extreme, naive and, perhaps regrettably, a little slow; to be blunt, the guy was not all there. None of this mattered, however, to either Charlie or me. Easy come, easy go, you win some, you lose some. Play with fire, you get your fingers burned. What did we care? We were pleasantly high, had just scored the easiest hundred bucks of our lives, and thought, walking back to the pool room, that life was indeed pretty good.

We had been back in the pool room perhaps twenty minutes when who walks in but the guy we had just ripped off. That Charlie and I had the audacity to return to the pool room like nothing had happened is almost beyond my own comprehension. Having absolutely no regard or concern for the possibility of this guy returning to the pool room in order to find us speaks volumes about the sheer arrogance of my character. Who was the sucker, him or me? Neither of us would have passed an intelligence test that night, I'm afraid.

I was sitting at a table with Charlie and a couple of other guys when our "friend" approached and asked how we had made out. I knew he had us cold, but I also knew he was in no position to say much without getting himself into a lot of trouble as well. Who could he go to? In five seconds I processed the situation and stood up to address him as quietly and quickly as possible.

What I said to this fellow was, absolutely nothing. Not a word. Zero. Zip. Just a stare and nothing else. He asked about his money and I stared at him, long, hard, silently, and with as much foreboding as I could. I gunned him off with a look that said far more than anything I could ever have articulated. The silence was deafening. You could cut the air with a knife. My silence, and the look of hatred I was giving that poor guy, told him in no uncertain terms that I was no longer interested in doing any business with him that night.

The signals I was sending him with my body language—the look on my face, my right hand clenched into a fist—were not unlike the way I must have appeared to those grade eight bullies when I'd finally had enough. All they had seen was full-blown rage and the realization that I was going to take things to another level, to a place they did not want to go.

So, too, did this gentleman standing in front of me, asking about his money, come to the same realization. All the fury, hate, and contempt I could muster was focused directly at him, on him, through him. In a moment it all clicked, and the realization that he had been taken and was powerless to do anything about it hit him with all the force of a tsunami. I was not his friend. I was not some easygoing, let's hang out and have a few laughs kind of guy. I was an angry, heartless street kid who couldn't have cared less about him, or anyone else for that matter.

He put his hands up, palms towards me, indicating he did not want me taking even one step towards him and said repeatedly, "Okay, okay, okay." With the last "okay" he turned and left the pool room, returning I presumed to his room, a little shook up and a little lighter in cash. Charlie and I agreed that perhaps we had better "get out of Dodge" while the getting was good and we left the pool room for the evening.

Walking down the street, Charlie commented that he had never seen me look the way I did when I had gunned our mark off in the pool room. He said I looked like I was going to kill him. I remarked that I had felt like I was going to kill him. Who did he think he was, I muttered, approaching me in front of my friends, questioning me about taking advantage of him? What a goof! Must have thought the pool room was filled with boy scouts.

I wasn't a boy scout. Nor was I just a little lost, searching for my place in the world. I had found my place in the world and it suited me just fine. I was a decent pool player for my age and would only improve with every passing month and year. At sixteen I could run thirty-five to forty-five points and more fairly regularly on the snooker table, and took to hustling like a fish to water. The potential to earn at the very least a part-time living playing pool was completely realistic.

I was also equally at home ripping people off and pulling small scores around town. I had found my niche and it worked very well for me. Pool hall bum, thief, two-bit criminal, whatever. It all worked for me. I saw no evidence that I was any worse off or any better off, for that matter, than anyone else. In fact, I reasoned, I was actually more content than most of the people I knew, had grown up with, both young and old. Morals? Principles? Please. This was how guys like me functioned, operated. I was a misfit, remember? I had concluded that something was wrong with me a long, long time ago.

My actions, choices, and lifestyle only affirmed, re-affirmed that I had been right all along. As long as I sold myself that bill of goods and ran with it I could live any way I liked. My own warped perception of myself gave me license to behave in any manner I chose, without excuse. I was free from all social restraints and responsibilities. The world was mine to do with as I pleased. My way or the highway.

The highway I was on, however, was going nowhere fast. I was on a highway careening headlong into a life that would only cause me to self-destruct and destroy those around me as well. I wouldn't stop until I was stopped. Until then, lady luck would remain on my side while those around me fell, one by one, going to jail, dying in car accidents, or being on the receiving end of a "tune-up" now and then by rivals on the street. Not me, though, never me. Everyone else, but not me.

***

The saga of the Black Donnellys, as they were called, has been a source of interest for thousands, perhaps millions of people around the world for decades. The true story of the Donnelly family is both fascinating and tragic. Many books have been written chronicling the life and death of this family, who were embroiled in what has come to be known as the longest, most violent feud in Canadian history.

Opinions are wide and varied regarding the Donnelly family in general. Were they a family of ruthless, wild, out-of-control hellions with little or no regard for anyone or anything, or were they the victims of unfortunate circumstances finding themselves in the wrong place at the wrong time? There are those who find their antics both disturbing if not downright revolting, and yet there are many sympathizers as well. How can this be?

That the Donnellys had a long history of run-ins with the law as well as neighbors and townspeople over a period of some thirty-plus years is without question. That the run-ins often resulted in one, or at times all, of the Donnellys pummeling their accusers senseless would also be acknowledged by both pro and con Donnelly factions. What is far more disturbing, however, is not the life that the respective members of the Donnelly family lived, but their death, or rather, and more to the point, the murder of several members of the family which included both the mother and father in an uncompromisingly cold, intentional manner that shocked the community and surrounding area for years.

Even more shocking was the trial, if one could call it that, which played out in the months to follow and was covered quite extensively by the local papers. The men accused of the murders of five members of the Donnelly family on the night of February 4th, 1880, were all acquitted, in spite of eye-witness accounts to the grisly murders. It remains almost beyond comprehension that the court, legal magistrates, judges, lawyers, and respected men and women in the community could "look the other way," as it were, while the murderers walked away free men. The story has all the intrigue, suspense, action, and drama of an Oscar-winning Hollywood movie, though one has never been made.

James Donnelly, along with his wife Johannah, arrived in the area of Lucan, just outside London, Ontario, Canada, from Ireland in the early 1840s. They had seven sons: James Jr., William, John, Patrick, Michael, Robert, Thomas and one daughter, Jenny. During a logging bee one day, the father, James, found himself in a heated argument with another of the group and ended the dispute by striking and killing the man with a fatal blow to the man's head. James was subsequently sent to prison, Kingston Penitentiary, and Johannah was left alone for many years to raise her children, on a farm, without the aid of her husband.

The boys grew up without a father and were often on the receiving end of verbal taunts and teasing by other children as to the whereabouts of their dad. Over time, the Donnelly boys responded to the insults by thrashing the daylights out of anyone who dared to challenge them in any way, verbal or otherwise. What started out as boyhood brawling in a schoolyard continued into their adulthood, with the brothers terrorizing the district for over thirty years in and around the town of Lucan, resulting in a deep-seated hatred between many of the locals and the Donnelly clan, who became known as the Black Donnellys.

One winter night, a group of men, including the town constable, came to the unanimous conclusion that enough was enough. Armed with an assortment of farm implements, clubs, etc., the group stormed the Donnelly farm house and murdered James Sr., his wife Johannah, their youngest son Tom and their niece, Bridget. After beating them all to death, the mob set the home ablaze, leaving nothing behind but the charred remains of four of the hated and feared Donnelly clan.

Not yet satisfied with their evening's work, the band of crazed, justice-seeking vigilantes continued on a short distance to the home of William Donnelly, the second-oldest of the boys, with every intention of cutting his life short as well. It was not William, however, who answered the door that night, but his younger brother John, who responded first to the shouts of "Fire, fire!" coming from outside the home, by opening the front door of William's house to see who was doing all the shouting in the middle of the night.

John never knew what hit him. Shotgun blasts tore through him, sending him back on to the kitchen floor where he died just minutes later. Believing him to be William, whom many of the townspeople feared more than any of the brothers, the killers departed, satisfied that they had taken quite a bite out of the most feared, dreaded and violent family in Canadian history. William, however, was very much alive, along with his wife in a bedroom just off the kitchen.

In the days that followed, all five of the murdered Donnellys would be buried in a single plot, on which stood a tombstone naming each family member killed and their respective dates of birth and death, followed by the word "murdered" after each name. The tombstone stood for many decades, but was slowly chipped away by tourists until a new one was put in place of the old, without the word "murdered." Seemed some of the locals found the word a bit offensive.

***

The story of the Black Donnellys was introduced to me when I was fourteen by my grade-eight homeroom teacher, Mr. Smitt, who was himself regarded as a somewhat questionable character by those on the school board—not by all, but certainly by some. Not only was he responsible for acquainting me with some very colorful Canadian history, he also introduced me to my very first visit to a court room, as a day trip. I sat and watched while one individual after another was led, some shackled, into the box used for holding prisoners. Once there, they listened while the charges against them were read out loud. Others simply stood where they were in the court room while they answered questions regarding their misdemeanor charges. Further to this, Mr. Smitt was also a snooker player and tried to arrange a trip to the local pool hall for an afternoon of playing pool, which was not approved by the principal of my junior high school. (I can't imagine why not.) I was disappointed in the decision, as I was already frequenting the pool rooms on occasion and looked forward to showing my teacher a thing or two about the game of snooker.

The Black Donnellys, a trip to the local court house (I'm still not sure today what the point was), and a proposed trip to the local pool room, all in the space of perhaps six months...*hmm*. Could Mr. Smitt have possibly known the impact he was having on me at that time of my life? No, absolutely not. Did Mr. Smitt influence me in a way that was marginally less than, shall we say, productive as far as normal (whatever that is) healthy behavior and growth is concerned in an average fourteen or fifteen-year-old mind? Yes. Absolutely, unequivocally, yes.

I was already beginning to feel a little restless, trapped perhaps, or just plain "antsy" about my life in general by the time I was in eighth grade. I felt very disenchanted with the whole school thing, and spent much of my time longing for a more meaningful and certainly more exciting life than what the classroom, and the people in it, could offer. I desired "real world" education and simply could not relate to or appreciate much of what I was being taught in school.

What did the depth of the Black Sea possibly have to do with me? Who cares? Algebra? I could count up the points I had run up on the snooker table just fine, thank you. How much moisture did a cloud contain on any given day? Please, will you give me a break! How did any of that stuff apply to me and how was it to be seen as relevant to me, personally? I simply could not reconcile myself to the fact that what I was learning was of any intrinsic value, in any way, shape, or form.

I would stand at my locker and watch the student body fill the halls between classes, some talking, some looking a little rushed or frazzled while making their way to their next class. Others looked a little downcast, alone, with the possibility of a bad day or a bad test written all over their faces. Others were always, and I mean *always* in the same group, just hanging out. These were the cliques.

I couldn't stand the cliques. I'm still not overly fond of cliques today. Often, not always but often, those who exist exclusively in these little groups are in great danger of becoming very gossipy, judgmental, and insensitive to the needs or overall well-being of those around them. Unfortunately, this is a problem within the church as well. "Christian cliques" abound, both inside and outside our sanctuaries. What I saw or more to the point, sensed, in school was a hall full of robots, all programmed to think the same way, do the same things, take the same subjects, play the same sports, and then? Brace yourself. Get up the next morning, and do it all over again. Awesome. Now that's living. Sign me up!

At times I felt like I couldn't breathe. I felt trapped in this lifestyle of mindless, aimless existence, of just going through the motions because everyone else was and it absolutely drove me crazy! I was filled with restless energy. I longed to break free from the status quo and discover life on my own terms, my way, in the real world. I can still see my mother shaking her head at my dissatisfaction of being just another "number in the system" and remarking to me on more than one occasion, "You just want to ride the rails and see the country... bum around the pool halls."

Oh, how true it was. What's wrong with that? I yearned to be out on my own, doing my own thing, which did not include working some menial job from nine to five or spending endless hours studying subjects in school that were of no interest to me. Perhaps I was beginning to exhibit the longings of my heart I had shared with my Sunday school teacher so many years earlier, when she asked me what I wanted to be when I grew up. To her horror and to my parents' horror as well, and much to the amusement of the rest of the kids in the class, I responded, "When I grow up I want to be a bum and drink beer." True story, with God as my witness. As it turned out, I was caught stealing beer out of my neighbor's garage when I was twelve or thirteen.

Organized sports were even becoming a little dull to me. At fourteen, I no longer drew much satisfaction from team activity. I had played both baseball and hockey for six years and was fortunate to be on some championship teams several times in both sports. In hockey, I was voted most valuable player in the playoffs when we took the league championship and in baseball I was the winning pitcher in the softball championships one year. Golf and tennis were also in the mix, but my enthusiasm was waning for those pursuits as well.

I had known the excitement, the rush of victory, and I had experienced the thrill of winning and all of the congratulations, the "way to go" pats on the back for a job well done on the sporting field, but I no longer cared for any of it. At fourteen, I had also experienced, in a limited way, the downtown pool room. I'd tasted the smoky atmosphere, the shady characters, seen money changing hands, heard lewd jokes, seen women coming and going, and they were nothing like the girls I knew in my classes. I wish. The scene in the pool room was electric, another world entirely, and stood in stark contrast to the world I and everyone else I knew lived in at the time.

And then there was Mr. Smitt, my grade-eight homeroom teacher. A man who had his own style, a teacher for certain but a teacher with a different approach, a different demeanor who seemed drawn, in some ways, to those who were willing to live outside the lines. He, like me, was intrigued by those figures who for one reason or another, in one way or another, just did not seem to "fit in." He spent his free time in the court house watching and listening to criminals and enjoyed a game of snooker in the pool room when he wasn't in school teaching. He loved westerns, both movies and books, tales of the lone gunfighters and recommended, highly, the book *The Black Donnellys* to his students.

I connected with Mr. Smitt in a way that I never had with any other teacher. I was both fascinated by him and a little afraid of him at the same time. Without realizing it, he encouraged my desire to live my life on my own terms. His enjoyment of the pool room re-affirmed in my mind that perhaps I was on the right track. Mr. Smitt held a respectable, responsible job with the board of education and saw nothing wrong with playing a little pool downtown, rubbing shoulders with an element of people who were a far cry from those he had coffee with on his breaks at school, and saw nothing wrong with it. If it worked for him, a grownup, a teacher, why not me?

As indirectly as it was, and certainly unintentional, Mr. Smitt was the nod of approval, the thumbs-up, go get 'em confirmation I had been looking for. He was an adult who had many of the same interests as I did and he fed, unknowingly, the darker, more rebellious side of me that had long ago come to the conclusion that grownups could not be trusted and that the "system" offered little if anything of lasting value. He pushed the envelope regarding acceptable or reasonable teaching practices and I admired him for it. If he could do it in his world, I reflected, then I too could do it in mine.

Through Mr. Smitt, I was introduced to law breakers in the court system for the first time and I was fascinated by the experience. In many of the accused, I saw bits and pieces of myself. They were individuals who, like me, were not interested in going with the flow. I realized in that court house that I was not the only anti-establishment figure walking around and I was comforted tremendously by that revelation. I was not just comforted, however, I was also drawn to them. We were kindred spirits.

As if that were not enough, I felt a certain connection to the Black Donnellys, that tragic, violent, misguided and, in some ways, misunderstood family from Lucan, Ontario. The Donnelly boys had grown up on the receiving end of many hurtful taunts and slanders against themselves and their family name. As far as I was concerned, this was not unlike some of the insults I had heard from a few of the adults I had known on the street I grew up on. Not long before discovering The Black Donnellys, I had made up my mind that I would no longer tolerate any teasing, bullying, threats, or insults of any kind, real or imagined. The connection I felt with the plight of the Donnelly boys was not unlike the connection I had experienced with those accused in the court house. I remember well the concern my parents had regarding my reading about the Donnelly family, and rightly so. I was heading down a dark road.

I do not believe it to be a coincidence that within two years of reading about the Black Donnellys, a family widely regarded and written about as the most violent in Canadian history, I would find myself associating with certain members of a family who were regarded and written about in the papers as Canada's most dysfunctional family ever. A family so steeped in criminal behavior, including murder, that it boggles the mind and I was playing pool with one of them regularly. In years to come, my cellmate in Toronto East Detention was considered to be one of the most violent criminals in the Canadian penal system, but more of that in the pages to come. Seems I was batting 1000 in all the wrong ways.

No, it was not a coincidence. Not in a million years. My life, my decisions, my outlook, my attitude, my choice of friends, associates, partners in crime, my behavior, none of it was a coincidence, not happenstance, not "it could have happened to anyone." I had become a product of my own thinking, my own thought process, and I take full responsibility for it. I created, if you will, who I was, who I became. I could have turned my life around on a dime but I simply didn't care to. No doubt, I was not mature enough. Maybe I had grown fond of the enormous chip on my shoulder, the one the size of a football field.

Proverbs 23:7 reads, *"For as a man thinks in his heart, so is he"* (NKJV). I was walking out, indeed living out, the absolute truth of that scripture. To be blunt, my thought life was in the toilet and had been for some time. A negative imagination, which many people do possess, can and will rule an individual's subconscious and, if left unchecked, can manifest itself in a person's life in very alarming, destructive ways.

Where I was concerned, my negative imagination was working overtime, all the time.

In his wonderful book, *The Strangest Secret*, which can be read in an hour or so, author Earl Nightingale compares the mind to farmland. The land, which is very fertile, produces whatever the farmer decides to plant. The land does not care what has been planted or who planted it. Its only concern is producing that which was placed into it in the first place and our mind, our brain, functions in the same way.

What goes in must come out, one way or the other. This is a universal truth and will bare itself out every time, without exception. Our brains quickly process whatever data they're being fed, whether it's positive or negative, and responds in kind; negative input equals negative output. Positive input, on the other hand, will produce positive output and even plays itself out in the type of questions we can ask ourselves. Ask yourself, "Why does this stuff keep happening to me?" and your brain will absolutely send back an answer something like, "Because you're an idiot!" However, ask yourself the more positive question, "How can I prevent this kind of thing from ever happening again?" and your brain will search out and help you to explore more positive answers. What had I been planting into the soil of my mind, my brain? The Black Donnellys? Criminals in the local court room? My brain food diet could have used a major overhaul.

SNAPSHOTS

"There is a way that seems right to a man,
But its end is the way of death."
—Proverbs 14:12 (NKJV)

I had known Joey for several years. In fact, Joey was one of my early snooker teachers. Although we were the same age, Joey had been playing snooker for years and was always giving me pointers when I began taking the game seriously. He was a fair player for his age and at the time was a considerably better player than I was. Joey was also an avid poker player and had quite a hand in dealing drugs in and around school, as well as downtown from time to time.

I first met Joey when I was about fifteen and still working part-time at a convenience store a block or so from my house. He would drop by the store several times a week to buy smokes and shoot the breeze a little before making his way to the pool room. I was just beginning my own love affair with snooker and the whole pool hall scene in general, and would envy Joey for being able to go downtown first thing Saturday morning and spend the entire day shooting pool while I worked behind the counter of a Mac's Milk.

I didn't mind the job and my boss was a great guy, but I just wanted to play snooker, which the part-time job provided the money to do. Knowing that Joey was out there where all the action was drove me crazy. At fifteen and sixteen, I had an insatiable appetite for "action" in the pool room, which nothing else could satisfy, and I mean *nothing* else. Joey appeared to have the kind of freedom to come and go as he pleased, a kind of freedom I longed for as well. He lived about five minutes from my house, which afforded us the opportunity to visit each other occasionally. On one such visit to his house, Joey brought me into his bedroom and removed a shoe box from his closet. In it was a roll of bills larger than I had ever seen and enough vials of oil to get half of the neighborhood high.

At sixteen, we had both quit school, with Joey packing it in first. I remember as if it were yesterday bumping into him early one school day morning and finding out he had quit. I was close to throwing in the towel myself, and realizing that Joey had done just that only heightened my desire to walk away from school once and for all. Within two weeks of that day I, too, had dropped out. My distaste for the "system" knew no limits. It had simply not worked for me at all, or rather I had not worked for it, but no matter. I was free from the restraints of mediocrity in the classroom and none too soon.

Over the next couple of years or so, Joey and I would play pool often but hung out together very little outside the pool room. He had his own circle of friends while I had mine. We crossed paths occasionally, but would not have been considered good buddies under any circumstances. Joey was dealing a lot of drugs once he had quit school and I was pulling nickel-and-dime scores around town. He had his crowd, a crowd who also sold and used drugs daily, and I had my crowd, criminals of a different sort.

I'm not sure where or when the animosity between us began, but it was very real by the time we were seventeen. We knew all of the same people and did associate in the same circle at times, but tension existed for seemingly unknown reasons, a certain amount of ill will perhaps, which on more than one occasion had left a bad taste in my mouth.

Joey wasn't a bad guy, and while I was certainly in no position to judge anyone else's behavior, I distinctly remember coming to the conclusion one day in the pool hall that I had had enough of his mouth. He was quick to fire biting remarks at anyone, for any reason, as we all were from time to time, but Joey's sarcasm seemed to be particularly potent when thrown in my direction. His specialty was trying to belittle me in some way, verbally, in front of others. Had it been one to one I may have dealt with it differently, but his doing so in front of the guys I hung out with, the guys I played snooker with, well that was crossing the line.

I made up my mind that he needed to be dealt with and the sooner the better. One evening, he remarked to a few of us playing pool that he was heading home. It was early, perhaps eight o'clock, and I commented to Joey casually that it wasn't like him to pack it in for the night so early. He just shrugged and off he went, not sensing that there was anything different between us, which he had no reason to. Until that night, everything was business as usual except that I had been waiting for the opportunity to administer a little payback and this was the night.

Within a half hour of Joey leaving the pool room, I informed two or three others that I'd had more than enough of his mouth and that it was high time to punch his lights out. Further, I told my pals I would take this fight to his own home, in front of his parents if need be, and asked them to come along if they weren't doing anything, which they eagerly did. I didn't have to ask them twice. I did not want them there to have my back. I wanted them there to add to Joey's humiliation: being beaten up in front of several of the guys he knew.

When we arrived at Joey's house, my buddies stayed back on the sidewalk while I approached the front door and knocked. It was not quite nine o'clock at night and I assumed everyone was still up. I had met Joey's parents several times—nice people. I heard footsteps inside and when the door opened there stood Joey, dressed as he had been less than an hour ago in the pool room. I could hear the TV but didn't know if his parents were around or not, nor did I really care.

I'm sure I was the last person Joey expected to see on his front porch that evening, or wanted to see for that matter. Seeing me standing at his front door would not have been a pleasant surprise for him, but it was shaping up to be a perfect evening for me. There he was, alone, away from his friends, his support group, the ones who gave him courage when he felt compelled to take a few verbal shots at me. Now it was just the two of us and he was anything but arrogant, or confident.

When he asked me what I wanted, I didn't answer right away but just considered him quietly for a few seconds and then responded, calmly, in a matter-of-fact tone that I was there to beat the living daylights out of him. I went on to say that this was going to happen one way or the other, even if it meant coming into his house to do the job, should he decide to not come outside. I asked him why it was he thought he could get away with talking down to me in front of everyone in the pool room. I told him he had crossed the line many times, but that I had let it go because we had known each other a few years, had some of the same friends, and we were neighbors. I went on to say none of that mattered any more, however, and that he might as well come outside and just deal with it.

Joey had been growing increasingly uncomfortable with my every word. He understood, fully, that I was not bluffing and that I really would come into his own home to take care of business if need be. That, I think, is what unnerved him more than the pending confrontation itself. Joey had been in a few scraps himself. He was no stranger to mixing it up a bit, but no one had ever come to his home, not caring whether his parents were there or not, to settle a score. Misunderstandings, arguments, and fights definitely occurred downtown on occasion, but it stayed downtown. It never followed someone to their home, right to their front door.

Staring at the floor for a moment, listening to me, Joey nodded his head a couple of times and then quietly motioned for me to go outside. It wasn't until we were outside and walking down his driveway that he spotted my friends standing on the sidewalk, down a couple of houses from his. He stopped, recognizing all of them and, in a heartbeat, feeling the embarrassment and perhaps shame of the situation. When he asked me why I had brought them, I reminded him of all the times that he had gone at me, verbally, in front of people with every intention of embarrassing me. What goes around comes around, right?

Resigning himself to the situation and the inevitable outcome, he said something I'll never forget. He asked me to promise not to punch him in the face. He told me to go ahead and do whatever it was that I was going to do, but wanted his face left alone. I said sure, whatever, and then let him have it with a hard right square in the face. Joey went down backwards and, hitting the ground, immediately curled up in a fetal position, protecting himself, waiting for the beating, a beating that never came.

I stood looking down at him, a big man with a lot of smart remarks in the pool room in front of his friends, now curled up in a ball at my feet. I was furious with him for not standing up and fighting and I loathed him, every ounce of him, for all of the snide, sarcastic remarks he had made at my expense. I was also enraged because, lying there curled up on the ground, he reminded me of myself years ago when I was on the receiving end of bullying at school. Finally, I was angry at myself for the type of person I was becoming, though no one would ever know of that inner struggle.

I never laid another hand on Joey that night or any other night, although we often found ourselves hanging out among the same circle of people. Once back on his feet, he made his way slowly towards his house while I rejoined my friends on the sidewalk. It had not been the altercation I was expecting, but I was still satisfied that Joey had been taught a lesson in humility, though the damage was far more psychological than physical.

He never, ever again spoke out against me in any way. Our acquaintance with each other, if it could be called that, was never quite the same, but no matter. It had to be done as far as I was concerned, and that was that. I've often asked myself over the years, however, who was the worse for wear that night, Joey or me? Joey, because he was humiliated publicly, or myself because I could see in my mind that picture of him lying on the ground, curled up in a ball, waiting for a beating to be administered by yours truly? That "snapshot" would come to haunt me years later and continue to do so for a very long time. It would anger me because I could not deal with how it made me feel about myself. At the time it was all about pride, power, and control, but it came with a heavy price down the road; simply living with it was a heavy.

It's quite a paradox, really. The more I lashed out, one way or another, at those around me, at society in general, at the "system" I had failed in so miserably, the more I just hurt myself. Whoever had coined the term, "fool for punishment" must have been looking straight at me for a little inspiration. A little piece of me died every time the demons inside reared their ugly rage, which ultimately meant I had a lot of dying to do before I would be fully spent.

***

Charley and I were long overdue for a wakeup call. We were both living, I believe, with a false sense of security. We had broken the law so many times while suffering no repercussions at all, none, not ever, that our lifestyles, which were as crooked as a dog's hind leg, seemed altogether normal for both of us. While we did do an honest day's work here and there, we predominantly made our way by indulging in a variety of nefarious scams and schemes which would put a few bucks in our pockets for a day, two days, a week maybe, but no more.

The on-again, off-again life of a thief I was living was not at all unlike the on-again, off-again life of a gambling pool player I had been living as well. Both persons, the thief and the pool hustler, worked very well for me and I was able to slip into either role at a moment's notice. I was well-suited to both roles, or personas, with little thought of consequence or danger. Anything and everything went, whatever suited my mood at any given time. I absolutely made money, regularly, playing pool, but just as regularly looked for an easy buck by engaging myself in less-than-honest activities.

All was fair on either the street or in the pool room, as far as I was concerned. The adage, "you can't cheat an honest man," was the gospel truth in my book. I rationalized or justified that every score, every hustle, every scam, and everyone taken was against someone who would "take" me, one way or the other, in the blink of an eye. I remember my mom asking me at one point, and rightly so, if I had any morals or principles at all. I was about sixteen at the time and I responded that I didn't even understand what those words meant. (I love my mom dearly today, and deeply regret being responsible for most of the grey hair on her head. She saved my life, literally, but more of that in another chapter.) Even if I had understood the meaning of the words, I doubt their meaning would have had much, if any, impact on me back then. What did I care? Very little for the most part.

The wakeup call I had long managed to evade was just around the corner, waiting for me shortly after turning seventeen. How close had I come to being busted up to that point? I was, in fact, pulled in and questioned by the police following a botched bowling alley robbery when I was sixteen that resulted in one of the group going away for about a year. While all of us were caught and rounded up the following day, the one sent away had quite an extensive record and took the fall for everyone. There were five of us involved, but only one did time. I and three others walked due to lack of evidence, though I was held and grilled over and over for about five hours at the police station.

I was seen frequently with known criminals by the cops who regularly walked the beat downtown, but they never had anything or enough on me to bust me. I knew everyone in the downtown core, but at the same time I wasn't really tight with anyone. It was safer that way, as the fewer people I dealt with directly, the less chance there was of someone "leaking" something to the wrong person, which could have resulted in my getting pinched.

One of the reasons I never indulged in the drug trade was that there were just too many people involved in order to score big. There's the supplier, the dealer, and the buyer, not to mention all of the people the buyer is getting high with, most of whom would point the finger at their supplier in a heartbeat if it meant saving their own necks if they were busted. Too many people and far too much paranoia for my liking. Granted, the money to be made in the drug business was and always will be astronomically high, but I could just never bring myself to trusting so many people to have my back. (One individual I came to know quite well and kept in touch with on and off until his passing in 2011 was busted for operating a forty-million dollar crystal meth lab.)

Charley and I were together one day in the pool room and were, as usual, broke. Getting a job was simply out of the question, which left us two choices. We could hang around the pool hall and get lucky with an easy game of snooker against someone who had no chance of winning (very important when one had no money to play with in the first place), which did happen on occasion, or we could pull off a score somewhere.

We opted for the latter, and staring at us directly across the street from the pool hall was a Bible store. It had, as far as we were concerned, "easy take," written all over it. What could be easier than robbing a Bible store? The owners would never suspect in a million years that a couple of young guys would walk into their store, in broad daylight, and fleece them for their money. Although the store was in the heart of downtown crime central, it would have been considered safe, as it were, from the "element" of characters operating their various businesses just an arm's throw away due to the very nature of their business. What could they possibly have to offer other than Bibles and some kindly, God-centered wisdom for those who wandered into their store?

Easy money, that's what, and it only took a moment for Charlie and I to make up our minds on this score. We walked across the street and, upon entering, saw that we were the only people inside other than the lady behind the counter. She was up in her years, sixty at least, and appeared to be the only one working at the time. I assumed the role I had played out so many times on other jobs and immediately began talking to the woman behind the counter. I explained to her that I was shopping for a Bible and did not really know where to start. She was more than happy to comply and began showing me an assortment of Bibles on the shelves, explaining what each one had to offer while I listened attentively to everything she had to say. The longer she took with her answers the better, as it gave Charley all the time he needed in the office at the back of the store.

At one point in our discussion, it dawned on that kind, unsuspecting lady that I had not entered her store alone, and she set off to find Charley. Actually, before leaving me she commented out loud that she had not seen my friend since we had come in and wondered what had happened to him. As she made her way to the back of the store towards her office, I did everything in my power, except shout out to Charley to clear out, to signal to him in some way to get out of the office immediately. The lady's back was to me as I jumped up and down, waving my arms in Charlie's direction hoping he would see me before she caught him in her office.

It didn't work. Charlie didn't see me. He was too busy looking for a cash box or money bag and did get caught, red-handed, by our unsuspecting Bible store employee, who turned out to be the owner of the store. Seeing her standing in the doorway of the office was my cue to get out, which I did, calmly and quietly. A second or two later, however, Charlie opened the door, frantic, and hit the sidewalk running, shouting at me to do the same.

Not knowing what had happened or why we were running, I followed my partner down the street and over several blocks until we found ourselves behind an office building a good two or three-minute run from the Bible store. Out of breath and a little confused, I asked Charlie what had happened. He looked upset, concerned in a way that was not typical of him. Whether a job went well or not had never really mattered in the past. A score was a score, period, and if it didn't work out, oh well, there was always tomorrow.

This time was different. Charlie explained to me that he hadn't found anything in the office, which I assured him was okay. No problem. That's the way it went sometimes, no big deal. No, Charlie said, it wasn't okay. He told me that when he had rushed out of the office, he had accidentally bumped into the sixty-something-year-old lady in his haste to leave and possibly had knocked her over. Charlie was seriously distraught. None of our little scores had ever involved anything physical, much less what would be considered assault on a senior citizen, and a female senior citizen at that.

The words were barely out of his mouth when I, too, began to feel a little sick to my stomach. I stood there trying to get my breathing under control due to running away from the scene, and trying to get my imagination under control at the same time. In my mind I saw that nice, sweet old lady lying on the floor of her store, hurt, confused, and alone. I was dying inside and so was Charlie. I asked him over and over if he had hurt her and he responded that he just didn't know; it had all happened so fast. We found out soon enough.

Within a minute or two of ducking behind the office building, a uniformed police officer came around the corner, as out of breath as we had been just moments before. He had us cold. He was out of breath but was just a few feet away, and we were in no mood to initiate another foot chase. The picture I had in my head of the old lady lying on the floor had completely taken the wind out of my sails and Charlie's as well. We were caught, we were guilty, we knew it, and in this case, deserved whatever the law or the storeowner decided to dish out.

Soon after the police officer apprehended us, a squad car pulled up and took us back to the Bible store where we were joined by another cop who pulled up in front of the store as well. Our arresting officer went inside to talk to the owner while we waited in the back seat, handcuffed and watched by the second officer. After what seemed like forever, the arresting officer walked out of the Bible store, alone, and returned to his car where Charlie and I had been waiting.

We were very fortunate indeed, the cop said after getting behind the wheel of the cop car. The lady was not interested in pressing any charges. She had explained to the officer that no harm had been done, nothing had been taken after all, and as far as being shoved a little, well, it was an accident. We weren't bad kids, we were just getting into a little mischief the lady had said, and she was concerned about our future. No, laying charges was out of the question. We had learned our lesson. What good could come of our going to jail?

While we were off the hook as far as being charged was concerned, the police assured both Charlie and me that they would be taking us home and having a word with our parents about our botched robbery and how fortunate we were to have had charges dropped. I would rather have gone to jail, I think, than face my parents. I felt like crawling under a rock. We had crossed the line. I had little doubt as to how my folks would take it. The only uncertainty remaining was my future at home.

To make matters even worse, I found out that lady's husband was almost blind. The guilt and shame I felt was all-consuming. I would have felt so much better if I had been charged and at the very least been fined or perhaps made to do some community service hours—something, anything, except walking away from this whole episode hearing, over and over again in my head, "They're not bad boys." Not bad boys? Are you kidding me? I was a creep. A lowlife. How could she not only forgive me but think I wasn't a bad guy as well?

My conscience was seared beyond repair and would remain so for a long, long time. If only she had thrown the book at me and let me pay my debt to society, I would have felt so much better about myself. If anyone didn't deserve forgiveness, it was this author. The guilt I felt turned to anger (as if I needed any more of that) at myself, as time went by. Self-loathing was at an all-time high in the days and weeks that followed, and I absolutely had no idea how to handle it or who to turn to. Who would someone like me talk to? I internalized it, as I had done with just about everything else up to that point, and simply continued along the same path.

Any lessons learned in all of this? No. None. At least not in a productive, learn by one's past mistakes kind of way. I did learn that lady luck was on my side. I learned that I could control the dimmer switch of my conscience. I learned that I functioned better on the street when the light was turned off completely. I learned that as long as I didn't spend too much time staring back at the reflection I saw in the mirror, I was just fine. I learned that there was no percentage in reflecting on one's choices, one's lifestyle, one's character.

Who I was, who I was becoming, had long ago been determined and I was just walking it out. I justified my actions over time with a simple shrug of the shoulders. This was how guys like me lived. I was an anti-establishment figure, a social reject. Individuals like me were not interested in living our lives between the lines. The world in general, I concluded, was not at all interested in having someone like me, a non-conformist, going with the flow, with them, beside them. I didn't get along with the world and the world didn't get along with me. The Bible store? That kind, forgiving, sweet old church lady behind the counter? Another "snap shot." Another condemning, accusing, unflattering, and wholly unforgiving picture to be developed, hung, clipped to a line and dried in my own private little dark room, the one nobody knew about, the one my partners in crime would tease me about if they knew it existed.

That line in the dark room of my mind would slowly fill up with other pictures in years to come. Pictures of people I had ripped off, hurt, hustled, misused, abused, or let down one way or another. Many pictures. Much regret. No one, *absolutely no one*, ever knew about my pictures. (I wonder if you who are reading this have a dark room of your own where unflattering pictures of your past are kept.) No one ever knew about my pictures because I never let anyone get that close to me. My own little dark room...taking me down memory lane—or in my case, loser's lane—over and over and over again.

HEY, LET'S JUST ROB A BANK

"Every way of man is right in his own eyes..."
Proverbs 21:2 (ESV)

The crowd in the pool room was typically scarce on Sunday evenings, and this one was no exception. I didn't find myself in this particular pool hall very often. The calibre of play was considerably less than the one I regarded as my home away from home, and the overall atmosphere was not conducive, in my estimation, to the serious snooker player. There was seldom any serious action on the tables, regardless of what time or day of the week it was. It just appeared to be more of a hangout than anything else.

Boredom had brought Charlie and me up to this second-floor, never much happening, it's better than nothing pool hall hoping to find something or someone to add a little juice to our eventless Sunday evening. We set the snooker balls up on a table in the back and started banging them around, neither of us putting much effort or concentration into our game. Perhaps, we thought, one or two of the regulars would wander in and join us for a game of something—follow, poker pool, bottle pool, 101, golf, whatever, it didn't matter to either of us. Anything was better than nothing.

After an hour or so of hitting the balls without much concentration, we both gave up for the night. With this room as well as our regular pool hall empty, we decided to hang up our cues and head home. I began packing up the balls while Charlie headed for the bathroom, telling me that he'd meet me at the counter to split the table time. My back was to him when he left in the general direction of the can, and I was surprised to see him re-join me just seconds later at the table.

Not sure what was going on but seeing a look on Charlie's face that I had seen so many times, I knew something was up. Charlie began speaking to me quietly, his back to the counter and the proprietor, as mine was, and shared with me what had caught his attention on the way to the bathroom. It was the fire escape at the side of the pool room, the one leading down to the sidewalk below. Not only had the fire escape caught his attention, but the window as well. A window either Charlie or I could easily fit through that led directly to the landing at the top of the fire escape.

If we chose to, we could be out the window, down the fire escape and on the sidewalk in seconds, rather than taking the stairs back down to street level. It was that convenient or, perhaps, accessible. If we could be out the window and down the fire escape in seconds, then we could also be up the fire escape and in the window in seconds as well.

Our quiet, boring Sunday night had just shifted gears. While there was no action on the tables, there might just be a little action in the pool room later on that night. Once the snooker balls were back on their tray and ready to be brought back to the counter, Charlie once again made his way to the bathroom and past the window, the locked window leading out to the fire escape. I paid for the table and bought a can of pop while Charlie lingered at the window, which was just out of site from the proprietor, and unfastened the lock, giving us an easy entry later on that night.

The second-floor pool room closed about 10:30 p.m., while our regular pool hall closed about midnight. We made our way back to our regular pool room, just around the corner and about a block away, to kill a little time before returning to our "about to be hit" billiard room. We felt good, confident of an easy take, a "candy from a baby" score which we hoped would line our pockets with a little cash. It would go down late on a quiet Sunday evening with no one around, giving us all the time in the world to fleece the place for anything our hearts desired. There were no alarms to be concerned with as far as we knew, and with the streets practically deserted, my job of keeping six would be a breeze as well.

Charlie and I made our way back to the fire escape around midnight. We were confident that everyone was long gone for the night. The fire escape ladder stopped ten feet or so above sidewalk level, which presented little trouble for us. We were both just over six feet in height, which gave Charlie an easy reach with me boosting him up a little. I crouched, interlocking my fingers while Charlie placed one foot into my cupped hands. Counting one, two, three, up he went, easily grabbing the bottom rung of the ladder and began pulling himself up, with me pushing and steadying his foot in my hands. In a moment Charlie was on the ladder and making his way up to the landing and an easy entrance through the unlocked window and into the pool room.

Mastermind criminals we were not. Looking back, I can only shake my head and, in giving myself an honest appraisal, have no choice but to come to the conclusion that I was just about as sharp as a bag of hammers. Why we thought that the window would be left unlocked for us is beyond me. No doubt, checking the window to make sure that it was secure before locking up for the night was something whoever was in charge of the pool room did every night before leaving. I'm confident that checking the window, which anyone with an ounce of intelligence would do, was the *first* thing secured every single evening, without exception, by everyone who ever worked in that pool room. They no doubt thought that no one would ever be stupid enough to climb the fire escape outside and try to enter through the window after they were closed, thinking that the window had been left open.

Maybe most guys were smart enough to know better, but we weren't most guys. Charlie and I really were dumb enough to think we were just going to walk right on in, through an open window at twelve o'clock at night and help ourselves to whatever we liked. Maybe the owner even put a fresh pot of coffee on for us to keep us awake while we robbed him! He probably just left all the money on the counter, stacked up for us and sorted in appropriate denominations to make counting easier. What would be the point in locking it all away in a safe? We were mastermind criminals and would just crack the safe in seconds anyway.

Within seconds of climbing up the ladder and reaching the landing, Charlie informed me about the locked window. The only thing in our favor was the deserted street. There wasn't a car or pedestrian in sight, which gave us ample time to think of plan B, should we decide to proceed. I suggested we call it a night, but Charlie was determined to see this thing through. He wanted something to break the glass with and, unconcerned with the possible noise, I crossed the street to find a rock.

The train station was a thirty-second walk from where Charley sat on the landing. It was dark and deserted at that time of night, and finding a stone suitable for breaking glass was easy enough. Just as I was making my way around the back of the station and onto the tracks, a cop car came around the corner and made its way down the street, driving below and right by Charlie who was lying down as flat as he could on the landing. With my "professional glass cutting kit" in hand, I walked back across the street and tossed the rock up to Charlie.

Removing his jacket in order to muffle the noise and to protect his hand from flying glass, Charlie smashed the jacket-enclosed rock into the glass and quickly reached in, unlatched the window and in he went, out of sight. Not knowing how long he would be, I lit a cigarette and walked slowly down the street, pausing here and there to look in store windows, scanning the street and intersections for any approaching cars or late-night strollers on the sidewalk. All was quiet, except for us.

Charlie stuck his head out of the pool room in a moment or two to see if the coast was clear, which I assured him it was, and quickly made his way back down the fire escape to the sidewalk beside me. Not only did he not have any money, he said, but he had cut his hand on some of the glass while making his way in. It was now about twelve-thirty at night, and there we were, hanging around downtown, two seventeen-year-old guys, one with blood dripping down his arm, standing below a fire escape covered in broken glass and drops of blood from Charlie's cut.

Down but not out from our botched robbery, we mutually decided that the night was young and held all the possibilities of another, more fruitful robbery elsewhere. We were not sure at that point just what that might be, but we were determined and began walking towards an all-night sub and coffee shop a few blocks away. We hadn't gone more than a block, however, when a cop car pulled up alongside us and one of the cops in the car asked us what we were up to. Each was eyeing us with a certain amount of suspicion, as they certainly should have been. (I eyed myself with a certain amount of suspicion regularly.)

We explained that we had just left the pool hall for the night, our regular pool hall that stayed open until midnight or so, and were heading to the sub shop for a bite to eat before going home. Our story was plausible enough and seemed to satisfy the officers, except for one thing. While explaining to the officers that we were on our way to the sub and coffee shop, Charlie had approached the cop car and, leaning on it a little, left some blood from his cut hand on the rear door handle! They didn't see it but we did and knew it would be discovered sooner or later. Charlie had simply wanted to appear as nonchalant as possible while talking to them, but got a little carried away with the act. What a night.

This second close call, the first one being when the other cop car had driven by us just prior to breaking the window, convinced us that it just wasn't our night and we decided to call it quits for the evening. We continued on, however, to the sub shop in case we were being followed or were checked out in a few minutes by the same cops to see if we really were there. Once inside we split a sub and had a couple of drinks, and Charley spent a bit of time in the bathroom cleaning his cut, which was a fair-sized gash, and wrapped it in some paper towel.

We parted company that night, after finishing our late-night snack, as we had on so many other evenings. We had talked about our day in the pool room, different sessions we'd played, how well we had or hadn't played, how much money we had or hadn't made, how our snooker game was improving, and how tomorrow was another day. Maybe we'd play some solid snooker and make some decent money.

We gave little or no thought to the events just prior to our meal in the sub shop. It was of no consequence one way or another. Pulling scores may or may not have been part of our day, and we gave it no more consideration than waking up every day, getting dressed, and heading to the pool hall for another day of "action" at the tables. Maybe our attention would be focused solely on playing and improving our snooker skills, which were considerable at that time for our age. Charlie and I could both build breaks of fifty points and more, regularly.

Maybe, however, we'd indulge in a little criminal activity if it appeared promising. Maybe we'd wander over to the strip club for a beer or two and play some bar pool for a change. Maybe we'd smoke a joint or two if it was made available, and, on occasion, maybe one of us would get into a scrap with someone who was annoying us for one reason or another, sometimes fighting in the alley beside the pool room and once, for me, under a bridge, secluded, not far from the pool hall. I would also sleep under the same bridge from time to time when I was sixteen. It beat following the rules at home, rules like getting a job, respecting others, helping around the house a bit—really crazy, unreasonable rules like that.

The evening of the botched robbery did indeed end like so many other evenings for Charlie and me, with each of us going our separate ways, but the next day did not begin, in the pool room at least, as so many other days had. I had only been downtown about an hour or so, playing pool, when I was approached by two uniformed cops who asked me to join them outside for a little chat. I was playing a game of follow with three other guys and after excusing myself, followed the policemen outside and into their squad car parked a short distance from the pool hall.

Once inside their car, the cops immediately informed me that they had picked up and charged Charlie with the attempted robbery of a pool room just around the corner from the one I was playing in. It was attempted robbery only in the sense that nothing was actually stolen. Charlie was also charged with break-and-enter, forcible entry causing damages over such and such amount, etc. When I asked what any of it had to do with me, the cops both responded, in perfect, matter of fact tones that they knew with certainty that I had been with Charlie the previous evening at the time of the break-in.

I kept my best poker face possible and insisted I had no idea what they were talking about. I acknowledged my friendship with Charlie and didn't deny our being seen around town together, but flatly denied having anything to do with some "pool hall break-in." The cops went on to say I had been positively identified as having been seen with Charlie the night before by the cops who had stopped us on our way to the sub shop. They had noticed Charlie's cut hand and did see the blood on the door handle at some point on their shift. When the call had come in about the break-in that morning, it wasn't long before Charlie had been fingered by the pool room owner who knew we had unlocked the window before leaving the night before and by the cops who had stopped us to have a chat. The investigating officers had also seen the blood, Charlie's blood, all over the broken glass at the top of the fire escape.

All was not lost, however, at least as far as I was concerned. Charlie had taken the rap for both of us. He insisted that he alone had perpetrated the break-in. He agreed that we were together before and after the break-in, but that it was he alone who had done the job. Charlie told the cops I had wanted nothing to do with it and that I was not involved in any way with the actual break-in. Charlie was a stand-up guy, solid, top to bottom, inside and out. He took the fall for both of us and went away for several months to do the time for a job we had both been involved in. The adage, "there's honor among thieves," never held more truth than in that instance. We had known each other since grade school, had played baseball together, and now he was doing time for of both of us.

No one had actually seen me with Charlie the night before when he was actually breaking into the pool room. Therefore, and for no other reason, I was not charged with the robbery attempt. The police knew I was a part of it but couldn't prove anything. I was free to go. Before I got out of the cop car that morning, the two officers spoke with me about my life and my future, for several moments.

With almost paternal concern, they encouraged me to think hard about the choices I was making, the people I was hanging around, and where it would all end up one day. They reminded me that others I had been seen with regularly were now in jail, and that jail time was inevitable for me as well if I didn't make some serious changes. Further, they informed me that I was well-known to the police, although I had never been officially charged with a single crime up to that point, and that it was only a matter of time before I would be spending my days behind bars with the others I hung around who had been busted for one thing or another.

All of this was shared with me for my own good. They let me go with a final caution to be careful. I thanked them and slowly walked back to the pool room. I knew they had my best interests in mind when warning me about my future. They had not been in any way threatening, but had gone above and beyond their duty to try and talk some sense into this hard-headed and hard-hearted writer. I thought about Charlie sitting in a jail cell, and the number of times I had been so close, so unbelievably close to getting pinched, or beaten up, badly, only to be spared somehow, in some way, by some last-second turn of events that spared me from a very unpleasant experience.

These and a multitude of other thoughts and concerns were swirling around in my head when I walked back into the pool hall and made my way towards the table where I had been playing follow. I knew everything the cops had said to me was true. I knew with absolute certainty that sooner or later my number would come up. I had just been lucky, I thought, incredibly lucky, time and time again. The guys at the table asked me if everything was alright. I nodded, answering that everything was okay. I grabbed my cue and went back to my game, thinking of Charlie, wondering how he was doing. As for me being alright, well, maybe at that precise moment I was, but down the road? I should have listened to those cops and taken their advice to heart. I should have listened.

***

I spent the latter half of 1978 and the first four months or so of 1979 free of any criminal behavior. I turned nineteen in January 1979, and had been living in the Colonial Hotel in Calgary for the past six months. I worked two days a week for an auctioneer, which guaranteed my rent ($27.50 a week), smokes, and food. I spent the other five days a week playing and watching snooker. When I played for money, I picked my games carefully, always gauging and calculating my opponent with great caution, looking for a potential steady mark while avoiding being taken for money myself.

It was an ideal situation for me, offering me the best of both worlds. The money I earned working two days a week removed any pressure I may have felt to have regular, solid paydays hustling pool to meet my basic living expenses. My paychecks left me enough money to get into a comfortable ten- or twenty-dollar game of snooker. If I had a bad week on the tables, no matter, every week was pay week from the auctioneer. I was never without money for long, and always had a roof over my head.

Why I began to feel a little restless at that point in my life, I'll never know. I was happy, perhaps the happiest I had been since living on my own. I lived a carefree, easy come, easy go, pressure-free lifestyle that was, in all aspects, custom-tailored for me. I worked just enough to pay my rent and spent the rest of my time doing what I loved more than anything in the world, playing snooker. Snooker fascinated, intrigued, and captivated my attention twenty-four/seven. If I wasn't playing the game I was studying it, as well as other, more skillful players I could learn from.

Living my life without breaking the law was a pleasant and refreshing change as well. Except for three days in jail for theft shortly after I turned eighteen, I had stayed out of trouble with the police in Calgary for the past year. I had indulged in a little shoplifting here and there, just some groceries, maybe a few items of clothing from time to time, but for the most part and certainly for the past six months at least, my life in Calgary had been lived on the straight and narrow.

Not long into my nineteenth year, however, I decided to head further west, to Vancouver for several weeks, with the possibility of crossing the U.S. border and continuing on to California for an undetermined length of time. The thought of hitchhiking my way from Calgary to Vancouver thrilled me. It offered everything I enjoyed in life: adventure, uncertainty, freedom, and dozens of pool rooms and bar rooms I had never played in. Maybe, I thought, I could make a buck or two along the way, all while experiencing some breathtaking country along some of Canada's most scenic highways.

Once the idea of a little travel had birthed in my mind, it was only a matter of a couple of weeks before I was ready to hit the road. My job was only part-time and I could easily be replaced. My room at the Colonial was rented on a weekly basis. I was free to walk away at any time without hassle. I had basically been living out of a duffle bag, which suited me fine, for the past eighteen months or so, which also made for an easy departure. I owed nothing and owned nothing, save for the clothes on my back. I didn't even own my own pool cue at the time. I had found a one-piece house cue months earlier that I really liked and had been renting it with my own cue locker for some time. Paying up my cue rent and returning the lock box key wrapped up my business in Calgary.

Hitchhiking was still an acceptable and inexpensive means of transportation in the seventies and eighties. I had little trouble hitching a ride, and there were times that the beauty of western Canada was such that I couldn't have cared less whether I was picked up or not. I had nothing but time and literally was not looking past the next bend in the road. The drivers who did pick me up were, without exception, decent people who not only provided me with free transportation but on a few occasions bought me a meal or coffee and in one instance even put a few bucks in my hand when we parted company.

While thumbing my way to the west coast, I stayed in a hostel one night and rented a motel room on the other. When I did arrive in Vancouver on the third day away from Calgary, I was only about twenty dollars short of what I had started out with after three days of travel, meals, lodging, smokes, etc. Not bad. I remember thinking that perhaps I would just stay on the road for a while, maybe hitchhike across Canada from coast to coast. My needs were as simple as always. A bed to sleep in—any bed, anywhere—and a meal in my stomach. As I've mentioned, I saw little if any evidence that my meagre, almost primitive lifestyle contributed in any way to my being any more or any less content than anyone else.

I had been in Vancouver about two weeks, staying at the Young Christian Men's Hostel, when I considered crossing the border into

Seattle and then on to California. I wasn't sure how it would go at the border and didn't really care one way or the other. Vancouver is a beautiful city and I was enjoying every day. I browsed the used book stores and pawn shops, read, and played pool. Every day was mine, around the clock. I even received food vouchers and meal certificates twice a week at the hostel, which allowed me to eat out at several low-key restaurants in the vicinity of the hostel for free. It was greasy bacon and eggs almost every morning for breakfast and a burger for supper, on the house, several nights a week.

As it turned out, I needn't have been concerned about the border. I didn't quite make it that far. On the day I had planned to continue thumbing my way into the states, I got no closer than perhaps twenty-five miles of the U.S. border when I noticed signs along the highway everywhere that said hitchhiking was strictly prohibited. No one was picking me up, and after an hour or so I called it quits and made my way back to the hostel to register once again for a bed and to take stock of my situation.

I still had about one hundred bucks in my pocket, which wasn't much less than when I'd left Calgary. A couple of guys in the hostel informed me that it was easy to hit up welfare for a Greyhound bus ticket and some start-up cash, in the form of a voucher that could be cashed at any bank (the system was so easy thirty five years ago), if a job search form was filled out by prospective employers to prove an attempt had been made to find work. It sounded good, but I wasn't quite ready to leave Vancouver. I wanted to stay for another week or so before making my way back to Calgary, and besides, I had noticed a flyer for an eight-ball tournament in the window of one of the drop-in centers not too far from the hostel. It was only two bucks to enter, with first prize being about two thirds of the pot, which would come to about thirty bucks. The tournament was a couple of days away and I figured I had a reasonable chance at some easy money.

The centre holding the tournament was clean, well-lit, and catered to what appeared to be many regulars. Most knew each other by name. After paying my two-dollar entrance fee, I grabbed a coffee and joined the group of participants waiting for the tournament to begin. The atmosphere was loose and non-threatening. I only mention this because in a drop-in centre the behavior of the guests can be varied to the extreme and things can become tense in a heartbeat, but all seemed low-key and laid back. It was only about noon when the matches began, which also meant that everyone involved was sober.

There were only about twenty of us playing on two bar tables, which meant the tournament wouldn't go on very long. A game of eight-ball on a bar table can be over in a minute or two and with two tables going, the elimination rounds leading up to the money matches would move very quickly. I did want the cash for first or second place, no doubt, but I was also having a good time with those guys. None of them posed any real threat as far as beating me was concerned. It was just a fun afternoon at the tables.

I continued drinking coffee and chatting it up with everyone and quickly found myself in the final. I won the match three to one without much trouble and, just as importantly, without ticking anyone off. After all was said and done, I was up about twenty five bucks at the end of the day. Not bad. I had all the free coffee I could drink, a few sandwiches provided by the volunteers, a fresh pack of smokes in my shirt pocket, a few extra bucks in my pants pocket, and a free, one-way bus ticket to Calgary waiting for me at the welfare office as soon as I filled out a job search form. Life was good.

***

I've never fully understood the conscious, sober decision I made to rob a bank. All these years later, thirty-three years at the time of this writing, it remains something of a mystery to me. I was not in a state of desperation, nor was I disenchanted in any way with my life or lifestyle. I was confident in who I was, in what I was, and thoroughly enjoyed the uncertainty of the day-to-day existence I typically experienced in that type of roller-coaster, you never knew what tomorrow might bring, lifestyle.

The trip to Vancouver had gone well. It was everything I'd hoped for. I saw a little more of Canada, met many fun and interesting people, made a few bucks here and there, and did score a free bus ticket back to Calgary. The job search had been a breeze, with the only snag being that the first place I walked into really was hiring and asked me when I was available to start. The last thing I wanted was a job. That would have ruined everything. How was I supposed to scam the welfare system if I had a real job? Just my luck, I thought, as I explained to the guy interviewing me that all I really wanted was a signature and the name of his company. He showed me to the door, minus the signature.

Other than that everything went without a hitch, and a week later I was on a greyhound heading back to Calgary. I had loved hitchhiking on my way out to Vancouver, but the bus was a welcome alternative, especially since I hadn't paid for it. The icing on the cake was the fact that I had, give or take, about the same amount of money on me on the way home as I had when I left several weeks earlier. It had been an all-expenses-paid round trip, including lodging and meals.

When I arrived back in Calgary, I left my duffle bag in a locker at the Greyhound bus terminal, as I was undecided about where I was going to live or what I was going to do next. The whole hitchhiking thing had added another entire dimension to my plans, as far as hustling pool and seeing a bit of the country was concerned. I had taken to it like a duck to water. I was tailor-made, I mused, for the bare-bones, living out of a duffle bag lifestyle that hitchhiking offered. As long as I was standing on a highway with my thumb out, I was free, totally free and detached from anything and/or anyone.

Those circles a friend had drawn on a piece of paper years ago, illustrating the world and my relationship to it, had been telling to say the least, and perhaps prophetic to a certain degree. As I moved further and further off the main trail or away from the flow of society in general, I felt less and less inclined to fall back in line with everyone else. I was living, I suppose, something of a self-imposed exile from the norm and most of what it offered. I wanted none of it, from anyone, period.

What had worked for me on the trip to Vancouver could just as easily work anywhere else, which opened up endless possibilities for travel and shooting pool on the road. The two worked perfectly together in my case, like a hand in a glove. There was much to consider and quite possibly plan as I made my way back to the old familiar pool room from the bus station in Calgary. With money in my pocket, I was ready for some action and looking forward to the possibility of a solid money match on a snooker table.

The "in the zone" thing I had experienced in my match with Big Jim was all over me from the moment I walked through the door and up the flight of stairs to the pool hall. It was only about ten o'clock in the morning but I knew, absolutely, that I was going to make a few bucks on the tables that day. It was my first day back in Calgary and, besides the bus station, the pool room was my first stop and would be, as it turned out, my only stop for the next fourteen hours or so.

The pool room was busy, very busy, and I was in a game within twenty minutes of buying a coffee and saying hello to several of the regulars whom I hadn't seen for several weeks. I was playing for a comfortable five bucks a game and for the remainder of the day and well into the evening I would play, nonstop, game after game, match after match, one opponent after another, for either five or ten dollars a game, hour after hour after hour until the pool room was empty and quiet, well after midnight.

Aside from going to the bathroom or grabbing a bite at the snack counter, I was at the snooker table, shooting, racking up the balls, and racking up a decent-sized roll of bills in steady five- and ten-dollar games for fourteen hours that sped by in what seemed like a fraction of the time. Walking back down the stairs at closing time, tired, shoulders aching, smelling like a dirty ashtray, and a couple of hundred dollars richer than when I'd stepped off the bus hours before, I wanted one thing: a long, hot soak in a bathtub, and I knew the perfect place. The Regent Hotel was just a block away from the pool hall and it was calling my name. Their over-sized, old-fashioned tubs were just what the doctor ordered and, after paying for a room for a week, I soaked in water as hot as I could stand, thinking about the great marathon I'd just been through on the snooker tables, as well as the trip I had just returned from and what the next day might bring.

The on-again, off-again, in the zone, out of the zone, flush with cash one day and broke the next cycle I had been living for more than three years at that point played itself out again, as it had on so many previous occasions. Within two weeks of my little marathon, I was once again broke and living in the hostel. The money had been spent on booze, decent meals, blackjack, and a hotel room I could no longer afford.

I was starting from scratch, again, for the hundredth time, but this time I wasn't in the mood to fool around with nickel and dime games of pool. I didn't feel like getting into another marathon for a couple of hundred dollars and I didn't feel like standing on the labour corner, hoping for a day's work. I was restless and a little bored of the routine. I did think about working for a couple of days and then hitting the road, hitchhiking around Alberta for a month or two, but then what?

One gentleman I had met in the pool room during my marathon a couple of weeks previously was feeling much the same way as I was. He had arrived in Calgary from Edmonton about the same time I had arrived back in Calgary from Vancouver. We had played snooker a few times, had a few beers together, and had both found ourselves broke, wondering aloud to each other what our next move might be. Neither of us was certain, but one thing we both agreed on was that we did not want a repeat of the past.

His past, what I knew of it, was nothing like mine. Up until that point, his life had been fairly typical, with its ups and downs, good times and bad, different jobs here and there, and he was moving on from a marriage that had not worked out. He loved to smoke pot, but had never been in trouble with the cops as far as I knew. He had an easy-come, easy-go way about him, and conversation between us was always relaxed and sprinkled with humorous stories about our respective lives, past experiences, and future plans.

We were sitting in the pool room one afternoon, having a coffee, just passing time when my mind began wandering back to the old days in my home town. I thought about the many times I had almost been pinched by the cops for one thing or another and the times as well that I had been seconds away from being "tuned up" by others for any number of reasons. I had stepped on a lot of toes, but lady luck always showed up just in time. As I shared some of my experiences of living on the street, my buddy remarked that it was a wonder I had never done time, other than a few days for shoplifting, to say nothing of the altercations I had been in over the years.

I agreed, acknowledging that I had always been very fortunate—a lucky criminal. I also shared that it had been some time since I had broken the law in any way. The past year had been a good one, with my job at the auction company and the steady stream of income from the pool tables. That and a cheap room at the Colonial had made for a comfortable year. Still, I thought out loud, it was time for something new, something that would yield some fast cash without the daily grind. We sat quietly for a time, lost in our own thoughts, both of us taking stock of our own situation, what we wanted and what we were willing or not willing to do to move on. We stared into our coffee cups for what seemed like a long time.

When the thought came, it came with all the clarity, certainty, and deliberateness of intention as when I made up my mind to travel west for the first time years earlier. I knew without question that what I was about to propose was not simply food for thought. In what seemed like mere seconds, I had just watched a movie of my life play quickly, in fast-forward, from the projector in my mind.

I saw the parents on the street I had grown up on who didn't want me on their property. I saw the bullies from school and the bullying I had subsequently engaged in, and the mundane days, weeks, and years in school that had not worked for me. I saw my school trip to the courthouse, the faces of the accused, and remembered seeing something of myself in several of them. I saw the faces and places of the past, people and businesses I had robbed. I saw the pictures in my dark room and I saw the hundreds of pool games I had played in for money, the winning and the losing and all of the dumps I'd lived in for the past three years.

I saw Charlie back home, taking the rap for me, and myself, lying through my teeth in court to get a couple of buddies off a burglary charge even when threatened with perjury by the prosecutor. I saw of all of it, in detail, and knew, in an instant, that what I was about to suggest had been coming for a long time, that it was just a natural progression of things, that my life had been heading, perhaps careening in a way, towards this moment for many, many years and that I would act without guilt, without question and without looking back. Sitting there in that pool hall in Calgary, nineteen, flat broke, ready and more than willing for a change, I looked my buddy in the eye and said in a matter-of-fact, no-nonsense way, "Hey, let's just rob a bank."

ON BORROWED TIME

"For I know that in me (that is, in my flesh) nothing good dwells."
–Romans 7:18 (NKJV)

One definition of courage reads this way: "A quality of spirit that enables you to face danger or pain without showing fear." Courage, then, is not the absence of fear necessarily, but the ability to keep it in check, if not hidden completely. The last three words, "without showing fear," would best describe that part of my character, if I had any at all, that had developed over the years of living on the street, pulling scores, staring down antagonists in potential altercations, and hustling pool. I had, out of necessity, mastered the art of hiding my fears. If Oscars had been awarded to me for best performance in the category of "hiding fear," I'd have a room in my home with nothing but shelves lined with those little statues, dozens of them, for showing courage, and I mean an unblinking, ice-in-my-veins, calm, cool, collected, I don't rattle, period, kind of courage when in reality it was all I could do to not have an accident in my pants in many situations.

Benny (The Jet) Urquidez, an incredibly gifted martial artist, boxer, and full-contact champion from 1974–1985, shared some insight in the area of courage to those of us who were fortunate enough to attend a training seminar held by him in the early 1990s. Benny, at one point in his professional fighting career, held an unprecedented six world titles in five different weight divisions. He was the first American to travel abroad and not only take on but defeat top-ranked Muay Thai fighters, including champions, on their home turf, in front of their fans, using their referees and fighting by their rules, which included the use of elbow strikes and kicking below the waist, something not yet seen or experienced at that time in North America. His heart rate was taken one time before a fight and it was noted to be that of a person sound asleep.

This fierce warrior, who had travelled the globe taking on and defeating anyone and everyone who stepped into the ring with him, answered a question regarding fear and pre-fight nerves in general, by one of the individuals attending his training seminar, and I've never forgotten his answer. To paraphrase Benny, he smiled and with sincere humility responded, "If the other guy in the ring had only known that I was dealing with my own fear, he would never have been afraid of me." Benny understood how important it was for him to show his courage and keep his fear to himself.

I was in my early thirties at the time, the year was perhaps 1991 or 1992, and I recall chuckling to myself and nodding in full agreement at Benny's answer. I could identify completely with what he said, as I had experienced the same emotions, in an entirely different way of course, so many times in my life.

Benny is also a Christian and mentioned that day, several times, the importance of having a relationship with God. That tough street kid and world champion carried himself with great dignity and humility. I saw in Benny that day many character qualities I admired. I believe God used him all those years ago to plant some significant spiritual seeds in the soil of my heart.

If I had a dollar for every time someone has said to me, "Man, that takes a lot of guts," about something I'd done or pulled off over the years, I'd be a wealthy man. I've never, however, thought of myself that way. I have definitely been in situations that required a certain amount of courage to be displayed to handle properly without yours truly getting hurt, but courage, as it has been described, is more about hiding fear than anything else and I was often—more often than not, perhaps—simply afraid.

With Benny "the jet" Urquidez, in shorts, and Bill "superfoot" Wallace, both undefeated full contact champions whom I was privileged to meet. Bill Wallace trained with Elvis and was the late actor/comedian John Belushi's bodyguard at the time of the actor's death. Benny trained actor Patrick Swayze for his role in the movie, "Road House."

113

I was afraid, at different times in my teenage years, of being caught by the police. I was afraid of losing face (being shamed in some way) at times, by others, in various situations. I was afraid that others, partners in crime, would know I was afraid during a job. More than anything, I think, at different times in my life, I was afraid to be honest with myself. I had been afraid, very afraid, to accept Jesus Christ as my Lord and Savior for many years, largely due to the fear of what others might think of me. Perhaps you, who are reading these words right now, have struggled with or are currently struggling with the same fear. Fear not, my friend. If this old bank robber can get down on his knees, ask for forgiveness and surrender his life to Jesus Christ, then so can you. You'll be just fine, I promise. The last fear, the fear of being honest with one's self, can especially have negative repercussions if not dealt with in an honest, mature fashion. Anger, rebellion, and a lengthy list of self-destructive habits such as substance abuse can be born from the place of not having the courage to really take a long, hard, honest look in the mirror.

Without question, showing courage, or perhaps in my case, a healthy measure of stupidity while keeping my fears to myself, was simply a necessary means of survival during my years of living on the street, living in prison, robbing a bank and even, to a certain degree, when I was hustling pool. Once, while waiting for breakfast one morning in the hostel in Calgary, a dispute broke out between two guys, resulting in one being stabbed a couple of times just two feet away from me. He fell to the floor, groaning, at my feet, while his attacker calmly folded his knife and put it back in his pants pocket before leaving the building. I stepped around the guy on the floor and made my way outside before the cops showed up. I lit a cigarette, my face—my emotions—betraying nothing of what I was feeling inside. Burying fear deep within me as well as displaying complete emotional detachment was a survival mechanism I had learned to turn on and off like a light switch when I needed to.

***

When I suggested to my buddy and soon-to-be partner in crime, in the spring of 1979, that we rob a bank, I was aware that life as I had known it up to that point was about to change, radically, dramatically, in the next twenty-four hours. I would no longer be a nickel-and-dime pool hall bum, scuffling along through life with a few bucks in my pocket, hoping for a decent payday sometime in the near future. While that had been primarily how I'd lived for the past three years, it had, almost overnight, become a vision of dull drudgery that sapped my enthusiasm. Perhaps it was the notion of scoring some serious cash in exchange for a few minutes of easy work that had made the thought of struggling for hours in a snooker game just to make a few bucks seem somewhat less appealing—for the first time, ever, since I first picked up a pool cue.

My partner, whom I'll refer to as Stan, answered in the affirmative when I suggested to him the possibility of hitting a bank. In fact, Stan said yes so quickly that it almost took me aback a little. I mean, he had barely drawn a breath before nodding in agreement, as though he had been waiting forever for someone to invite him along to just rob a bank. I'm not even sure if I was one hundred percent on board with the whole thing at the time of the proposition, but upon hearing Stan's immediate, "Let's do it," I too was all in.

I've reflected on that moment, the moment of our mutual agreement to rob a bank, many times over the years. To my knowledge Stan had never been in trouble with the law, and I've always wondered, as I'm sure others have, who was influencing who in our friendship. We'd only know each other a few weeks. Stan had little to no history in criminal activity and I had been out of the game for many months myself, and yet, without hesitation, there we were, sitting in a pool hall, planning a bank job without the slightest concern for our future. It all seemed as though it was the most natural thing in the world. In fact, not doing it, not following through, seemed altogether unimaginable. We didn't have to talk each other into doing it. We would have been hard-pressed to talk each other out of it! Very strange. I've never fully understood the dynamics of the situation or our friendship, and I suppose I never will. One thing was certain: my life was about to change forever.

Eighth Avenue in downtown Calgary, otherwise known as Eight Avenue Mall, was situated about six blocks from the Greyhound bus terminal, or about a ten-minute walk at a steady, unhurried pace. Putting as much distance between us and the bank we were going to rob, immediately after the robbery, was critical. In fact, we wanted to get as far away from the city of Calgary as possible, as quickly as possible, directly after the hold-up. Eighth Avenue was lined with banks in the late 1970s, with one or two on every corner for a mile or so, which made the job of selecting one to rob the least of our problems.

Once the bank to be robbed had been chosen, Stan and I went through the motions of robbing it, a rehearsal if you will, beginning inside the bank the day before we actually hit it, and timed ourselves to see how long it took us to walk to the bus terminal. We then checked the bus schedules for buses leaving town—any bus, going anywhere, as long as it was away from Calgary. We didn't want to wait more than fifteen minutes or so for our pre-determined bus once we were inside the station.

We also left our duffle bags, each containing a fresh change of clothes, in a locker, to be accessed just prior to boarding the bus. The clothes we would wear when robbing the bank would be discarded in the men's washroom before boarding. A change of clothes, including a cowboy hat on Stan's head (everyday wear in Calgary and Stan often wore one) and a baseball cap on mine, which neither of us would be wearing at the time of the robbery, would complete our "after" look, in case the cops showed up at the bus terminal to quickly scan faces or appearances matching any descriptions from the bank employees.

It was not, by any stretch of the imagination, an elaborate getaway plan. Simple had always worked well for me up to that point in my on-again, off-again criminal career, not that I had a lot of other options in terms of how I did things in those days. I don't think I had the brain power to operate in any other way but simply. The subtle changes in clothing along with the respective hats we'd be wearing just minutes after the job would be, we were sure, just enough of a change to make a quick ID difficult. At the very least, the change of clothing gave Stan and me a greater sense of confidence in getting away, should we even get as far as the bus station after the job. Was I hiding my fear? You better believe it.

On May 3, 1979, at the age of nineteen, I walked into a bank on Eighth Avenue in Calgary, Alberta, along with my partner Stan, and relieved the teller of $1,810. I cannot, for the life of me, remember the name of the bank I robbed that day. I've made every attempt, through the local police and the RCMP, to obtain the information through their database, but without success. Court records reveal the date, the exact amount of money taken, the street the bank was on, even the name of the teller I robbed, but the name of the bank is not on record. Up until the time of writing this book, I had not thought about the robbery in any detail for a long, long time and after thirty-three years the bank's name has simply slipped from my memory.

Neither Stan or I anticipated any resistance from the bank tellers, and we were not disappointed. We each approached a teller at about the same time and very quietly, casually, went to work. I handed my teller a withdrawal slip with the following words written on it: "This is a robbery. I have a gun. Put all the money in the bag." I waited a few seconds for her to read the note and allow what was happening to sink in before handing her a brown lunch bag that had been folded up in my jacket pocket.

My right hand was hidden inside my jacket as though holding a gun, and when the teller's eyes looked up from the note and met mine for the first time, I simply nodded a couple of times and suggested she get busy filling the bag with all of the money from her till. Those were the days when each teller kept money in a cash drawer right in front of them, making it easy to comply with my wishes. Today, with the tellers having to leave the customer momentarily at the counter in order to obtain the cash desired from another employee stationed elsewhere behind the counter, my approach would have been impossible.

Were I to do it today, I would have had to vault the counter, which some bank robbers do, bypassing the teller altogether in order to gain immediate access to the individual handling the cash. Given the fact that I got a C in gymnastics in school, I'm not sure how that would have worked for me. I can see myself in mid-air, halfway over the counter, when suddenly my foot catches on the edge and down I go, head over heels, landing on the floor in a heap behind the counter, where half a dozen employees calmly make a citizen's arrest while waiting for the police to arrive.

Before the teller began to place the money from her till into the bag, she looked directly into my eyes for a few seconds to see, I suppose, if what was happening was real. I smiled at her, not arrogantly or menacingly in any way, but in a casual, friendly, "How are you doing today?" kind of way I hoped would relax her as much as possible. It was my sincere desire, from beginning to end, to have any employees of the bank with whom I dealt during the robbery to feel as unthreatened as possible under the circumstances.

Stan and I were not there to unnecessarily intimidate anyone. The job was not personal. We simply wanted the money, period, as quickly, quietly, and painlessly—for everyone, including ourselves—as possible. While smiling at the teller, I began to speak to her in a quiet, firm, no-nonsense tone, reminding her that it was not her money I was stealing and that it was in her best interests to comply with the note and begin to fill the bag, which she did without uttering a word. As she was putting money in the bag, I encouraged her to do it as calmly as possible as though simply complying with the instructions of any other customer.

I glanced to my right and saw Stan doing just fine with his teller as well. We each stood, leaning against the counter, watching the tellers fill our brown lunch bags with money, while stealing casual glances around the bank, watching the faces of the other employees as they went about their business, oblivious of the fact that their bank was being robbed. So, too, were the other customers in line behind Stan and me, in the dark about what was taking place just a few feet in front of them.

The entire robbery played itself out in a very composed, unhurried fashion, without any undue excitement, agitation, or frantic body language from either us or the bank staff involved. Casually walking in off the street without masks or disguises of any kind allowed Stan and me to pull off the job casually and, even more importantly, without any drama. Had we walked in wearing masks and displaying firearms, we would have been on the clock immediately, every second counting while trying to keep everyone in the bank, including the customers, calm. That's just not my style.

While many bank robbers do work that way, it's just not how I saw myself pulling it off. For me, I saw many similarities between robbing the bank and hustling someone out of their money on a pool table. In each scenario it was me against another individual, a battle of wits, each gauging each other, reading each other, one trying to keep their money and one trying to take it. Whether I was hustling an individual in a game of pool, leading the person to believe I wasn't much of a player in order to, in the end, walk away with their money, or leading a bank teller to believe I had a gun in order to walk away with her money; it was all the same to me. A con was a con, with the only difference being that one involved prison time if caught.

The psychology used in both scenarios was basically the same and did not go unnoticed by me shortly after the hold-up. I could, should I feel so inclined, slip in and out of character, so to speak, as that of either a pool hustler or bank robber in a moment's notice. The bank job had taken only a few hours to plan when robbed the way we did it, without the use of disguises or weapons, and without the use of physical violence, which was important to both of us. There was a bank on every corner of every street in the country and I realized, in the weeks following the robbery, that I was every bit as at home walking out of a financial institution with their money in my pocket as I was walking out of a pool hall with someone else's money. I reasoned that the two scenarios paralleled and complimented each other beautifully, except for the consequences.

Stan and I had discussed, before robbing the bank, the very real possibility of being caught and what that meant for each of us. In a word, nothing. Getting nailed and subsequently doing time just didn't seem to matter much to either of us. We were both willing to take the risk and didn't consider the possibility of spending a couple of years in prison as necessarily meaning the end of the world for either of us. I had already spent a few days in jail and had been associating with criminals for several years. What side of the bars I stood on was of no consequence. Either way, it was the same people, the same environment basically, and the same twenty-four hour day to spend one's time. What did it matter? I did not care, end of story.

Once the bank employee had finished her job and handed the bag back to me, I looked towards Stan who was just stepping back from the counter as well. Before turning my back on the teller and walking away, I suggested she not move or say a word until I had left the bank and with that I walked out the door, joined by Stan, and began making our way, on foot, down Eighth, around the corner and towards the bus station, several blocks away. The bags filled with money were inside our jackets, out of sight from what would be, in seconds, the eyes of cops racing past us in cop cars, lights flashing, sirens screaming, heading towards the bank we had just knocked off.

Our approach to the job had been unconventional in several ways, which Stan and I had counted on to aid us in not only robbing the bank but in getting away as well. As mentioned, we had opted against wearing masks of any kind, as this would only have alerted everyone in the bank that a robbery was taking place. We were not at all concerned with being identified because no one, except for the two tellers involved, knew the bank was being robbed, and they were too busy complying with our demands and trying to stay calm to pay attention to our appearance. At least in any kind of detailed, exact height, weight, color of eyes and hair, incriminating way that could have resulted in our being caught. Not wearing masks allowed us to conduct ourselves like any other citizen walking into a bank to make a withdrawal, no muss, no fuss.

Also, the location of the bank made it difficult for the police to reach by car. Eighth Avenue mall was (and is) an outdoor shopping strip in the heart of downtown Calgary and was busy, very busy, with people out walking, shopping, meeting friends, having coffee or a bite to eat from morning to evening, seven days a week. While the police could drive down Eighth Avenue mall, it would take some time because of the crowds milling about, the very crowds of people Stan and I blended into just seconds after leaving the bank. At best, the police would have to park their cars a block or so away from the bank and walk the remaining distance, which gave Stan and I more time to get away. Every second gained in our favor was a precious second that could make or break us one way or another.

The fact that we were on foot avoided the possibility of a car chase or of being seen and identified by someone as the car sped away from the bank after the robbery. Not having to ditch a car or change plates was just a lot less to worry about and no one, including the police, would ever suspect that two guys strolling down the street, apparently in no hurry, had moments ago robbed a bank. Just being ourselves, wearing ordinary clothes, along with our casual behavior and our nonchalant body language, was the best disguise for the job.

Seconds after rounding the corner off Eighth and knowing we were out of sight of the bank, I turned around momentarily, walking backwards for a pace or two, looking for any signs of someone following us or a cop, or cops, approaching us on foot. The coast was clear. We continued on our way towards the bus terminal while the inevitable sounds of wailing cop cars got closer and closer until they were speeding past us, one car after another, racing towards the bank we had just robbed while looking—for who, what? They didn't have a clue, at least not yet.

Within ten minutes or so, Stan and I were inside the bus terminal. After retrieving our duffle bags from the lockers we had rented the previous day, we changed into new sets of clothes, complete with a cowboy hat on Stan's head and a baseball cap on mine. After throwing the clothes, including the jackets, we had worn in the bank just moments earlier into the garbage, we purchased two one-way tickets to Edmonton and stood in line, waiting to board the bus.

Edmonton was our temporary destination only because the bus going there was the next one out of the station and we wanted to leave Calgary behind as soon as possible. I half expected the police to come bursting through the doors of the bus station at any moment, guns drawn, yelling at us to freeze, but all was quiet. Time never stood more still as it did while waiting to board that bus. Every second was an eternity. We stood in line, not speaking to each other, both lost in our own thoughts, digesting what we had just done, what had just taken place and knowing, without saying it out loud, that our lives would never be the same again.

We had crossed the line, and there was no turning back. We would live on the run as bank robbers or we would go to prison, one or the other. I had an awareness of the situation and the inevitability of it all before we were even on the bus to Edmonton. I wasn't being paranoid, fatalistic, or melodramatic but knew, with certainty, that we were on borrowed time. We were on borrowed time because I had left the note with my instructions to the teller in the bank and it had my fingerprints all over it!

I became aware of what had happened while changing out of my clothes in the bus terminal bathroom just moments before. I checked and double-checked all of my pockets, making sure I had transferred everything over to my new pants, shirt, and jacket and everything was there, except the note. When I had handed it over to the bank teller, she had placed it down on the counter in front of her and I was so focused on her staying calm and filling the bag with money that I had forgotten to simply reach across and take the note back while she was putting the money in the bag.

Realizing I had left the note behind and understanding, fully, what the implications were, left me with a feeling of profound doom. It was only a matter of time before the note was fingerprinted and there would be my prints, glaringly clear, unmistakable, like a neon billboard advertising yours truly, the master bank robber for all to see. They would be matched up right away to the fingerprints of me already on record and bingo, the cops would know exactly who they were looking for and what I looked like.

I explained the situation to Stan shortly after boarding the bus but he did not seem to be concerned about the note at all. He was too busy counting his money and thought that the chances of finding a decent print off the deposit slip were slim to none at best, given the fact that many others had handled the piece of paper, one way or the other, before me. I wasn't as confident as Stan, feeling that the success of the robbery had now been greatly compromised, but I was relieved that

Stan wasn't sweating it. He was experiencing too big of a rush at having pulled off the job to let anything bother him and suggested that I just take a breath, relax, and enjoy the sound of the bus pulling out of the station, leaving Calgary, the bank, and the note behind.

RUNNING ON EMPTY

"We can't run from who we are.
Our destiny chooses us."
–Rounders

"I knew what I was going to be when I was
fourteen years old."
–Ted Nellis, 2012

Stan and I should have split up once we were in Edmonton. The likelihood of the police not getting a print off the note was slim indeed as far as I was concerned. While I was just as elated as Stan to have pulled the job off, I could not escape the sense of foreboding, which quite honestly overwhelmed me at times, I felt regarding the note. How could I have been so careless? The scene between the teller and me played itself out over and over again in my mind. I should never have even handed her the note but kept it in my hand while she read it and then placed it immediately back in my pocket. It should be noted that not once, at the time, in replaying the scene in my mind, did I regret robbing the bank. Had I the power, then, to turn back the hands of time, would I have still robbed the bank? Absolutely. It wasn't robbing the bank that was stealing away my peace of mind, it was forgetting the note.

Stan did not have a police record. He had never indulged in any criminal activity to speak of up to that point in his life. Although he was about ten years older than I was, it was me, not him, who was the bad influence. Many people assumed that because of the age difference, with Stan being older, that it was he who had led me down the wrong road but that was simply not true. It was I, not Stan, who had been tempting fate, criminally speaking, for many, many years. Stan was just an easygoing guy who was somewhat "in between" things in life when we had first met in the pool hall. Had we never met, I'm quite sure he would never have gotten involved in anything like the bank job we had just pulled.

I, on the other hand, had been in and out of trouble, one way or the other, for at least the past five years, maybe longer. The truth of the matter was that I had always been a thief, to some degree, for most of my life. I remember shoplifting, just for kicks, when still in grade school. There was a Zellers store not far from the street I grew up on and I regularly shoplifted out of that place.

On one occasion when I was about thirteen, I was stopped by a plainclothes store detective on my way out of the store because he thought I had lifted a few things while wandering through the aisles. I reacted in a very offended, loud, "you've got to be kidding" manner and invited him to search me. Somewhat taken back at having the tables turned on him, the store detective declined the invitation, apologized, and remarked that he was just doing his job. We parted company, my hands on the stolen handkerchiefs in my coat pocket (I needed them for a magic trick I was working on at the time) and a smile stretched from ear to ear on my face, unseen by the detective as I made my way outside, my back to him.

Larceny came as easily and effortlessly to me as drawing breath. I was a natural born con from my youngest days. Stealing, robbing, hustling, and conning were just part of who I was, what I did, and I was good at it, very good. By the time I was in my late teens, I was a well-dressed, well-spoken thief always on the lookout for an easy score or an easy mark in the pool rooms and bar rooms across the country. When I had watched the movie *The Flim-Flam Man* as a young boy I knew, with certainty, what and who I wanted to be when I grew up. That I found myself in Edmonton, at nineteen years of age, on the run from a bank job was no surprise to me. It had been coming for a long time.

My only real regret at the time was involving Stan and I told him so on more than one occasion. He assured me over and over again that he was not sorry for what he had done, but I wasn't so sure. How different his life could have been, while mine had been careening down a one-way street named, Rip-Off Avenue for a long time. Had we parted company in Edmonton, Stan could have gone on his merry way in relative safety and with a strong sense of security of not being caught. He was unknown to the police and would remain so as long as he was on his own.

In the event of me being caught, I would have very little information to give to the cops regarding my hold-up partner in Calgary. I wouldn't have had to lie, much, because I really didn't know a whole lot about Stan. I had no idea where he was from or where he had worked prior to us meeting in Calgary. His personal background was, for the most part, a mystery to me and just as well. Had we split up, we would not have told each other where we each were headed, allowing both of us to handle any future interrogations with an honest, "I don't know." That, as well as a less-than accurate-description of Stan's height, weight, hair color, even his real name, etc., and the likelihood of him getting away with the robbery would have been relatively high, provided he kept his mouth shut.

As clichéd as the following statement might sound, there really was "honor among thieves," at least in my experience of living in that life. We really did have each other's back as far as looking out for each other went. Either Stan or I would have, in a heartbeat, taken the fall for the other person had it come to that. Neither of us would have aided the police in any way, regarding the apprehension of the other, should we have been pinched separately. Others in times past had taken the heat for me and me for them, including coming very close one time to going to jail myself in order to get two brothers off a charge of robbery, but that's just the way it was.

As it turned out, however, we did not split up. We stayed in Edmonton for a couple of days, buying new clothes, planning our next move, and keeping an eye on the news and newspaper accounts of the bank robbery. Our instincts about not being concerned with solid descriptions from the bank employees in spite of not wearing a mask or disguise had proven correct. The descriptions of us in the paper, what there was of them in print, were not even close. Being identified by anyone was the least of our worries. Our only real concern, if there was one, was what to do with ourselves and where to go next.

British Columbia was a consideration, and should have been our choice. Aside from the beautiful scenery, we were both somewhat familiar with Vancouver and felt very much at home there. The city of Vancouver, particularly the downtown core, was very transient in nature which would have afforded an ideal backdrop for Stan and me. Incognito was the password of the day for both of us and the busy city streets of Vancouver, a sea of faces coming and going daily, in and out of the city, was perfect. We could, if we chose, remain lost in that sea of faces forever.

Vancouver was also the home of a few of Canada's top snooker players in the 1970s and '80s. Seymour Billiards was a who's-who of talent in those days and I would have been more than content to just lay low, play a little pool, maybe win a few bucks here and there and watch some of the best players in the country play snooker on a daily basis. It looked good and sounded good but such was not to be the case. We did not head to the west coast but rather, for reasons I'm not entirely clear about to this day, opted instead to make our way east, right back to my hometown.

Returning to my hometown in 1979, on the run, presumably, from the police, wanted for bank robbery or, as far as the law was concerned, possible armed robbery, had to be, in the annals of dim-witted criminal escapades, right up there at the top of the list for, shall we say, questionable thinking. Okay, who was I kidding, I could be, at times, as dumb as a bag of hammers. I mean, honestly. Really? What was the thought process there? Oh yeah, I forgot, there wasn't any. What happened to incognito? I did not have both oars in the water the day I decided that my hometown might be the best place for us to lay low.

The idea could only have come from me. Stan had no idea where I lived and even if he had known, I'm confident that he would not have suggested that the safest, wisest, course of action for both of us would be to stick together and head for my hometown where everyone, and I mean absolutely everyone in the downtown area knew me, especially the police. Why didn't I just suggest that when we arrived back home in Ontario, I report directly to the police station and let the boys in blue know I was back in town just in case they were looking for me?

Almost beyond belief, we did in fact board a train in Edmonton with a one-way ticket back home—my home, not Stan's. In my defense, there were one or two solid reasons for heading back to Ontario. We were putting a lot of miles between us and the bank in Calgary, which was a good thing, and my hometown was not far from Toronto, the capital of Ontario and the largest city in Canada. As was the case in Vancouver, had we gone there, we could easily have remained lost, so to speak, among the two-million-plus people on the busy streets of Toronto.

There was also a lot of action in Toronto, in and out of the pool rooms and of every conceivable type one could imagine, should either Stan or I have been looking for a little entertainment, legitimate or otherwise. When I was sixteen, my buddy and I both blew the last of our money in a massage parlor, of which there were many in the 1970s, in downtown Toronto. We spent three hours afterwards panhandling enough money to get back home on a Greyhound. We each conceded, once safely on a bus heading home, that it had been well worth the trouble.

One other plus, if one could look at it that way, to being back home was that I did know a lot of people who could line us up with a score of some kind if we decided to pull one. Looking back, I don't think there was ever a doubt that there would be another score, another bank to be specific, at some point in the future. It wasn't so much a question of if, but when and where. Neither Stan nor myself were about to settle down into a nine-to-five lifestyle any time soon. We lived day to day for the most part, knowing very well what the future meant for both of us sooner or later.

I believe that deep down I also wanted to spend a bit of time with my parents. I'd seen them very little in the past three years or so and knew that any day, or at any moment, I could be arrested and taken away, perhaps back to Calgary, for an undetermined length of time. That I could be picked up, right in their hometown, which would make my arrest so much worse for them, in so many different ways, was lost to me at that time. I was, at times, the epitome of young and stupid.

But well-dressed? Absolutely. I often wore dress slacks, dress shirts, and expensive shoes. I looked, when I chose to be, like a young, successful businessman. Well-spoken? Yes, for my age and considering I had little in the way of any formal education. Walter Scott, a card sharp of considerable renown among his peers, magicians, and sleight-of-hand experts of the mid-twentieth century, was a gentleman whom many considered the most gifted second and bottom dealer ever. When sharing a little about his background to an interviewer, he explained that he was indeed well-educated, but not from being in school. He said he learned from reading books, and knowing the world he lived in. I could well identify with Walter's words. As far as using a little common sense from time to time, however, ah, no. I was living out my days following the bank robbery in Calgary with reckless abandon which not only resulted in my being arrested in my home town, but right inside my parents' home.

***

Just going through the motions of day-to-day living since the bank job in Calgary with a strong, persistent sense of being on borrowed time was taking its toll on me. The year was 1979, and I was nineteen years old but felt like I was thirty-five on a good day. I'd been living hard for several years and I was tired, more from looking over my shoulder than anything else. Every time I spotted a cop car or saw a policeman just walking his beat, I braced myself for a potential altercation. What exactly I would do in the event of being identified, how I would react, I couldn't be certain. There was one thing, however, of which I was certain. The time had come to give some serious thought about pulling another job and getting out of town.

Weeks of partying, gambling, and travel had depleted our funds and it was time to make some cash. Stan and I had each left Calgary after the bank robbery with just under two thousand dollars, which went a lot farther back then than it would today, but still, we had managed to blow most of it in about six weeks, maybe even a little less. I'd racked up quite a tab just in the bar car on the train back to Ontario, to say nothing of Stan's hotel bills and the cost of some weed here and there. Life in the fast lane really meant just going broke fast, because we didn't have a solid plan for how and where we were going to live between jobs.

I spoke to a couple of guys around town about the prospect of working together on a couple of different scores, one being the possibility of hitting a jewelry store in Toronto, but after some consideration Stan and I decided to handle the next job ourselves. We worked well together, understood each other, and most importantly, trusted each other completely. I knew, without a doubt, that I could count on Stan to hold up his end in any situation, under the most trying circumstances and he felt the same way about me. He was an easygoing, happy-go-lucky kind of a person, but when it came time to get down to business, he was as solid and dependable as anyone I had ever known or run with in those days.

We spent one day in Toronto looking at various banks, planning different escape routes, and considering travel plans and possible destinations after the next robbery. Toronto was a big city and we could have remained in my hometown after knocking off a bank or two for an undetermined length of time had we chosen to do so. For that matter, we didn't have to leave Toronto at all after the robbery. We could have simply stayed put and worked the city and its thousands of banks until our hearts were content or we were caught, whichever came first. Every prison in the country is filled with men and women who thought that they would never get caught. For most, if not all career criminals, doing time is the inevitable outcome and for many it's just an accepted part of the lifestyle they've chosen.

In the end, we opted out of hitting a bank in the big city. I'm not sure what it was that had both Stan and me second-guessing ourselves, but after spending an entire day in Toronto and looking at a dozen possibilities, we called it quits and made our way back to my home town feeling a little restless and eager, in a way, to get on with the next job, whatever that might be. We had even entered a bank in Toronto with the full intention of robbing it, but at the last minute, while standing in line, just seconds away from confronting the tellers, we had changed our minds. Something deep down in my gut hadn't felt right and we walked back out, not quite sure what had happened.

Once back home, life continued as it had for another week or so, with neither of us doing much from day to day. We met regularly in the pool room, played a little snooker, each of us getting into a money game here and there, but shooting pool felt more like a distraction than anything else. Both of us knew what we were really after and it wasn't a little cash from some sucker in the pool hall. We were both preoccupied with one thing and one thing only. Finding a bank that felt right to us, robbing it, and getting out of Dodge by any means necessary.

I reflected often on the bank job in Calgary. It had gone so smoothly from start to finish with neither of us feeling, even for a second, that we were in over our heads in any way or that we'd bitten off more than we could chew. Not once had we second-guessed ourselves, the bank we had chosen to rob, our escape route, the time of day we had robbed it, the busy location with lots of pedestrians milling around just outside the bank's front doors; all of it had felt right.

The thoughts racing through my mind pertaining to the impending second bank job centered on the idea of finding a bank that offered some of the advantages Stan and I felt we had with the first bank. Our biggest advantage in Calgary, I thought, was the busy street. Eighth Avenue mall in Calgary was always so crowded with people that it made it easy for Stan and me to get lost in the crowd quickly after leaving the bank, while at the same time making it a little tougher for the police to reach in good time.

Getting away—or disappearing, so to speak—quickly, quietly, smoothly, and immediately after robbing the bank was our key consideration and one I felt I finally had the answer to. I was looking for a bank to hit in a very busy part of town. I wanted to blend in with people, lots of people, within minutes of the robbery. Getting out of town right away was not as big of a consideration for me as simply getting out of sight from the bank after hitting it. Sometimes the best place to hide is right under the nose of the people looking for you.

I used and played on reverse psychology often when hustling pool or pulling a score. The very thing that no one thought would or could ever happen or that I would or could do was, in fact, the very thing I did that allowed me to come out on top of many situations that could have gone either way. The incident with the store detective when he had wanted to search me was a prime example of reverse psychology working in my favor.

Had I reacted to the detective's request in a nervous, guilty, or frightened manner, I'm sure I would have been pinched for shoplifting, but when I invited him to search me in an offended manner, the situation turned around entirely, leaving the detective somewhat taken aback and me with the upper hand of confidence. The short version is I had simply bluffed the store detective right out of his boxers, and I had used the same ploy many times in many different situations over the years. I felt I'd come up with a ploy now, for the next bank job, that would work just as well for Stan and me getting away cleanly, or rather, hiding right under the noses of the police who would be looking for us.

There was a bank in my home town situated directly across the street from the University campus. The little plaza the bank was in was not busy necessarily, nor the street it was on, but the campus, just a baseball's throw away across the street, was indeed very, very busy with people, hundreds, perhaps thousands of people, young and old, students, professors, and university employees by the hundreds milling about on campus, going to and from class and to and from work.

If we could make our way over to the campus immediately after the robbery, we would be lost in plain sight. The police and bank staff would assume that with every passing minute following the robbery, the robbers would be further and further away from the scene of the crime, probably heading out of town, but we would be right across the street, having a beer and something to eat in any one of the dozen or more pubs on the campus, just biding our time, waiting for the commotion to die down, watching the news about the bank robbery calmly on TV along with all of the other hundreds of young and old patrons who frequented the campus pubs daily for a bite to eat and a cold one.

With my baseball cap on and a backpack over my shoulders, I would look like any other student walking across campus for another day of classes. No one, absolutely no one, would look at me or my partner twice. Even though the campus was just a minute or two from the bank, it was an entirely different world and the last thing the cops would think of doing was swarming the campus and begin searching students who fit the descriptions of the two bank robbers. It just wasn't going to happen in a million years.

The more I thought about it the better it felt, and when I ran it past Stanley he felt the same way immediately. The campus even had a billiard room where we could hang out following the robbery and play some pool until things outside had quieted down a little. Once on campus, the choice would be ours as to how and when to make our exit. City buses drove through the campus regularly and cabs were always parked at various locations, waiting for fares from students and faculty. Getting off the campus would be the least of our worries after we had robbed the bank. It was getting across the street from the bank, unnoticed, onto the campus, after the robbery, that would prove to be a bit tricky but I felt I had that figured out as well.

I explained to Stan that once we had left the bank with the money, we would walk, just as we had in Calgary, away from and behind the bank, out of sight from any of the employees, a couple of blocks down the street—a suburban street with houses on either side. No one would give us a second look as we casually walked down the street away from the bank. None of the neighbors who happened to be out would ever suspect that the two guys walking down the street, past their house, smoking cigarettes and just chatting away nonchalantly had just robbed the bank a stone's throw away. There was a place to cross the street onto the campus a few blocks down from and out of sight from the bank. I figured Stan and I would be at that crossing point just as the police would be arriving, by the dozen, at the bank.

By the time the cops had our descriptions from the bank employees, which we were not remotely concerned with, and were beginning to trace our steps as we left the bank, we would be across the street and long gone, on foot, somewhere on the university campus. The police would assume we were already out of town at that point, which would give Stan and me all the time in the world to relax, count the cash, have a few beers and decide where we'd like to travel to next.

Stan was as confident in the overall plan as I was. Neither of us were concerned with either the robbery or the escape and had only to pick a day to get it done. We went through the motions of the robbery, timing the walk away from the bank to the point of crossing the street, which was just a few minutes away, and felt good about our chances. There was, however, just one little piece of information I had withheld from Stan regarding the bank itself. It was the bank where my mother and father did all of their business. It was my mom and dad's bank!

***

Willie Sutton was known by the F.B.I. as a disguise artist, escape artist, and master bank robber. During a twenty-five year period, from the early 1920s through the early 1950s, Willie robbed a staggering one hundred banks or more. He was highly esteemed by both law enforcement agencies and the criminal underworld for entirely different reasons and was, by all accounts, a quiet, unassuming, modest individual, given his extensive record of both bank robberies and successful prison escapes. He spent most of his adult life in prison and when questioned about his decision to rob banks for a living, he was known to respond with the brief answer, "That's where the money was."

His response was both profoundly simple and simply profound, depending on one's perspective. Beauty is indeed in the eye of the beholder. One would expect that someone who had managed to elude the police, on and off, for about twenty-five years, rob the number of banks he robbed, and escape from some of the toughest prisons in the United States would be, perhaps, marginally more animated in his response to the many questions asked of him by law officers and fellow criminals regarding his colorful criminal career.

Willie Sutton was, however, an uncomplicated, "I know what I want and I know where to get it, period," kind of a guy. No apologies, no explanations, no right or wrong, good or bad, should I or shouldn't I dilemmas running around in his head. He robbed banks because he could, end of story. His life, how he lived and why he did what he did was something of a mystery, it seemed, to everyone but him.

My decision to rob the bank situated across the street from the university campus did not come from a place of long hours spent on the whys, how-comes, and what-fors of life. It was not a "deep" decision. Following the same vein of thought as Willie Sutton, that particular bank was chosen because it was where the money was and it worked to our advantage regarding our means and chances of getting away. The layout of the bank itself, the number of tellers, employees, security, etc. never factored into our thinking at all. Walking in and robbing the bank was the easy part. Walking back out with the money and getting away, without anyone getting hurt, was really what the game was all about.

That the bank just happened to be where my parents did their banking had nothing to do with my choice of hold-up locations. I understand that my thinking at the time gave new meaning to the adage, "too close to home," but my parents hadn't factored into my choosing that particular bank. It looked good to me, period, and I was determined to take it, and besides, I was already on the run. There was no turning back and I wasn't about to turn myself in. I was low on cash and it was time to hit another bank.

To give my partner Stan credit, he urged me to reconsider what we were about to do. He reminded me that there were a million banks in a thousand different cities across Canada to hit. He suggested we hold off for a couple of days to think about it. The thought of robbing my parents' bank made him very uneasy, for a number of reasons, not the least of which was the fact that my parents simply did not deserve it. He was absolutely correct. My mother and father did not deserve what I was proposing to do.

This was, without question, the most difficult portion of the book to write. In fact, I simply stared at the keyboard for two weeks without typing a single word, not knowing how to articulate, in words, the horrendously hurtful, almost diabolical decision I made all those years ago. How do I rationalize, adequately, the decision I made to rob that bank? It can't be done. The shame, embarrassment, and self-loathing I felt for twenty years following the incident returned to me with the force of a tsunami every time I attempted to write about it for the purpose of this book. My parents have forgiven me though I do not, in the natural course of things, feel I deserve it. God as well has forgiven me, and given me the grace to forgive myself and move on.

Unfortunately, it being my parent's bank was not the end of the story as far as making a "questionable choice" was concerned. I was also planning on using their home, located on the street directly behind the bank, as a place for Stan and me to change our clothes immediately following the robbery, before making our way over to the university campus, which also happened to be where both my mother and father worked. Could all of these factors lead one to conclude that the bank job was just a little too close to home? Ah, yeah, one could reasonably say I was pushing the envelope a little. Did this deter me at all or give me cause to possibly reconsider my options? No, not for a second.

I had long been an anti-establishment figure. I had turned my back, completely, wholly and without compromise, on everything and anything even remotely connected with "normal life," including everyone and anyone in it. My mom and dad were just two more people living their lives in a world I had very little respect for. As odd as it may seem, the bank job, their bank, was not personal. It was just the right bank at the right time for me, and who or who did not do their business there was of no concern to me, even if it was my own parents.

Likewise, as far as using their house as part of the getaway plan was concerned. It was just a stone's throw away from the bank. What could be better? After the job, while pandemonium would be ensuing throughout the bank, Stan and I would be safely inside my parents' house, calmly changing our clothes and keeping an eye outside for any police activity just up the street. That I was indirectly or perhaps directly involving my parents by using their home in a bank robbery was completely lost on me at the time. The selfishness of my thinking knew no limits and as far as consequences went, I didn't care, period.

My parents both left for work about the same time every morning and wouldn't be back until after four-thirty in the afternoon. This gave Stan and me all the time in the world to hit the bank, change clothes afterward, and just relax as long as was necessary in my mom and dad's house before making our way across the street and on to the campus. By the time my parents arrived back home from work we would be long gone, out of their house, off their street, off the campus and out of the city with enough cash to keep us going until, until it would be time to rob another bank, and then another one, and another.

One day, I knew, I would be caught. Everyone, or almost everyone is, sooner or later. When that would be, what city I would be in, what part of the country, whether I would be on my own or still with Stanley, I couldn't be certain. My life had become not just a day-to-day existence but a minute-by-minute existence much of the time, which is what wore me down mentally. As it turned out, I needn't have worried about which city I would be living in when I robbed the next bank or what part of the country I would find myself in either. The bank job I was about to pull, at the bank where my mother and father did their business, did not go exactly as planned. Less than thirty seconds after robbing the bank tellers, everything, and I mean *everything*, went very, very bad.

***

On the morning of the bank robbery, I awoke in my parents' house and went about my business as usual. I said goodbye to my mother and father as they left the house to go to work, remarking that I'd probably just go downtown for a while and that maybe I'd see them later at dinner, maybe not. They both walked to work because they lived so close to the campus, and as I watched them walk down the driveway I became acutely aware, perhaps for the first time since planning the job, that I would not see either of them again for a long time, if I did see them again at all.

The thought also struck me, while watching them leave home that morning, that they would know immediately who had robbed their bank when the news broke. That I would suddenly disappear, without a goodbye, on the same day that the bank had been robbed would not go unnoticed for a minute, and then? What would they do? How would they handle it? My actions would, without question, place my parents in the worst possible position imaginable. They would be faced with, sooner or later, the decision to remain silent, which in effect would be helping me to get away, or to go to the police with the knowledge they had concerning the robbery and who had done it: their own son.

To say I would be putting my mom and dad between a rock and a hard place would be a top contender for understatement of the year. They would, within hours of leaving their home that morning, find themselves in the middle of one of the worst scenarios possible for any parent. Next to dealing with the death of a child, I can't imagine being in a more painful or difficult situation than the one that they would find themselves in very shortly, through no fault of their own. If they looked the other way they would be implicating themselves in the robbery by aiding and abetting a felon, to say nothing of living with a conscience exploding with guilt. Or, they could go to the police regarding their own son and his activities.

Stan showed up at the house shortly after my parents had left. I made us each a cup of coffee which we drank outside on the back deck, neither of us saying much between sips of coffee and long drags on the cigarettes we were smoking. Stan once again asked me if I wanted to reconsider our situation. If my memory serves me correctly, he strongly suggested that I not do the job. I felt, however, that I had reached the point of no return and that for one reason or another, it was that bank, that morning, or nothing. That's where the money was. Now or never. No looking back. Do or die. Within a couple of hours of sitting on the deck that morning, I would be wishing that I had, in fact, died.

On a warm, pleasant summer morning in 1979, around 11:00 a.m., Stan and I walked into the bank a block or so up the street from my parents' house, across the street from the campus where my parents were working, and once again handed our respective tellers notes informing them that we were armed and wanted their money. We carried out the holdup exactly as we had in Calgary, handing each teller a brown paper bag while keeping the other hand inside our jackets, as if holding a gun.

This time, however, I hung on to the note and put it back in my pocket after the teller had read it.

The teller looked me square in the face for a second after reading the note to see if it was not some kind of joke. I calmly and quietly assured her that it was no joke and, nodding to the "gun" inside my jacket, I reminded her that it was not her money and was not worth getting hurt over. I encouraged her to begin filling the bag, which she promptly began doing without giving me another look. I glanced across at Stanley who seemed to be doing just fine. All was quiet in the bank. Another moment or two and we'd be long gone.

When the tellers had finished emptying their cash drawers into our bags, Stan and I quietly walked out of the bank, across the parking lot and...then it happened. The unthinkable. The one thing that I never, ever, could have prepared for in a million years. The entrance door of the bank burst open and the manager, a wannabe hero in his nice suit and polished shoes, shouted the proverbial, "hold it," and then, incredibly, advanced towards us. This guy, whoever he was, was breaking every rule in the book pertaining to co-operative conduct during a robbery. From what I understand, he was seriously reprimanded for his actions by the police afterward.

I could not believe my eyes. There were two of us, possibly armed, and out comes Mr. Bank Manager, a.k.a. Dirty Harry, all by himself and warning us to...what? What did he think we were going to do? Apologize and hand back the money? "Sorry about that. No hard feelings, okay? Here's all your money, we'll just call it even Stephen." Gimme a break. Didn't he know he was screwing up my day? But it didn't end there. It gets even better. When we turned and ran, he chased us.

If anyone reading this has ever run while either very angry or very frightened, you know just how fast you really can run when either or both emotions are fueling your adrenaline. I mean, I was superman that day—faster than a speeding bullet, able to leap tall buildings in a single bound, you know the drill. Stan and I took off like two Olympian gold medal winners with Dirty Harry right behind us.

Planted down the side of my parents' house, separating one side of their home from the street, was a six-foot high privacy hedge. I went over that hedge, as did Stan, like it wasn't even there. We both hit the ground running, now inside my parents' backyard, and in another moment we were up the steps of the back deck, where just a short time ago we had been drinking coffee. Yanking open the back door off the kitchen, we stepped inside where I immediately opened up a drawer and pulled out a large carving knife. Spinning around to deal with Dirty Harry once and for all, I realized, gratefully, that he was nowhere to be seen.

We assumed he had called it quits when we had jumped over the hedge. He would have had no idea that the backyard we had escaped to belonged to my parents. We found out later that after seeing us disappear over the hedge, the bank manager had returned to the bank, assuming we had just kept running, cutting through one backyard after another, I suppose. Would I have used the knife on him had he been right behind me? No one will ever know for sure, including me.

Stan and I stood in the kitchen for a few moments, catching our breath and processing what had just taken place. Realizing we were no longer in any imminent danger, I put the knife back in the drawer and got my breathing under control. I chanced a peek out the living room window, which faced the street we had just moments ago been chased down, and all was quiet. No one there. Nothing going on. The street was normally fairly quiet, with little traffic and even fewer pedestrians, and that morning all appeared as usual outside. I began to breathe a little easier.

As incredible, as precarious, as the past fifteen minutes had been, it looked as though we had pulled it off. We had been chased by an unbelievable, "You won't get away with this," type of a bank manager but had still managed, barely, to escape. The bank manager, whoever he was, was no doubt just as surprised at his own behavior as we were. I'm quite sure he had simply been motivated into action by white-hot adrenaline, just as we were, although for entirely different reasons. Today, all these years later, I can only shake my head incredulously at his decision to chase after us. Whatever his motive was, whatever he was thinking, well, it's one for the books, that's for sure.

It was only about eleven-fifteen in the morning. Stan and I had the house to ourselves for at least another five hours before my parents would arrive home from work, which gave us plenty of time to relax a little and look for an opportunity to make our way down the street, which was only about fifty yards or so, around the corner and then over onto the university campus, where we would blend in and go unnoticed for as long as we felt necessary until we made our exit out of town.

We had no way of determining how much the police knew as to our whereabouts. I hadn't realized that the bank manager had stopped chasing us until I had turned, knife in hand, to deal with him seconds after entering the kitchen. How far he had actually chased us was not clear. Perhaps he had been right behind us until we had jumped the hedge or maybe he had only run a hundred feet or so from the bank before calling it off. I just could not be certain of anything. We had no way of knowing if the bank manager actually knew which backyard Stan and I had disappeared in.

After making sure both the front and back doors of the house were locked, we went downstairs, away from the main floor windows, to collect our thoughts and to count the money. No sooner had we started to sort the bills, however, when the doorbell rang, not once, but several times in rapid succession, as though the individual outside was impatient or just very determined. Seconds after the doorbell began ringing we heard footsteps, lots of footsteps, directly outside. Also, we could clearly see through the basement windows the shoes and pants of uniformed police officers. They were all over the property. So much for the notion of the bank manager not knowing where we'd gone.

Stan continued counting and sorting the money while I sat, quietly, in a corner chair in the basement, my wheels turning, trying to come up with plan B. Hadn't I been hitchhiking through the mountains in British Columbia without a worry in the world just a few months previously? From where I was sitting at that moment, in the basement, in the dark, in a house that was crawling with cops outside looking for yours truly, my old room at the Colonial Hotel in Calgary and a nice, comfortable, five-dollar game of snooker looked very pleasant indeed.

Had I been able to go back in time, at that moment, to the fateful meeting with Stan in the pool room in Calgary when I had suggested we just, "rob a bank," I would have, in a heartbeat. I imagined that

Stan, after hearing my proposal, had just laughed and said something like, "Ted, why don't we just hit the road and hustle some pool?" How different everything would have been. Did my regret come from a place of actual remorse over the choices I had made, or was I just ticked off because the present situation offered little hope of a positive outcome? I'll leave that question to be answered best by you, the reader (perhaps one day we will meet and you can share your thoughts with me).

We still had time on our side. It was just past noon, which gave us the better part of the afternoon to somehow get out of the house—in fact, out of the neighborhood altogether. I hadn't heard any voices or footsteps outside in several minutes. Perhaps, I thought, the police had concluded that no one was home and that their best bet would be to return later in the day when the homeowners had returned from work. Had the police thought, even for a second, that Stan and I were actually holed up in the basement, they would have been through the doors, guns drawn, long ago. I couldn't see what exactly was going on outside but I was certain that the cops would be canvassing the entire area, looking for any clues as to our whereabouts and asking neighbors if they had seen anything.

The situation, I thought, could have been worse. My mom or dad could have come home unexpectedly for lunch or perhaps because they had simply forgot something, only to find Stanley and me sitting in their basement, in the dark, money everywhere and their entire block crawling with cops. That would have been perfect. "Oh, hi Mom. You're home early. What's new with me? Not much. Just robbed your bank up the street. Things are a little crazy right now, but as soon as the commotion dies down we'll get out of your hair. What's new with you? How was your day?"

My mom did come home that day at lunchtime. She did come downstairs and she did see Stan and me sitting in the shadows of the basement. Almost beyond comprehension, my mother came home from work early that day, that one day, which did, if it was possible, make the situation far, far worse than it already was. Could anything else go wrong? The events, as they played out that day, were simply unbelievable.

An awkward silence followed when my mother realized I was not alone. She had not yet noticed the money Stan had been counting, but commented immediately on the number of police and cop cars in the area as she had made her way home from work. She asked me if I had any idea what was going on, but before I could say anything, I could see by the look on her face, her expression changing from confusion to concern to downright horror when she realized that all of the commotion outside was somehow about me. The police, everywhere it seemed, uniformed and plainclothes, cop cars parked all over the place, the news media milling about…and me, sitting in her basement in the dark with someone else she had never met and a lot of money on the floor at our feet.

The phrase, "you could cut the air with a knife," could never have been more aptly applied than to the scene that began unfolding that day in my parents' house. There are bad days and then there are *bad*, and I'm talking about *really bad*, days that words can simply not describe. Following a moment of complete silence that ticked by in excruciatingly slow motion, a moment that had my mother simply staring at me with the most desperate look on her face imaginable, I slowly began telling her everything.

I told her that it was me and Stan the police were looking for and I told her why. After filling her in about the bank robbery down the street, I told her I was on the run from a bank I had held up out west as well. I told her that as soon as things died down a little outside, I would be on my way and that I would never come around and bother either her or my dad again. I apologized for turning out so bad and then there was silence. Long, painful, agonizing silence, our eyes locked, my mother taking in, processing, if possible, what I had just said, trying to make some sense out of a senseless, awful, horrible, unexplainable situation. I believe that my mother died a little that day, as did my father and I as well.

Turning slowly away from me, my mother left the room without saying a word. I heard her footsteps as she ascended the stairs back up to the main level of the house and then all was quiet for a moment or two. My partner and I looked at each other, neither of us certain of anything at that point. As awkward and emotionally trying as the ordeal had become for my family, I believe that the whole scene was just as difficult for Stan as well, in a different way. He, too, had witnessed the shock, pain, and disbelief on my mother's face. We had all gone a little numb.

The house upstairs was not quiet for long. Within minutes of my mom going back upstairs, the front and back doors of the house filled with both uniformed cops and plain-clothed detectives. They swarmed the house from every side, preventing any possibility of escape. Above the sound of loud footsteps resounding from a dozen or more pairs of police shoes on the floor upstairs, I could hear, from the basement, my mother franticly shouting, "Put away your guns, he's my son, he's my son!" Seconds later the basement filled with cops, guns drawn, aimed at Stan and myself. The cops crowded into the room, their eyes locked on our faces, then to the money still clearly visible on the couch and floor and then back to our faces again.

I just sat, looking at the guns drawn, wondering where my mother was. I hadn't heard anything from her since the initial shouts from her informing the police that I was her son. I told the police that we were not armed and, after they frisked us, we were cuffed from behind and led back upstairs into the kitchen. I caught a glimpse of my dad, now home from work as well, standing down the hall with my mom. I can only imagine the emotional turmoil and stress they were dealing with at that moment. There stood their son, cuffed and surrounded by police, right there in their own kitchen, on his way to prison.

The police's only objective up to that point had been to apprehend my partner and me, which they had done. Their only objective now was getting us out of the house and into one of their cars and down to the police station as quickly and quietly as possible. I mention quietly because there were a lot of people standing around outside the house, curious to find out what all of the commotion was about or to catch a glance at the two holed-up bank robbers inside.

At that point, none of the curious bystanders outside knew anything about the connection between the bank robbers and the home they had escaped into after the robbery. As far as anyone knew, we were a couple of armed bank robbers on the run and hiding out in their neighborhood, which was pretty sensational stuff for a small town. It was definitely not the normal, day-to-day routine for anyone involved, including the police.

Not wanting to create a media circus while escorting Stan and me to a police cruiser, which was as much for my parents' sake as anything, the police decided to use a decoy rather than have us walk out the front door and face reporters and camera crews. A couple of plainclothes officers were used in our place. They were led out the front door and across the front lawn by a couple of uniformed officers towards a waiting cruiser. Once they were out front and had drawn everyone's attention, Stan and I left the house, cuffed and with several plainclothes officers on either side of us, by the back door, across the backyard and into an unmarked vehicle parked at the side of the house.

It was over. Curtain down. Lights out. Check-out time. The only one not surprised, I suppose, at how my life had turned out, was me. It is true that we really do become what we think about. I was a living, walking, talking example of that train of thought. I had not thought about anything but hustling, conning, ripping people off, and stealing for several years, nor had I fed myself, my mind, my imagination, my spirit, with anything even remotely resembling honest, clean, decent, positive material as far as influences went, be it books, movies, television, or just role models in my life. I had lived, ate, slept, and breathed the con, the hustle, the quick buck, the fast, easy and often dishonest cash, while the nobler of the virtues like integrity, honesty, sound principles, and morals had been absent from my character for years.

My lack of respect or regard, if you will, for the "system" and everyone in it, was full-blown at the time of my arrest. The utter contempt I felt for everyone and anyone in general knew no bounds but was nothing when measured against the contempt I felt for myself. I was a colossal disappointment to myself. I had become someone I did not care for. It had not happened overnight, but over a period of many years of harboring negative, angry feelings and/or emotions towards life in general, people in general, and towards myself specifically.

That nineteen-year-old kid in handcuffs being led out of his parents' backyard on his way to prison that day had been a person in the making for a long time. It had not been an overnight journey, and it would not be an overnight journey when attempting to live a different life, to be a different person. Growing into an individual who loved life, people, and most importantly himself, would not just take a couple of years, but a decade or two, and would involve a cast of characters unimaginable, unthinkable at the time. Prison would not be the end of me but rather, would lay the foundation for a life that would really begin to manifest itself in a productive, positive manner almost twenty years later.

GUILTY

"I didn't stop robbing banks because I became a nice guy,
I just hated being in prison."
–Ted Nellis, 1982

My relationship with the police had never been antagonistic. They did their job and I did mine. We were on different sides of the fence obviously, but I did not view law enforcement as the enemy. Never once during my on-again, off-again criminal lifestyle did I harbor feelings of resentment towards anyone carrying a badge. The old, "you'll never take me alive, copper," hissed though the teeth of some gangster in an old black and white movie was never who I was. It wasn't me against them. It was me against myself, but isn't that the case, in an entirely different way of course, with so many of us at different times in our lives?

I was not a product of my environment. I had not been dealt a bad hand in life. I was not some unfortunate victim of unpredictable, unforeseen circumstances that would make life in general very difficult for me one way or the other. I had turned my back on everything and everyone I'd grown up with, determined to live life my way, by my rules. It was me against the world and I would win, period. I understood, clearly, that I had chosen to walk a difficult, hard road which could result in severe consequences should things go wrong, which they inevitably do sooner or later.

When I was being led away from my parents' backyard, in handcuffs, on my way to prison for an as-yet-undetermined length of time, the only thought in my mind, quite honestly, was that I had done this to myself and now I was going to pay the price, big time. I don't remember being particularly angry or resentful towards anyone, except myself. I had set out years previously to become a pool player, to travel around the country hustling pool, moving from town to town at will, shooting pool and enjoying life, enjoying the uncertainty and adventure of it all, seeing the country and making a few bucks along the way and most of all, enjoying the incredible freedom that such a life would offer.

I had tasted it from time to time. I had certainly caught glimpses of that life here and there, and I had seen a good portion of western Canada along the way, but not anywhere near to the extent that I could have. Somewhere in the grand scheme of things, I had allowed a lot of negative, destructive thinking to influence, shape, and warp my perception of myself and the world I lived in. As a result, not only was I not living with any real sense of freedom, but I would soon live my life, for the next couple of years at least, in a tiny concrete cell with nothing but memories of what I almost was.

Believe it or not, through all of this, the one thought in my head that dominated all other concerns was the note. The note, or rather, deposit slip I'd left with the teller in Calgary still haunted me. There I was, sitting on a steel bunk frame in a concrete cell at the police station, my life, for the time being at least, flushed down the toilet, and all I could think about was that note. Did they or didn't they, the cops that is, have that note? At that time, in that moment, even with all that had happened, leaving that note behind was still my greatest regret. The "if only I'd…" scenarios played over and over again, endlessly, in my mind. It absolutely drove me crazy and had since the day of the robbery in Calgary.

My mind was put at ease, mercifully, soon enough. Just moments after being led into an interrogation room, the plain-clothed detective handling my case asked me if I had ever been in Calgary. I responded that I had never been to Alberta and inquired as to why he asked. Looking me in the eye and with a trace of humor in his tone, he told me that the Calgary police were in possession of a withdrawal slip that had my fingerprints all over it. A withdrawal slip which also instructed a bank teller to hand over all of the money.

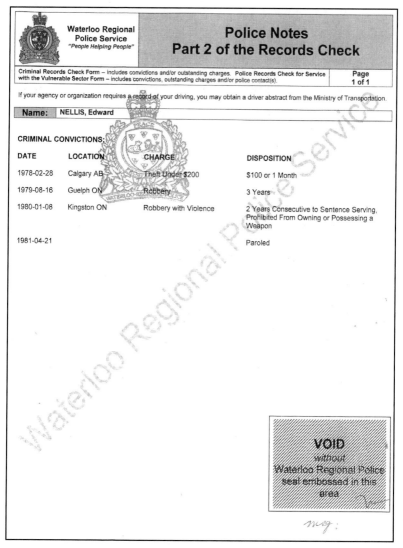

My criminal record as it stands today.

Silence filled the room after his last remark. He was sitting on the corner of a desk looking down at me, his eyes locked on mine. I sat there, handcuffed, so caught, but not giving him the satisfaction of looking away. I stared right back at him, giving away nothing in my expression, two fighters trying to stare each other down in the middle of the ring right before the first round. I knew it was over but did not want to throw in the towel.

After a few seconds of playing the stare game, the detective, in a very matter of fact, almost paternal tone, told me I was screwed. He explained that they had me cold for the Calgary bank job and that they wouldn't hesitate to fly me back out there to have the teller make a positive identification if I did not co-operate. He also assured me that the Calgary police would come down on me very, very hard, to the full extent of the law, should I refuse to talk but instead take my chances in a courtroom in Calgary.

It didn't end there. He told me they were also looking at me for a dozen or so other unsolved bank robberies around the country, including a couple more in Alberta. With that, he suggested I think things through and then walked towards the door of the interrogation room. Up to that time, there had been no mention of a lawyer from either of us. One had not been offered, nor had I requested one. Before walking out the door, he looked me in the eye and suggested, in a non-threatening way, that I not think about the situation for too long.

I knew they had me. I also knew there was no point in dragging the situation out forever. I was going away to prison for an undetermined length of time whether I co-operated or not, and I was not likely to tell the cops much of anything they didn't already know anyway. Any information I could give them regarding the bank job in Calgary was almost redundant at that point, at least as far as their investigation went. If I cooperated with the police, however, it could work in my favor when the time came to be sentenced. Also, I really didn't relish the thought of flying back out to Calgary, handcuffed to a couple of plainclothes detectives during the entire trip, with the other passengers on the plane staring at me, wondering what I had done to warrant the escort service.

I was between a rock and a hard place and I was tired of fighting. Not in the physical sense but emotionally, mentally, psychologically. I had been fighting against the system for what seemed like my whole life. I had made up my mind years previously that I would live my life my way or not at all and it had definitely taken a toll on me. I was becoming old way before my years. The "me against the world" mentality was a drain. It was a tough way to live and I didn't have it in me to play up the tough-guy role to the cops. They had me and that was that.

Moments after leaving me alone in the room, the detective returned and asked me if I'd like a cup of coffee or something cold to drink. I responded that I would love a coffee and wouldn't mind a cigarette if it was possible. He replied in the affirmative and once again left me alone with my thoughts for a moment or two before returning with a coffee and cigarettes and with another detective as well. As I've stated earlier, there was no animosity between us. My job had been breaking the law and theirs had been to try and catch me, which they certainly had.

After lighting a smoke and taking a few sips of coffee, I asked the detectives how Stan was holding up. They told me he was okay. He was being held in another room, undergoing some questions and, they emphasized, co-operating. It made no difference to me whether Stan was co-operating or not. I was not even remotely concerned with anything that Stan shared with the police. He had his future to think about, as did I, and had to do whatever seemed right. After finishing my coffee, I leaned back in my chair, my handcuffed hands in my lap, looked the detectives in the eye and asked them what they wanted to know.

***

I was relieved that it was over. No more looking over my shoulder every time I saw a cop car drive by. The nagging, gnawing feeling in my gut that I was walking around every day on borrowed time had finally come to an end. It had only been two, maybe three months since the bank job in Calgary, but it felt like I had been on the run forever. Regret about leaving the deposit slip behind with my fingerprints all over it had been robbing me of a decent night's sleep since pulling the job and I was more than happy to just confess and be done with it once and for all, which is exactly what I did.

I've often wondered how different my mindset would have been at the time of my arrest in my parents' home had I not left the note behind in Calgary. Sure, they would have had me for one bank, but not the one in Calgary. I can only imagine that my confidence level would have remained quite high even though I had been caught. I could have, and most certainly would have, chalked up the whole incident of being nailed for robbing my mom and dad's bank as being one colossal fluke on the part of the police force for being able to apprehend me. Had the bank manager not chased us, which never happens, and my mother not come home from work early, which also seldom, if ever, happened, I would have been long gone.

Incredibly bad luck, not bad planning, I would have reasoned, had gotten me pinched. Again, any remorse I felt at that time had nothing to do with robbing the banks. The feelings of remorse and guilt existed only because of the people I had hurt over the years. I made no apologies for who or what I was, or who I had become, but readily apologized to those around me for hurting them so deeply. I felt little, if any, regret at all regarding the bank jobs or any of the other scores I'd pulled, but did regret, profoundly in some cases, the innocent people hurt by my actions along the way.

It was all something of a quandary. I would not, in a million years, apologize to the president of the bank for robbing his place of business but I would, without hesitation and with absolute sincerity, apologize to the bank teller for causing her any upset or anxiety during the robbery. I felt nothing but contempt for the wannabe hero who chased Stan and me from the bank, yet at the same time hoped that the tellers inside the bank were okay—strange.

This is to say nothing of dealing with the fact that I had completely derailed my parents' life. Not only had they found out that there was a little more going on in my life besides playing pool, they had found out in the most awkward, painful, and humiliating way possible. Talk about "right in your own backyard." My life and ultimately theirs as well had blown up, literally, in their own backyard. It wasn't hurting myself or putting myself in tremendous jeopardy that haunted me, but hurting others in the process that caused me endless grief.

What kind of thief was I? Was I a thief with a conscience? Ridiculous. Could I rob someone out of their hard-earned money, whether on the pool table or by criminal actions, while simultaneously hoping that they were alright emotionally during the process? Oh brother, I was losing my marbles. I knew one thing for certain. No one, absolutely no one, would ever find out about the internal struggle that I worked through from time to time. I was too proud and far too independent to ever admit to anyone that I regretted my actions or questioned the choices I'd made over the years.

The life I had chosen to live left little, if any, room at all for second-guessing or doubting one's actions. Any doubts I was experiencing at the time of my arrest would remain the best kept secret in town. I had long ago mastered the proverbial poker face, and used it to my every advantage whenever I felt it was necessary, particularly when being questioned by the police or interviewed by criminal psychologists.

My distrust of everything and everyone far eclipsed, however, any feelings of regret I might have had towards individuals who may have been hurt by my actions over the years. I was nineteen, but in many ways I was still that angry kid in school who swore that no one would ever hurt me again. I was still the guy who did not fit in. I was still the guy who kept those around him at arm's length, due to trust issues and a fear of being hurt. I was still very much the guy who didn't get along with the world, nor did the world get along well with me. The world and I were totally at odds with each other.

As extreme as the situation had become, I still felt no inclination at all to change. Even though I would be spending the next couple of years in a tiny concrete cell, there was nothing within me that cried out for what? A better education? A trade? A chance to do it all over again? Not at all. I wanted out of jail, but only because of a yearning to return to my first love: hustling pool. I considered the bank jobs to be nothing more than a little "slip" of sorts. Next time I went bust in a pool game, I thought, I'd just go back to the old hostel and start over the way I had always done.

While sitting in a jail cell was less than appealing and the immediate future did indeed look rather bleak after my arrest, it did nothing to make "normal" life seem more attractive to me. School had left a bad taste in my mouth that remained, as though I had just dropped out that week. I had no desire, even in my worst days, to return to those corridors, the cliques, the shallow dating scene that was more about head games than anything else, and the inevitable schoolyard or neighborhood tough guy who thought he was the baddest dude on the planet. The only thing really bad about most of it was my attitude.

**

There were four of us in a tiny cell block. Three of us had our own cell, while the fourth had his cot out in the common area, which was perhaps eight by twenty feet. My cell was maybe five feet wide by about ten feet in length. The jail itself was very old and musty, with dripping, stained sinks and leaking toilets. There wasn't much for the eyes to take in but steel bars and concrete floors, walls, and ceiling. I had zero view of the outside, none. The food was palatable, just. The attempted suicide and suicide rate of the old "county bucket" I was being held in was high enough to result in more than one investigation. I was there in 1979, and it closed down within a couple of years, I believe, of me being shipped out to Kingston.

Although I had not been home much for two, maybe two and a half years, I knew several of the guys doing time in the county jail. Stan and I were referred to as "Butch and Sundance" more than once by both the guards and the other inmates. It didn't bother me. I got along with everybody and spent my days, while waiting to go to trial, rolling cigarettes, reading, and watching TV. We were only allowed out in the exercise yard once or twice a week.

I was grateful for the visits I had with my mom and dad. One can only imagine how difficult it must have been for them to see me under those conditions. We sat on either side of a solid Plexiglas window and spoke through a telephone-like system that was functional at best. Time allotted for visiting was limited and crude in its surroundings, and this after my parents were searched and questioned before even seeing me. Not easy, to say the least. Life for my parents in those days was extremely difficult. They too, were paying the price for my choices. In some ways, they were doing much harder time than I was.

I ran into one guy shortly after being incarcerated whom I had known very well from my younger days. I had played a lot of snooker with his older brother, when he wasn't serving time. Our paths, mine and both the younger and older brother, had crossed constantly before I had moved out west. They, as well as their other brothers, four in total I think, were always in the local paper for one thing or another and were described at times, in print, as being Canada's most dysfunctional family.

Their crimes were varied, from smalltime break-and-enters and burglary to assaults and, finally, murder. While I had been out west they had beaten to death a young lady who was to testify against them in court for a number of charges. I'm glad I was out of the province at the time, as I was often seen in their company, usually in the pool room. Three of the brothers were given life sentences and were, last I'd heard, deported out of the country, back to England where they were originally from.

Such is the company one keeps in jail. It wasn't much different from the company I had been keeping for years, except now I was on the other side of the bars, the inside. I did about three months "dead time" in the county bucket while waiting to be sentenced for the hometown bank job. Dead time is time served while waiting to go to trial and can be looked upon by a judge as time already served, before sentencing. I was anxious to get on with the whole thing. The sooner I was sentenced and began serving out the sentence, wherever it was they were going to send me, the better. Going away for a few years was inevitable. I just wanted to get the show on the road, serve my time, and get back outside, playing pool.

After several brief appearances in court, a date was finally set for sentencing, which couldn't come soon enough for me. I'd grown weary of discussing my case with my lawyer, who was court-appointed. Though she certainly had my best interests at heart, the endless questions pertaining to method and motivation were largely inconsequential to me. I believe that I was something of a mystery, a "grey area," if you will, to both my lawyer and the court-appointed psychologist, who had interviewed me for the benefit of both the prosecution and my lawyer.

Given the rather serious nature of the crimes and my age at the time, nineteen, those involved in my case seemed confounded, both prosecution and defense. Trying to profile me, get a handle on me, as it were, was not especially easy. What was my childhood like? Great, played lots of sports, had lots of friends on the street I grew up on. Did I grow up on the wrong side of the tracks? No, middle class, quiet street and neighborhood, hardworking parents. Did I have a drug/substance abuse problem, was I sober when I robbed the bank/banks? Yes, I was straight as an arrow at the time and no, I didn't have a drug problem. Was I aware of the seriousness of the consequences involved for committing a federal offense? Of course I was and thought it strange that they should ask.

Then there was the million-dollar question. The question everyone, my parents, the arresting officers, my defense, the psychologist, other inmates, I mean absolutely everyone asked, "Why did you do it?" What made me decide to start robbing banks? The answer remains as uncertain today, thirty-three years later, as it did then. I robbed banks for the same reason I hustled pool: because that was what I did. That's what worked for me. It was a good fit at the time. That is where the money was and that was how I chose to make money. Period.

To my way of thinking, all those years ago, why would I have gotten a job? Please! For what? So I could fall in line with everyone else and spend the rest of my life going through the motions of modeling the American dream? Maybe one day if I worked really hard I could own my own home and then I could mow the lawn and trim the shrubs in my spare time. Sign me up! At nineteen, it wasn't so much why would I, but why wouldn't I rob a bank that better answered the question as to my motives. My response, of course, was somewhat unsettling to those handling my case, but I was who I was.

Was I experiencing any sense of remorse for having robbed the banks? Not particularly. I felt tremendous remorse about those I had hurt, but in terms of simply feeling guilty about breaking the law, no, not at all, no more than I felt guilty about having a good payday in a pool room. Had I not been caught, I would have absolutely robbed another bank. That's what guys like me did. My situation was not an overly complicated one to figure out as far as I was concerned, but seemed to be a bit of a head-scratcher to everyone else. Did I enjoy robbing banks? Yes, every bit as much as I enjoyed playing pool for money, but in a different way. Did I, however, enjoy being in jail? No, and therein lay the problem. One walked hand in hand with the other. What was I to do?

The judge knew what he was to do. I pleaded guilty and in the fall of 1979, at nineteen years of age, I was sentenced to three years in prison, for the bank job in my home town, to be served in a federal penitentiary. As I was being led from the courthouse, in handcuffs and leg irons, to an awaiting police van, my mother appeared and begged the police escorts, who were on all sides of me, for thirty seconds before I was taken away. With tears streaming down her face, she hugged me and told me that she loved me. I told her that I was sorry to have caused her so much pain, to have been so much trouble. The police gently pulled my mother and me apart and led me away to begin serving my sentence in Kingston. Before stepping into the awaiting police van, I chanced another look over my shoulder. There stood my mother, helpless, weeping, sure that she would never see me alive again.

PRISON

"I was in prison. I have been in handcuffs and leg irons,
but I can say, with certainty,
that millions of people today, including professing Christians,
are also in prison, mentally, emotionally, spiritually,
handcuffed and chained to a past that debilitates,
deadens, and destroys
both their present and future."
–Ted Nellis, 2012

I only shared a cell with one man during the two years I was incarcerated, and even then it was only for three days. Those three days were in the fall of 1979. The cell was in the Toronto East Detention Centre, a maximum security facility, and the man on the bottom bunk of the tiny concrete cell I was sharing was Serge Leclerc.

Serge commanded a certain amount of respect by both the inmates and the guards. His body language, his manner in general, the way he carried himself, told me and others who may not have been familiar with him all we needed to know, without knowing much of anything at all. Serge was, in every sense of the term, a hard case. He carried with him a certain air of authority—not arrogance, but a quiet, controlled degree of rage that could, I suspected, be unleashed without forgiveness on an unsuspecting inmate or guard if either crossed his line.

I knew nothing of Serge when we met, if one could refer to it that way, in Toronto East. One did not ask questions of other inmates and, for me at least, I went out of my way to mind my own business. I was cautious as well of simply looking someone in the eye the wrong way, at the wrong time, or for too long. "Gunning someone off" or looking someone in the eye was grounds for an altercation, and altercations on the inside often erupted quickly, explosively, and violently. No thanks.

Just as I had done dozens of times over the years in pool halls with prospective marks I was considering hustling, I sized up, gauged, and read the body language of every inmate and guard within fifty feet of me. This was a habit I'd learned and honed to near perfection as a necessary means of not only making money hustling pool and pulling scores but of, at times, survival. I carried out this practice silently, unobtrusively, inoffensively, and efficiently, storing away and processing any information I could regarding a guy's posture, whether his hands were open and relaxed or clenched most of the time, the pace of his gait, whether his eyes looked straight ahead or down at the floor, etc. All body language and mannerisms told me something, in some way, and everything about Serge told me to be very careful.

We spoke to each other only once in those three days. We had just been locked into our cell for the evening and each of us had a cup of tea. Coffee was not available and I hated tea. I offered it to Serge, and after taking it he suggested I develop a taste for it as that was often all there was. I asked him if there was anything else he could tell me. He asked if it was my first bit (first time in the pen). I nodded, to which he responded that I should just keep my mouth shut and mind my own business and I'd do fine.

I had no trouble doing both. Keeping my mouth shut and minding my own business came easily, though I couldn't say the same thing for everyone in there. Some found out the hard way how important it was to mind one's own business, but it was second nature to me. Serge and I never exchanged another word until months later, though we followed each other from Toronto East to Kingston and finally to Collin's Bay, where I served out the bulk of my sentence.

We had no reason to speak to each other, or to regard each other in any way for that matter, other than the fact that we were both serving time. Serge, I was to find out as the months went by, was indeed a hard case and no stranger to incarceration. He was a millionaire drug lord, heavily connected in South America and other parts of the world. He had done a lot of serious time, including almost six years' worth of solitary confinement. He had organized-crime status with the underworld and had been investigated for his involvement in several prison murders.

I had known guys like Serge on the outside and was grateful for that, under the circumstances. Though it was my first time in the penitentiary, I was not new to criminal behavior. I knew the unwritten rules playbook by heart and was much, much older than my years. Being around guys like Serge in the pool room was one thing, but sharing a tiny cell or simply living among those guys twenty-four hours a day was something else altogether. The years I'd spent on the street prior to being in prison had taught me a great deal and I was thankful for it.

It's 10:30 p.m. on Tuesday, May 15, 2012 as I write these words, about thirty-three and a half since I shared that cell with Serge in Toronto East. He didn't know me, but I surely knew about him, quickly, because of his reputation. So often over the years I've wondered about the odds of sharing a cell with him, of all people and of all the jail cells and prisons across Canada, why that one cell, that one time? Furthermore, we went to Kingston together, at the same time, on the same day, and then on to Collin's Bay together, on the same day, at the same time. Why?

God was, once again, intervening on my behalf, that's why. I absolutely believe that. I know now, with certainty, that all those years ago, God was beginning to move the pieces of the puzzle of my life together in a way that, even today, seems almost unimaginable. God was making himself known to me in that cell in Toronto East, I just didn't know it. How could I? Who would ever believe it? My being in that cell in Toronto East with Serge was not a one-in-a-million chance encounter. It was not just one of those things, or an oh well, life's like that sometimes type of situation. It was the first of a series of events and encounters so incredible that even today I can barely manage to get my thinking around it. In fact, I can't at all, at least not in the natural sense of things.

Remember that name, Serge Leclerc. He will appear on the scene again some fourteen years later. Another chance encounter, but more of that to come. For now, at that time, I was on my way to Kingston and then to Collin's Bay penitentiary to begin a three-year sentence for the bank job in my home town. I still had to deal with the one in Calgary, which would inevitably mean more time, and I wasn't sure whether I would be in court for the Calgary job here, in Ontario, or in Alberta. I'd find out and be sentenced soon enough, just before my twentieth birthday.

***

Kingston Penitentiary, or KP as it is often referred to, opened in, or about, 1835. It's a maximum security prison located in Kingston, Ontario, and is, according to Wikipedia, one of the oldest prisons still being used in the world today. Some of the country's most notorious criminals have served time there. The institution has survived more than one riot, the last one being in 1971, I believe, about eight years before I was processed in the old, "Grey Rock Hotel." Before the riot of 1971 was over, two inmates had been killed and much of the prison was in complete shambles. When I was escorted through the entrance of Kingston in the fall of 1979, at the age of nineteen, I was, to the best of my knowledge, the youngest inmate in the penitentiary.

At that time, KP served largely as a reception centre, the first stop for convicts serving federal time in Ontario. The duration of my stay there was six weeks, as was my partner Stan's, after which we were shipped out to serve our sentences in any one of the area's other penitentiaries, of which there are at least five, ranging from minimum to maximum security. Kingston was, absolutely, the most old-school type of facility I've ever had the displeasure of serving time in. I've lived in some holes in my time, but nothing quite compares to that armpit of a prison.

Much has been made in the press of the notoriety of many of KP's inmates over the years, including Paul Bernardo and, most recently,

Russell Williams. While I was there, I worked in the laundry during the day, cleaning and distributing the inmates' pants and shirts. One day, the guards warned all of us not to say a word to any of the inmates about to line up and receive fresh clothing for the week. They were the boys in PC, short for Protective Custody. These guys were segregated from the main population of the prison for their own safety, twenty-four hours a day, seven days a week.

Standing there in front of me, on the other side of the counter with thick Plexiglas between us, were the Paul Bernardo's of the world. There was a widow cut out in the Plexiglas just big enough for me to push the clean laundry through. Any communication at all between me and any of those guys, the slightest jeer or hint of a threat, would have resulted in my being tossed into the "hole" for a few days. They weren't worth it. Rapists, child molesters, child murderers, stool pigeons, or just guys who were afraid for their life for one reason or another walked past me, received their clean duds and kept going, surrounded by guards, not saying a word.

In 1977, a young boy whom I will not name was sexually assaulted, repeatedly, over a twelve-hour period before being strangled and finally drowned in a kitchen sink in a dumpy little apartment above a massage parlor on Yonge Street in Toronto. The boy was only twelve and was seen regularly shining shoes on what was then a rather seedy, sleazy strip of downtown Yonge Street near Dundas. The city was shocked, stunned really, at the appalling brutality of the crime. That part of Yonge had long been known for its wild, rather unsavory entertainment scene, but the violent death of that innocent, twelve-year-old shoe-shine boy was an embarrassment, a black eye to the entire city, and changes were soon made to the downtown core.

One by one, the massage or "body" parlors were closed down along with many of the other adult entertainment establishments in the area. The shoeshine stands, of which there were several in the area, were closed down as well before, during, or shortly after the trial. The three men responsible for the heinous act were caught, tried, and each given a life sentence with no chance of parole for at least twenty-five years. They will never be released. One died of cancer in 2003, and the other two are still incarcerated.

Two years after the incident, the three men responsible for brutalizing and murdering that boy stood four feet away from me, waiting for their clean laundry. I had been in several of those body houses when I was sixteen and seventeen, before I had moved out west. I used to take the greyhound into Toronto on a Saturday and put in the whole day on that adult strip. I loved the action. The three convicted men worked in those parlors during my ventures to the big city. It could have been me they jumped any number of times. I was often alone on that strip, shooting pool, hanging out and just growing up way too fast.

I do not doubt for a second that I walked right past them, on different occasions, just an arm's length away as I entered and left those dens of iniquity. They worked the doors of those dumps, keeping things under control, when they weren't satisfying their own appetites one way or another. Fast-forward just a couple of years and there we were: them on one side of the glass and me on the other. What does evil look like? It looks just like you and me, with a monster inside.

I've had the privilege of sharing the gospel with folks many times in the past ten years in that area of Toronto, particularly at the corner of Yonge and Dundas. I've been told it's one of the busiest intersections in North America. It amazes me, endlessly, God's ability to change the heart condition of one who is truly born again. For those of you who may be reading this and wondering what the heck that born again stuff is all about, it simply means, in its most abbreviated sense, an invitation to Christ to come into one's life, literally, for real, and thus be "born again" spiritually, just as we were once born in the flesh.

What I once loved now turns me off, if not flat-out repulses me, and what I once disliked or hated, I now love. Incredible really, mind boggling, a miracle in its own way. Where I once spent endless hours and dollars, enjoying the action along that seedy strip of Toronto, I have, since becoming a Christian, spent hours sharing the gospel open-air, feeding the poor, and simply praying for those who are lost in a sea of iniquity.

***

Within a couple of hours of settling into the cell I'd been assigned, I was approached by a guy who suggested I cover the wire-meshed hole on the back wall of my cell with tightly packed, watered down toilet paper. When I asked him why, he said it kept the mice from crawling through the little holes in the wire mesh and spending the evening in my cell with me.

He had a somewhat amused look on his face while bringing me up to speed concerning my little nighttime cellmates, and I disregarded his suggestion with a "yeah right, okay," type of response. I should have listened. Within an hour of "lights out" on my first night in Kingston, noisy, squeaking, scurrying mice or sewer rats, whatever they were, were indeed coming into my cell through the little hole in the back of my cell. The Single Men's Hostel in Calgary, with its stinking, snoring, and occasionally vomit-covered homeless men passed out on the floor for the evening was looking more and more appealing by the minute.

Sitting up on my cot, careful not to step on one of the tiny rodents navigating its way around my cell and through the bars of my cell door out to the range (the common area that all cells lead directly to), I turned on the desk lamp, standard issue in every cell, and simply watched, fascinated, grossed out, and ticked off all at once. Anyone with a fear of disease-carrying, dirty little four-legged creatures would not do well in that environment. It is, however, incredible what we can adapt to in a relatively short period.

Mice can squeeze themselves through a pinhole-sized opening if necessary, and apparently they found it necessary to do just that in my cell during my first sleepless evening in KP. Not only were they coming and going through the wire-meshed hole on the back wall of my cell, I could see and hear them scurrying about along the range. The adage, "when the cat's away, the mice will play," certainly held true in that hole of an institution.

I was in that place because I had to be. I was serving time. I've often wondered, however, why anyone would chose to work in such a dark, dank, depressing atmosphere as the one offered in that old facility. Folks find it hard to believe, when hearing or reading about this, concerning the mice. They think I must be describing some sixteenth-century, subterranean gulag in a faraway land somewhere, but I most certainly am not. Anyone who has ever had the misfortune of vacationing for a time in the all-inclusive resort of Kingston Penitentiary, or worked there, can readily attest to the furry little friends coming out to play every night after lock up and lights out.

Needless to say, the next morning after breakfast, the fellow who had advised me to wad up a thick layer of toilet paper and cover the wire mesh in my cell asked me how I had slept. The grin on his face was considerably broader than it had been the day before when he'd suggested I get busy putting up the makeshift barricade. I answered him, while rolling a cigarette and using very colorful language, exactly how I had not slept much at all, thank you.

On my second night, well before lights out, I was busy in my cell soaking thick wads of toilet paper in water and packing it tightly against the wire mesh. I was determined to get the better of the rodents and wadded up enough toilet paper to keep every mouse alive in the city of Kingston and surrounding area out of my cell. It worked, though in the morning I could see partly chewed bits of the toilet paper scattered about on the floor. Rolling cigarettes and wadding up toilet paper, day in and day out—pretty exciting stuff.

***

Stan and I were on the same range, which allowed us to hang out a little every day after work detail. He was holding up fine. Same old Stan. Easygoing, didn't complain. Stan went through the day-to-day with an "oh well, that's life," kind of attitude. He didn't pose a threat to anyone and his easygoing nature allowed him to get along easily and comfortably with those around him. If several of us were sitting around the table and he pulled out his tobacco and papers to roll a cigarette, he was quick to offer it to anyone else who may have wanted to light up.

Three or four of us were doing just that one day when the guy sitting beside me was suddenly attacked. I didn't see it coming and neither did the unsuspecting guy to my right who was on the receiving end. He was in charge of cleaning the range every day—sweeping and damp-mopping the floor, wiping down the tables, etc. Apparently one of the other inmates whose cell was on the second tier of our block was not impressed with the cleaning.

The attacker put a choke-hold around the cleaner's neck that I thought was going to decapitate him altogether if he didn't let up. In no uncertain terms, he explained to the cleaner that not everyone was just passing through, that some of the guys *lived* there, permanently, and that he had better start taking his cleaning responsibilities a little more seriously. The attacker relayed this information while continuing to squeeze the life out of the cleaner, who was now flat on his back on the concrete floor, not moving a muscle.

The attacker's face was just inches from the cleaner's, watching the life slip out of him, and then, just as suddenly, he released his grip and walked away. The cleaner didn't move for several minutes and only sat up with the help of a couple of us who had been sitting with him before the assault. Shook up, stunned, and grateful to be breathing at all, he finally took his seat at the table without saying a word.

I only mention the incident, one of many I would witness, some far more violent than this one, because of my encounter with the same attacker the following day. I was sitting at a table on the range by myself the day after the incident when the guy who had almost choked the life out of the cleaner approached me and asked if I needed any tobacco or papers. I responded immediately that I did not, but thanks anyway. I absolutely did not want to be in debt to a guy like that, a guy who by all appearances was "connected" in some way, a guy who obviously had some clout and was treated with respect by the other inmates. He would, I was certain, call in the favor one day, no thanks.

He sensed my reservation but assured me that it was okay and motioned for me to follow him to his cell, which I did not. He turned and looked at me, asking, "Look, do you want some tobacco?" Still not sure whether I was walking into something, I followed him to his cell, wondering what was up and getting ready to be jumped. It didn't happen. He walked into his cell and took a pouch of tobacco off a stack of at least six or more other pouches and handed it to me.

Uncertain as to what was going on, I did not take the pouch from him but stood, just outside his cell door, regarding him, wondering what his trip was. Following a few seconds of silence he again told me it was okay and offered the pouch for me to take. I did not sense any imminent danger but read a level of sincerity, for unexplainable reasons, in the gesture, in his mannerisms, and on the look on his face. I took the tobacco, along with some rolling papers and a couple of books of matches and, looking him in the eye, thanked him.

I had no idea who he was, but he did definitely live there, as opposed to just passing through. He had enough tobacco, papers, matches, etc. in his cell to open a convenience store, as well as a stack of books and magazines for his reading pleasure piled up on a corner of his table. Before parting company that day, he asked me if I was alright, to which I responded in the affirmative. He then told me that if I needed anything, to not hesitate to ask. Very strange. Why me? What was going on? We never spoke to each other again, nor did he regard me in any way when we saw or passed each other in the range or in the chow lineup at dinner time.

It would not be the last time a "heavyweight" in the joint—and I'm not referring to body weight—would inquire about my well-being. All these years later, some thirty-three years later, I consider those bizarre, unexpected, and brief exchanges with a sense of wonder, curiosity and, without question, gratefulness. Aside from my partner Stan, only one other inmate in Kingston knew me, though only in passing. Serge Leclerc.

Serge was going through the same processing drill as the rest of us, or most of us, before leaving to serve out our time elsewhere. Serge, as previously mentioned, was a man of influence, of a certain rank if you will, within the penal system. In fact, he was regarded as one of the most violent inmates in the Canadian penal system at the time and he and my tobacco supplier knew each other. The big boys all knew each other, either from the street or from having served time together previously in another institution, or simply by reputation.

Could Serge have had something to do with Mr. Heavyweight giving me tobacco and inquiring about my well-being? It seems highly unlikely, at least on the surface. I was a smalltime nobody, a virtual unknown among the other convicts, and I preferred to keep it that way. I hadn't the slightest desire to get in tight with anyone. I was a loner, except for Stan, in the truest sense of the word. I wasn't in there to make friends, make connections, make a reputation or make anything else except parole, at the earliest possible date.

Yet, I can't help but think that somehow, in some way, Serge had something to do with the unusual gesture by Mr. Tobacco. Random acts of kindness with no strings attached are not the norm in prison. These are not boy scouts looking to do a good deed. I can't prove my theory, of course, and would have never asked any questions at the time, but still, it just doesn't make sense, at least not in the natural.

Given my relationship with Jesus Christ today, however, I do find myself leaning towards divine intervention regarding the tobacco incident. To be candid, it could only have been divine intervention, though I certainly did not look at the situation from that point of view all those years ago. It's been well said that an individual with an experience is never at the mercy of an individual with an argument. You may argue away, but at the end of the day I *know* what I experienced.

About six weeks into my time at KP, I received word that I was going to Collins Bay to serve out the remainder of my sentence. Stan was being sent to Joyceville, a medium security facility just north of Kingston, Ontario. After parting company in Kingston, we would never see or hear from each other again. I understood from my parole officer a few years later that Stan had violated his parole and was sent back to serve out the remainder of his sentence behind bars. I have no way of substantiating that report and can only hope that today he is well. I'm not sure if I would recognize him today if I did see him.

Leaving Kingston was a blessing all the way around. The regimented protocol in general left little to be desired. I was ordered out of the supper line once for not having the back of my shirt tucked into my pants. Had I given the guard any attitude at all, I would have been in the hole (solitary confinement) for a day or two I'm sure. I was sick of working in the laundry and was just anxious to get to wherever it was I was going to so I could settle in and begin serving out my sentence. I didn't care where, necessarily, I just wanted to get it started.

Anything, I reasoned to myself, had to be better than the almost two-century-old abode called KP that was showing signs of decay. Collins Bay was to be my home for the next couple of years, and I was happy to have received my marching orders. Saying goodbye to my furry little friends of the night was easy to take, as well as the daily chore of putting up my little toilet paper barrier. One can grow a little weary of such a monotonous, dreary day-to-day existence. It can be a little depressing and, for some, an outright killer. If I remember correctly, the guy a few cells down from me hung himself shortly before I left for Collins Bay.

COLLINS BAY

"Do not be envious of evil men,
Nor desire to be with them;
For their heart devises violence,
And their lips talk of troublemaking."
–Proverbs 24:1–2 (NKJV)

An online article posted by ottawacitizen.com titled, "A normal night on Unit One," addresses the death, or rather, murder, of a young, white twenty-seven-year-old male on Unit One in Collins Bay Penitentiary. It seems, according to the article, that the murder victim did quite well in keeping himself alive for six months on Unit One, otherwise regarded by some of the staff in the penitentiary as "the zoo."

The article goes on to describe the unit where the victim lived and, unfortunately, died, as being in a state of shambles after a riot had left it in serious disrepair. Only fifteen or so men were still living in Unit One after the riot and most of them, reportedly, were black with the exception of the lone white male who found himself on the receiving end of "jailhouse justice," as I call it.

Call it what you will: payback, evening the score, settling the score, setting things straight, sending out a message, whatever. The result of the beef, whatever it may have been, was found with the discovery of the body of the twenty-seven-year-old victim stuffed under his bunk in his cell, a plastic garbage bag wrapped around his head, his torso covered in multiple stab wounds, blood splattered on the walls of his cell, and his few belongings scattered about during the fight.

Just hours earlier, the young victim had apparently spent the afternoon with his girlfriend, who may have travelled some distance to visit him and had no doubt assured him that all would be well one day. She would have tried to encourage him with words of comfort like, "just hang in there, one day we'll be together." (Visits in prison were great. Saying goodbye was never so great.) She could never have known what was waiting for him later that evening, nor perhaps could he. The article mentions the fact that as his body was being wheeled out of Unit One on a stretcher, several of the other inmates on the unit began cheering and clapping their hands. Such is prison life, at times.

The young man in the online article was regarded as "lucky" by fellow convicts and, I suppose, a few of the guards as well, to have stayed alive as long as he had on Unit One. He had held his own for six months, probably the longest six months of his young life, before coming to a violent and in all likelihood senseless end.

Late in 1979, just several weeks away from my twentieth birthday, I began serving out my sentence in Collins Bay. I was assigned a cell on Unit One. The deceased gentleman in the article had surprised those around him, both convicts and guards, by remaining alive on a tough cell block, situated in what is thought of as one of the toughest prisons in Canada, for a whole six months. He had been twenty-seven. I was nineteen when I was shown to my cell on Unit One and, except for one other young man in the penitentiary who was about my age, I was, again, the youngest inmate in the Bay at the time. Was I apprehensive? Yeah, you could say that.

Just hours after being shown to my cell on Unit One, I was walking up and down the range when I observed a cell on the top tier that appeared to be a little gutted. The interior had been stripped bare, completely—no desk, no metal cabinet for belongings, no cot, nothing. And the walls were blackened as if by a fire. I climbed the stairs to the upper tier of the range for a closer look and it did indeed appear to have suffered the effects caused by a fire.

Back on the main floor of the range, I asked the cleaner what the story was with the upper, blacked-out cell. He stopped his mopping and explained that it had just happened a night or two previously. When I enquired further, the cleaner told me that the guy in the cell had been "torched." He had been set on fire after being locked in his cell. The layers of old paint on the cement walls and floor of the cell went up like an inferno with a little gasoline and a match. It was not an altogether uncommon form of payback.

Home sweet home.

***

I settled into Collins Bay, grateful in a way to be in the penitentiary where I would serve out the remainder of my time. The Bay was the fourth correctional facility in five months for me and I'd had enough of the processing rigmarole that accompanied each first day or first few hours of the initial admitting procedure at each facility. I had begun serving time initially in my home town jail and from there it was Toronto East Detention and then to Kingston and, finally, to Collins Bay.

Give or take, every one was the same, at least on the inside. Concrete and steel bars, convicts dressed in the same prison garb with uniformed guards all looking alike, some easygoing and some not so much. The one thing that did separate Collins Bay from the others was the yard, the prison yard that is, where the cons could spend some time outside, away from the main housing building. The yard was a good size, with a running track, two handball courts, two tennis courts, a weight-lifting pit of sorts, a heavy bag and speed bag station, and a baseball diamond and bleachers.

With approximately four hundred inmates living in the institution at any given time, with close to ten percent of them serving life and another fifty percent or so serving more than forty months, it was home, literally, for many. The variety of sport and recreation options provided a productive "outlet" for the guys, both mentally and physically. The facilities in the yard in general, as well as the equipment in use, were hardly state of the art but did suffice, and I for one was grateful for them.

During the summer months, particularly on the weekends, the yard was heavily used by a significant portion of the prison population. One guy was a long-distance runner and on the weekends would run the track for two to three or four hours at a stretch, as well as shorter durations on weekday evenings as time allowed. Others were serious weightlifters, moving a lot of iron using old rusted barbells, dumbbells, and plates. There was also a weight room inside but in the good weather many of the regular lifters preferred to work out in the fresh air.

Rest assured, dear reader, though it may sound or, in this case, read as a little expansive or luxurious, it was still very much prison. Yes, I spent as much time as possible outside, but even outside my view of the real world was curtailed, abruptly, by high walls and guard towers where armed guards, always visible, kept an eye on everything and everyone. Though fresh air and exercise were welcome for a number of reasons, one never lost sight, for a second, of the reality of one's surroundings.

On January 8, 1980, three weeks before my twentieth birthday, I received an additional two years in a Kingston courthouse for the bank job in Calgary. This brought my sentence in total to five years. I considered myself lucky to have been given only two years for the Calgary job. My lawyer had urged the judge to consider my being just nineteen years old before handing down my sentence, and reminded him that I was the youngest inmate in Collins Bay at the time. My age was being used for leverage and my lawyer unabashedly appealed to the judge to consider the long-term consequences to my mental, emotional and physical well-being before handing out the sentence. He repeatedly reminded the court that I was not yet "institutionalized" and that a harsh sentence would only hinder my chances at rehabilitation (rehabilitation is, for the most part, a joke).

Had I been ordered to stand trial in Calgary, I would not have fared as well. This was the consensus of all who were involved in my case, both the prosecution and defense. While the judge agreed that my being just nineteen did allow for a more positive future, if I so desired, he could not, on the other hand, dismiss entirely the seriousness of my crimes at such a young age, which did concern him a great deal. When his gavel came down, he ordered that the two years for the Calgary bank job be served consecutively, meaning in addition to the three I was already serving.

My age had been brought up many times during my incarceration, both in court and in prison among staff at different times, during meetings with me for one reason or another. The nature of the crimes I had committed and the consideration on the part of law enforcement that I had quite possibly committed many more robberies, of which they were unaware, at just nineteen years of age, was very disturbing to all who were involved with me at that time.

I was young it seemed, to everyone but me. Age really is just a number, insignificant and inconsequential in so many ways. I felt much, much older than my years and generally carried myself as one considerably beyond his teenage years. Perhaps this worked to my advantage as far as being left alone was concerned, while I served out my time. It certainly didn't hurt.

Young and innocent? When? I couldn't remember. Did I belong in Collins Bay? Was Kingston, stark, militant and rat-infested, fair and just punishment for one as "young" and, in some ways, I suppose, naive as myself? In a word, yes. I was just nineteen, but I was going on forty and I'd left a trail of robbed, conned, hustled, ripped-off, lied-to, deceived, swindled individuals and businesses from Ontario to Vancouver and back. Yeah, I belonged in prison.

Incarceration had been just around the corner, waiting for me, for several years. I'd done well to have avoided serving time up to that point and the only reason I was no longer indulging in criminal behavior in some way, at some level, was because I was behind bars. I did not spend my time feeling sorry for myself or making excuses for my choices, actions, and lifestyle. I was what I was and I was neither embarrassed nor ashamed, for the most part, of myself or my life.

I had regrets, certainly. My little dark room did haunt me on and off at different times but much more so as I got older. I knew right from wrong. I just didn't seem to care most of the time and that, in a nutshell, would be my greatest challenge. Would I ever care enough about myself, my circumstances, my life, actually, to make a conscious decision to change? That was the question of the hour.

For that matter, would I ever care enough for others, for human beings in general, for my family, my mother and father, to change who I was, what I had become? I'm referring to change in a very real, permanent, radical, dramatic, no-looking-back kind of way that could be regarded by others as positive, productive, and undeniable. In early 1980, serving five years in Collins Bay, surrounded by and living with every type of deviant individual known to mankind, it did not seem likely or even, to be perfectly candid, possible.

***

Edwin Alonzo Boyd robbed what might have been his first bank when he was about thirty-five years of age. That bank was located in Toronto, Ontario. The year was 1949. Over the next two years, Edwin was thought to have robbed at least six more banks in and around the city. He was written up in the local papers as daring, if not downright flamboyant, because of the way he vaulted over the counters, landing squarely on his feet, gun drawn, facing the tellers and calmly emptying the cash drawers before making his exit with just as much self-possession and composure as he had displayed while initially leaping the counter.

Not only did Boyd have a talent, if one could refer to it that way, a certain knack, if you will, for taking down banks with a bit of flair, he was also something of an escape artist. Eddie, as he was commonly known, also escaped from Toronto's Don Jail twice during his years as Canada's most wanted and colorful bank robber. The largest manhunt in Canadian history resulted after one of his escapes, with Eddie being tracked down and eventually sentenced to eight life sentences. His crime spree, including dozens of bank heists, a Toronto police officer gunned down and murdered at the hands of one of his gang, and two members of his gang, the Boyd Gang, being hung, ended the same way most if not all criminal careers end: in death and/or serious jail time.

The Boyd Gang's exploits have been written about at length in at least two books, and at least two movies or documentaries have been made and produced for TV. Edwin Boyd's escapades are the stuff of folklore and he was looked upon by the masses of Canadian populace and beyond as Canada's own Dillinger, the famous U.S. depression-era bank robber. At one time in his criminal career, Eddie was Canada's most wanted and the newspaper accounts of his bank heists and jail breaks could be seen and read in every newspaper across the country.

Colorful? Yes, Eddie was colorful and was, as well, seen by some as a somewhat romanticized figure. Boyd was looked upon by many a common laborer at the time with a certain amount of envy or even admiration for his brash, brazen, "living life on his own terms" lifestyle. But at what cost? A Toronto police officer had been gunned down in cold blood. Dozens of innocent bank employees threatened and intimidated during the holdups, a wife and children at home whom Boyd would seldom see and many, many years spent behind bars. The same bars I was now spending my time and wasting my life behind.

I came across a book detailing the life of Edwin Boyd and what would come to be known as The Boyd Gang while serving my time in Collins Bay. I happened to see it one day while perusing the bookshelves in the institution's library. It was in the same library where I found the biography of Willie Sutton, another "master" bank robber referred to earlier in this book. I've always possessed a healthy appetite for the written word, though as one can readily see, my choice of literature did not always benefit me in a positive way.

As is the case with most of us, I chose reading material I could relate to in some way, and the more I could identify with the main characters in the book, the better. I tended to lean towards books, fiction or non-fiction, where the main characters were depicted as loners, outcasts, misfits if you will, misunderstood and unaccepted by the mainstream of society. That was precisely how I saw myself, how I had felt about myself for a very long time, and I gravitated towards those of the same ilk, male or female, in books, on TV, in movies, and in real life.

The Edwin Boyds of the world, the Willie Suttons, the hustlers, the con men, the gamblers, the mobsters and the murderers did not simply live within the pages of some book or on a movie screen where I was concerned, but were living under the same roof as I was, eating across from me at the dinner table, walking beside me in the prison yard, and living, if one can call it that, in their respective cells on the same range as me.

Those colorful characters we see in movies and read about in books and newspapers were now my roommates and every one of them had one thing in common: prison. Professional bank robbers, maybe, but they, as well as myself, were in prison. Master thieves, safe-crackers, etc., and there they were all behind bars. Drug lords, presidents of motorcycle gangs, millionaire mob figures—all spending, some far more than others, the best years of their lives behind bars. Some were living out the final years of their lives doing time. It gave me a lot to think about.

Perhaps the benefits of turning pro, so to speak, were not all they were cracked up to be. I was surrounded by professional, career criminals. Crime was their chosen career and with it, doing time. Had I become a career criminal? I wasn't so sure. Was being in prison okay with me? No, not by a long shot. Not by any stretch of the imagination, and yet a part of me was marginally comfortable with prison life.

I recognized, almost from the beginning of my being caught and incarcerated, that my biggest challenge in prison was the battle within myself to not give up, give in, and resign myself to my surroundings. The voice inside my head that kept reminding me over and over again that, "It's not so bad in here, three squares a day, a roof over your head, beats working for a living doesn't it?" was my biggest and most doggedly determined enemy I had to face. The greatest threat to myself while I was incarcerated was me.

***

I didn't get along with the world, remember, and the world didn't get along with me. The truth is, I was more at home in some ways with the guys inside than I was with many of the people I had known on the outside. I could relate to the guys inside. I understood the life, the psychology, the unwritten rules, the dos and don'ts of the criminal and the world they lived in. As warped, if you will, as it is to admit and as bad as the environment in prison was, or at the very least could be, I was, in a way, in my comfort zone.

My own prison experience has given me an understanding of sorts, of women, for example, who go from one abusive relationship to another. It's all they know. Even though they may have a clear understanding, as I did regarding my own situation, that the relationship they're in is bad for them in so many ways, on so many different levels, it is, in the end, what they know, and in some cases all they know. The abuse is familiar. In a terrible, sad, and desperate way, the abusive relationship is in their comfort zone, just as being in prison was in mine.

I had to face the fact that I got along better with the guys in jail than I did with a lot of the guys I had known while growing up and going to school. I had also fit in easily, effortlessly, with the men and women in pool rooms across the country, while trying to get along or attempting to find common ground with men and women in the "mainstream" of life, just normal, working, everyday people, had been largely an exercise in profound futility, or so it had seemed to me. I didn't know what it was to just have a cup of coffee and an easy conversation with a girl my age, either in school or in the working world. But a cold beer or coffee and a little chit chat with a stripper or a lady of the evening? Well, that was as easy and as comfortable a fit for me as a hand in a glove.

What to do? I simply did not know. Did I go back to hustling pool when I got out, maybe rob a bank or two when I needed some start-up capital? I had a lot of thinking to do and plenty of time to do it. A season of honest, tough love to myself, of deep, objective soul-searching, was paramount to having any chance at all of turning my life around. Did I really want to turn my life around? Did I carry within myself a profound, all-consuming desire to turn things around, no matter what, kind of determination?

I don't believe I did. Too much work, way too much. Turning one's life around is "hard labour." It is painful, emotionally, spiritually, physically, and intellectually. And dealing with one's conscience? That can be heavy. Far too heavy for many folks to deal with. It's much easier to just turn that old dimmer switch down and leave those painful, difficult, embarrassing, no one needs to know moments, situations, and circumstances in the dark where they belong. No easy answers I'm afraid, but then there seldom are in the areas of life that matter the most. Hence, much thought and contemplation about my future.

Returning to crime seemed a long-shot at best. I would never return to smalltime stuff. Going from banks back to nickel-and-dime boosting didn't make any sense at all. If I were to become active again, criminally speaking, it would be banks or nothing. I had spoken to a couple of guys about the possibility of taking a Brinks truck, but it just wasn't my style. With armed guards inside the truck and a team of us just as heavily armed, if not more so, outside the truck, the possibility of someone being shot and/or killed during the job was just too high for me.

Banks, done quietly, inconspicuously, were far more in keeping with my personality. But the consequences, if I was nailed again? That was something very real to consider. Were I to be arrested again for bank robbery, I would be looking at a bare minimum of six years for one count, and in all likelihood ten years could be closer to the mark. There would be no leniency or sympathy on the part of the judge the next time. My age would be a non-factor in any courtroom in the country, of that I was certain.

Any time spent thinking realistically about resuming my old life on the run, while in prison, was fueled only by my ego. In my mind, what there was of it, I had never really been caught. Out of legitimate, genuine fear and concern for my life, my mother had told the police that the person they were looking for was her son. It was the right thing to do, the only thing to do. Still, I had not been caught, not technically, by the police. I had gotten away, as crazy as the scene had been following the last bank job, even after being chased.

It was irrational, nonsensical thinking, absurd in the highest degree, and yet, such were the thoughts of a young, brash, social rebel with far too much time on his hands. Were I to once again rob another bank, or banks, and be apprehended, say at the age of thirty for three more counts, I would be realistically looking at serving another sentence of at least fifteen years, *minimum.* I wouldn't be out again until I was about forty years old.

Looking at the situation from that perspective brought it all home. There was no way. The price was just too high. Resume pool hustling?

Travel the country again playing snooker? Once again be out on the road as a wandering pool hall bum? Yeah, absolutely, but robbing another bank? No. It wouldn't happen ever again. I was done as a criminal and I knew it deep down. Not because I had an epiphany or a moment of profound understanding of who I was and what I was all about.

My conscience was not suddenly seared, resulting in sleepless nights and endless walks around the yard, weighing out the options of one as lost and forlorn as myself. No, I simply hated being in prison. It was just that simple. Career criminals understood the consequences of their actions and just did their time. It came with the territory. I, however, could not accept that. The thought of spending a good portion of my life locked up was not acceptable to me. When I looked at my future as a criminal, honestly, with open eyes and a little common sense, my days did indeed look very bleak.

I had no idea what I would do when I was released from Collins Bay. As grim as life could be on the inside, the thought of going straight, I mean all the way straight, squeaky clean, when I got out did cause me some anxious moments, to say the least. Where would I live? How would I live? Return to what? I'd been living in hotel rooms, hostels, and jail cells for the past three years. Would I actually get a job? Punch a clock, become a nine-to-five guy and perhaps go to a movie on the weekend? Oh brother. Maybe jail wasn't so bad.

ME, A SINNER?

"For the ways of man are before
the eyes of the Lord,
And He ponders all his paths."
–Proverbs 5:21 (NKJV)

"What's so sinful about wanting a cold beer
and a warm woman?"
–Ted Nellis, Collin's Bay Penitentiary, 1980

I'd been in Collin's Bay perhaps four months when a guard approached me with an appointment slip in his hand. When I enquired about the nature of it, the guard explained that the prison chaplain wanted to see me. I had never spoken with a chaplain before. In fact, I wasn't entirely sure what a chaplain even was. I had a vague idea that he had something to do with God, but in what capacity I hadn't a clue nor did I have the faintest idea why he wanted to see me. Actually, I wasn't sure how it was that he even knew I existed.

I had seen a few of the other inmates coming and going from church on Sundays, some with a Bible in their hand, but I had no real concept of what they were doing or where, for that matter, the church was located. I was neither for it or against it. Going to church was not a part of my routine, but I was in no way down on those who did attend a service on Sunday. To each his own. Religion was, in general, something of a mystery to me. I believed in God, always had, but simply did not understand how any of it applied to me personally.

Common sense, if I had any at all, told me that we could not have come from some faraway explosion in space. When was perfect order ever the result of an explosion? A "big bang" and just like that, here we are. I had some family issues but no way was my great, great, great, great…great, great grandpa an ape. No, I don't think so. For me, it was always an either-or choice. God the Creator or evolution, one or the other, and I just do not recall ever giving evolution and the Big Bang theory much, if any, thought at all.

The idea of God and a created order always made more sense to me, always, even in my darkest days. It's not that I didn't believe in Jesus Christ and that he was crucified, I just didn't understand what it had to do with me on a personal level, nor did I care to know. I had enough problems as far as I was concerned, without trying to figure out God and whether the Bible was real. Please. What did any of that have to do with me playing snooker for a living when I got out?

And church. People singing, shaking hands with one another, all happy and dressed up. What a disaster. Who would want to spend their day off being told what to do by some guy standing up at the front wearing robes? Why would I have any desire at all to put my "hard earned" money into a collection basket and then watch some stranger walk away with it? Besides, I didn't give money, I *took* money. It was all upside down.

The whole church, God, Jesus, "the chaplain wants to see you" thing was definitely not for me. Still, I would have to keep my appointment with the chaplain, pastor, minister, Father, or whoever he was and find out what he had to say. If nothing else, it would be a break in the routine. I had nothing better to do and nothing to lose by stopping in and saying hello.

As it turned out, the prison chaplain, whose name I have long forgotten, was in fact a decent guy. He was older, maybe sixty or so, with grey hair and a sincere, warm, smile. His manner in general, his approach and tone of voice were very gentle and nonthreatening—a welcome change in prison. I liked him, even if I wasn't on board with everything he had to say about God and how I could be forgiven of my sins. What was so sinful about wanting a cold beer and a warm woman? I didn't get it.

I spent twenty minutes or so with the chaplain that day. He told me that he tried to meet with every inmate, sooner or later, during their stay in the penitentiary. After asking me a few questions about my background, where I was from, where I went to school, whether I had ever attended church growing up, did I believe in God or give much thought to eternal matters, etc., he assured me I was more than welcome, any time, to attend one of his services on Sunday morning.

I thanked him for his time, shook his hand, and remarked that who knows, I could show up in church some Sunday morning. I must admit, my wheels were turning a little as I made my way back to my range. Church, eh? God could and would forgive me if I but asked him, the pastor had said. I wasn't so sure. I had a lot to be forgiven for and just like that, poof, I would be in the Almighty's good books for saying I was sorry? It sounded like a good deal, just a little too good to be true, I concluded.

There was no denying I had enjoyed my visit with the padre. He had seemed genuinely pleased to meet me and I sensed that he really did care about me. I had noticed, immediately after being shown to his office by a guard, that he had not been the slightest bit uncomfortable around me nor did he appear to be even remotely concerned about our being alone during the meeting. The guard had left at once after showing me into his office.

He had been completely at ease with me, surprisingly so, since we could not possibly have had less in common. He walked with Jesus. I ran with the devil. I had complete disregard for the law, while he revered and upheld, lovingly, God's laws. I conned, lied, hustled, and robbed. He implored, pleaded, reached out, and gave. I carried a pool cue. He carried a Bible, and yet, I felt as though he had understood me in some way.

Was he hustling me? No, very unlikely. He was the real deal. No false airs. He had not been simply putting on a show, posturing for my benefit. To what end? I had nothing to give, nothing whatsoever to offer. Why go to the trouble, unless he really did care about me and my eternal well-being? Still, I would have to think long and hard before taking in a service any time soon. Deep down, I trusted no one, not even a man of the cloth.

I kept everyone at arm's length, at a distance, out of reach, so to speak, from who I was, what I was all about, what made me tick and had been for years. No one got close. Ever. Not on the outside and especially so while doing time inside. Trust, faith, love, hope, forgiveness, in a church, with strangers, and in prison of all places? Couldn't be. Didn't add up. It wasn't that part of me didn't want it or at the very least wasn't a little curious. I just did not believe that real change, internally, was possible for me. For others, maybe, but not me. If I could be forgiven, truly forgiven, as the pastor had said, if I could feel a sense of peace about myself, about God, about who I was and where I was going, well, I suppose that would be a miracle.

***

The days, weeks, and months passed by, as did the changing seasons, winter giving way to spring, spring to summer and summer to fall, each one noticed and noted in a way, as though to help me keep track of time. I would walk around the track, play handball, and lift weights on and off in all elements of weather. I spent as much time as possible outside, often spending the entire day on the weekend sitting out in the yard with a book, minding my own business, just doing my time.

I kept to myself for the most part, bothered no one and no one bothered me. I was not a threat to anyone and went about my business as low-key and unobtrusively as possible. Those who did know me at all knew me as something of a lone figure bank robber, which made me okay in the books of anyone who mattered in prison. I saw Serge Leclerc every now and then, and would exchange a few brief words with him before going our respective ways.

One guy I did hang around with a bit had some solid connections into the drug scene. Black hash was never in short supply, particularly on Saturday, which was the busiest visiting day in the pen and I found myself, as often as possible, smoking up and getting high on Saturday night either in my cell or my buddy's, whom I'll refer to as Brian. Brian knew where and with whom to score the stuff which made him my go-to guy whenever I wanted to score a little dope.

Some weekends, Brian would score a little and other weekends it would be me, but regardless of who had it, one always got the other high as well. There may very well be more drugs per capita on the inside than on the street. Grass, hash, uppers, downers, whatever, it was all there and available for cash, which was also obtained from visitors whenever possible.

More than once during a visit from my family, my dad would slip me a twenty-dollar bill which I would then hide in one of my socks before leaving the visiting room. Fortunately for me, I was never strip-searched after a visit. A quick pat-down and I was on my way back to my cell, twenty bucks richer. Twenty dollars, in 1980, in prison, could buy a pretty fair chunk of black hash, or hashish, my substance of choice.

My father had no idea what I was going to do with the money. (He does now!) It didn't always go towards drugs. On one occasion I used some of it to buy a radio and on another a couple of speakers. Brian, who was serving fifteen years for attempted murder, had a pretty decent stereo system in his cell. Many a Saturday evening was spent in his cell, smoking hash, playing backgammon and listening to tunes.

Regardless of what one's routine was, at the end of the day, it was all about doing the time. I worked out because it helped put in the time. I read books because it passed the time. I got high because it was a mental escape from doing time. I minded my own business because doing so meant doing easier time. Time is indeed the substance of which our lives are made and is so easily taken for granted until it represents a number that separates one from freedom.

***

Another birthday passed by, my twenty-first, and was just as non-celebratory as the previous one I'd seen come and go in Collins Bay.

At the ripe old age of twenty-one, I was no longer the youngest inmate in the penitentiary. In fact, I may not have been after I turned twenty. Another young man, who looked to be about seventeen and was perhaps one hundred and fifty pounds soaking wet, now claimed the title of "youngest."

I felt bad for him. I say he looked about seventeen but that was stretching it. He was as thin as a fence post and baby-faced, not a winning combination as far as being "left alone" in a penitentiary was concerned. I had no idea what he was in for or for how long, but thought it would only be a matter of time before he was "preyed" on for one thing or another. By all appearances, it seemed inevitable.

One young man, about my age, approached me out in the yard one day while I was walking around the track. I'd seen him around but knew nothing about him, including his name. He introduced himself and asked me if I minded him walking with me for a while. I rolled a smoke and, after offering him one, continued walking, wondering what the guy really wanted. I was ever cautious, perhaps a little paranoid, whenever I was approached by another inmate I didn't know very well. I'd seen seemingly casual conversations between a couple of inmates become suddenly explosive, sometimes violent, in a heartbeat, more than once. My guard was always up, so to say, psychologically as well as physically.

It didn't take long for the young man to get to the real reason for our walk and talk. He was being stalked and didn't know what to do about it. Upon returning to his cell, he had found canteen items on his bunk on a couple of occasions. Items like chips, chocolate bars, cans of pop, etc., which could be purchased by anyone at the canteen, had been left for him on his bunk in his cell by someone, anonymously, in return for…use your imagination.

Of an even greater concern to him, and for good reason, was him getting "piped" over the head a week earlier, an attack that had resulted in several stitches in his skull. He had no idea who had done it, as he had been blind-sided from behind while leaving his cell. He was clearly agitated, more than a little concerned for his well-being and wanted to know if I had experienced anything like it myself, which I had not. He also asked for my advice.

During our conversation, my eyes had never stopping scanning the yard. I was looking for anyone or any group of inmates who appeared to be overly curious about my connection to this guy. I didn't have one, nor was I looking for one, particularly with someone who was in trouble, and this guy was in a bad situation, the worst as far as I was concerned. There were no easy answers to his dilemma and I told him so. He could stand his ground, ask to be put into PC, short for protective custody, ask for a transfer to a different institution, or—the unthinkable—accept the bribes in exchange for whatever the stalker or stalkers wanted.

I wanted nothing to do with the guy. I did not want whoever was after him to think we were pals. We were not. I was not his friend or his buddy, and more than anything I was not his protection. He was on his own as far as I was concerned. He was between a rock and a hard place and I told him so. The only advice I gave him was to think clearly before he made a move of any kind and to be very careful. It wasn't much but what more could I say? We never spoke again. I saw him around but I had no idea whether his situation had been resolved in his favor or not, nor did I really care.

I did my time, no one else's. Such was prison life. I wasn't there to counsel, care for, consult, or consort with anyone. Other than Brian, who for the most part was a quiet, unobtrusive type of guy, I had very little to say to anyone and those who did know me at all respected and acknowledged my somewhat quiescent demeanor. The one and only time I was approached by anyone, for anything shall we say, unconventional, was far more comical than threatening.

Several cells down from mine was a gentleman whose name was Sam, or Samantha, as he was otherwise known. To be truthful, he was known as Samantha, period. Samantha was openly, brazenly, unabashedly, gay. Samantha didn't walk. He strutted, strolled, pranced, swaggered, and sashayed around the place for all to see and admire. Samantha would, on occasion, wear his white, sleeveless undershirt like a strapless female top covering only his chest. Oh yeah, high fashion.

I made small talk with Samantha from time to time, his sexuality of no concern to me or, like everything else in there, none of my business. I walked passed his cell several times a day while coming and going from mine and we would exchange "hellos" and "how's it going?" as was required. My behavior towards Sam was no different than it was with anyone else. He did his time and I did mine.

One evening, while walking by his cell, Samantha set aside the top he was sewing and asked me how I was doing. I told him all was well and politely asked him how he was. He responded that he was just fine and then, in a sincere, hushed tone, divulged what was truly on his heart. Samantha thought I was adorable. In fact, he thought I was downright gorgeous and he had been dying to tell me so for some time.

Samantha went on to say, in a somewhat coy fashion, that if I ever needed anything, *anything* at all, I was not to hesitate to ask. In plain English, Samantha was there for me, any time, for any reason, no strings attached. I thanked him for his offer before returning to my own cell, *alone*, assuring him that should I ever feel the need for a little company I wouldn't hesitate to look him up.

Sam never brought it up again or crossed the line with me in any way. We had an understanding and that was that. I appreciated his respect for my position and my space. Not he or anyone else ever laid a hand on me. I was never threatened, mistreated, abused, or harassed by another inmate or guard, ever. Others, however, were not so fortunate.

Back in my cell, drinking a cup of coffee and smoking a cigarette, I thought about Samantha's offer, grateful that the nature and tone of our conversation had been amicable. For all his effeminate posturing and overt homosexual manner, Sam could also hold his own, in a confrontation, with anyone. I saw him remove a ten-inch shank from under a heat register on the range one time and, after concealing it under his jacket, head off out of the range at a steady gait, a look of murderous rage on his face.

I also thought about the meeting I'd had with the prison chaplain and the invitation to stop by the chapel one Sunday morning for a visit. How is it that I could live in relative comfort among inmates in prison as well as homeless individuals in hostels and yet experience a feeling of tremendous discomfort at the thought of being among peaceful, welcoming, warm, sincere, forgiving church folk like the pastor I had recently met? What was I afraid of? God? Myself? Who I really wanted to be? What was I running from?

I was twenty-one and had been living either on the street, so to speak, or in prison for the past five years. I'd been keeping regular company with hustlers, thieves, drug dealers, pimps, mobsters, and murderers both inside and outside prison since I was fifteen and almost incredibly, I wasn't any worse the wear for it—except for being incarcerated, of course. I'd never been stabbed, shot, beaten into a coma, hospitalized, molested, betrayed, ripped off, or ratted on.

The many faces of violence and deviant behavior had been all around me for years. I had been so lucky, so many times, to have never been seriously injured, if not killed on a couple of occasions. Even while in prison, surrounded by and living with human nature at its darkest, I had gone about my daily business without the slightest hint of trouble from anyone. It just didn't seem to make any sense. Maybe someone or something had been protecting me all along.

Perhaps a visit to the chapel wouldn't hurt. A couple of songs, a prayer or two, a sermon of some kind. What the heck. Besides, there were no bars in the windows of the chapel and they supplied all the fresh coffee one could ever drink during the service. As if that weren't enough, there were even female singers in the worship team. Not a bad bargain and God forgiving me, too! Why not, I'd tried just about everything else. Maybe an hour of church once in a while wouldn't be so bad.

***

In mid-April of 1981, I received word from the parole board that I would be paroled, day paroled to be specific, to a halfway house in Calgary, Alberta. About twenty months after being sentenced for the Calgary bank job, I was just a couple of weeks away from walking out of Collins Bay, at the age of twenty-one. I felt much, much older.

I was surprised, stunned really, upon learning that I had been approved for day parole, given the fact I had served just less than two years of a five-year sentence. The chances of my being paroled at such an early date and at my first parole hearing were apparently very slim. So slim, I was told by several inmates, that I should not get my hopes up. Someone or something, however, was looking out for me again. Seemed I was still a "lucky thief."

It's so easy now, all these years later, to recognize that divine intervention was actively, miraculously at work on my behalf, in so many ways, on so many different occasions. From narrowly escaping more than one vicious pummeling on the street, to serving relatively easy time in a couple of the toughest prisons in Canada, to being granted parole after serving the bare minimum time required, all without a hair on my head being harmed.

I did eventually, before being paroled out, find my way to a chapel service one Sunday morning and to my surprise I did enjoy the experience. The coffee was good, and the females singing songs were a pleasant change, and escape from the day-to-day life experienced in prison, but there was more, much more. I enjoyed the environment in general and would go back many times, perhaps a dozen or so in total, and always left feeling somehow refreshed.

The padre spoke often about the forgiveness one could find in Christ, regardless of one's past, if one would simply ask and receive Christ as savior. He assured us, over and over again, that high walls and steel bars could not keep God out of our lives or from restoring lives and mending hearts. I didn't understand all of it but I listened, always, to every word and I believed it.

The padre was not there for the good of his health. He was not getting rich quick, coming into prison to speak to a room full of convicts about God, glory, redemption, and who knew what else. We had nothing to give and he asked nothing of us but to examine ourselves in truth and to think about how we were living and where it would all take us eventually, eternally. I was damned and I knew it.

At the conclusion of every service, there was an opportunity given for anyone and everyone to step forward and receive Jesus Christ as Lord and Savior. I was close to doing just that so many times, but was afraid of what others might think. I didn't want to give the impression to any of the other inmates that I was weak or getting soft. One Sunday, however, I did go forward and asked God to forgive me of my sins.

I was shaking like a leaf. When the chaplain placed his hands on my shoulders and began praying for me, I thought I was going to go down. It was all I could do to stay on my feet while he prayed up a storm on my behalf. Afterwards, making my way back to my chair, I experienced a sense of peace and well-being that was, at the very least, euphoric.

Again, I knew very little, if anything about Christianity or religion in general and had never read a single page of the Bible, but I had always known deep down that God existed. After the experience of being prayed for in the prison chapel that day, I knew and understood beyond a doubt that God was very real and did indeed hear and answer the heart cry of a human soul. I felt a profound sense of rejuvenation and elation inside that day as I made my way back to my cell.

Although I did not become what is known as a born-again believer in prison, I did experience enough of the reality of forgiveness, the existence of God, and a relationship with Jesus Christ if one so desired it during those chapel services in Collins Bay to know it was there for me and that it could be life-changing if I really wanted it. The Sunday services had been positive, rather than dreary and negative, which is absolutely what I had expected.

Attending chapel service in prison had not been a waste of time. Productive seeds had been planted, though it would be many years, if not a decade or two, before those seeds would begin to bear fruit. On April 21, 1981, I was paroled. I walked out of Collins Bay, never to return. The spiritual awakening of sorts that I had experienced while behind bars would have to be put on hold, however. I was out.

God, Jesus, church—that was all well and fine inside, but now I was back on the street with a plane ticket to Calgary in my pocket. It had been almost two years since I'd held a pool cue. Two years since I'd been in a money game or just spent an entire day watching snooker being played brilliantly, by some of the best players in Canada. I wondered if the snooker scene was just as hot in Calgary as it was when I had left two years previously on a greyhound bus with a sack of money courtesy of the Eighth Avenue mall bank. I'd find out soon enough. Just hours after leaving Collins Bay, I'd find myself back out west in my beloved pool rooms and bar rooms. I was still a pool hall bum. I had no desire to be anything else. I didn't know how to be anything else.

TED NELLIS

26 Yetta Shepway
WILLOWDALE, Ontario
M2J 1X9
499-8799
ACTS MEMBER
924-9947

c/o Mr. & Mrs. R. Nellis
29 Moore Avenue
GUELPH, Ontario
N1G 1R6

Height:	6'2"
Weight:	185 lbs.
Hair:	Blond
Eyes:	Blue

Theatre

Enemies	Kvach	Inner Stage	Cecil O'Neal
Birdbath	Frankie	Inner Stage	Craig Duffy
Dream Play	Various	Inner Stage	Harry Lane
Curse of the Werewolf	Dr. Bancroft	Act One Co.	Rex Buckle

Training

Mime, Clown, Masks:	Adrian Pecknold
Advanced Scene Study:	Rex Buckle, A.C.T.S.
Scene Study:	Equity Showcase, Simon Johnston
Voice:	Maggie Bassett, Ann Skinner
Theatre Crafts: Lighting, Sound & Set design:	University of Guelph
Scene Study Workshop:	University of Guelph, Edward Albee

Special Skills

Most sports, juggling, snooker champion

I narrowly escaped going back to prison to serve out the remainder of my 5 year sentence several times during my first six months out on parole due to various violations while I was in a halfway house. Because of serious concern for my future, I dropped out of sight, disappearing altogether from my beloved pool rooms and bar rooms which had for so many years served as my "office," or my "place of business," if you will. What to do? I moved back home, moved in with my parents and disappeared in to the world of theatre, helping to construct sets, learning a little about lighting and sound and as well, I became an amateur actor. My years

TED NELLIS

spent hustling pool served as an excellent training ground to hone my acting ability and I thought that the switch from the pool hall to the stage would be an easy one. It was. I put in my remaining years on parole studying the craft of acting in my hometown as well as in Toronto. It kept me out of trouble and I discovered a world far removed from the streets, pool halls, bars, hotels, hostels and prisons that had been my life up to that point. The "head shot" is a publicity photo. I was twenty-three years old at the time and still on parole. The shot of me sitting on the stool is from a one man, one woman play called Birdbath in which I played Frankie Basta, a struggling New York writer and alcoholic. The role suited me just a little to well. I laughed when I saw the words "snooker champion" on my resume. While I did play in and win a few small tournaments, I was certainly no champion. I was the quintessential "pool hall bum" but champion? Hardly. I hoped that the mention of my snooker prowess could help me land a spot on a beer commercial of some kind. I did do a commercial, a "talkie," for Rogers in the early Pay for View days while I was in Toronto. All the world certainly was a stage for me in my early twenties until just before meeting my first wife.

UNIVERSITY OF GUELPH
UNIVERSITY CENTRE

GUELPH, ONTARIO, CANADA · N1G 2W1
Telephone (519) 824-4120

Rerum
Cognoscere
Causas

March 1, 1984

Dear Ted:

We are happy to have you participate in the All Ontario Inter-Varsity
Snooker & Table Tennis Tournament to be held at the University of
Western Ontario in London on Saturday, March 3 and Sunday, March 4/84.

Arrangements for transportation and accommodation are as follows:

Craig Martin will be in charge of transportation which will leave the
University Centre main entrance at 7:30 a.m. on Saturday, March 3.

Accommodation is arranged for Saturday evening at the old Holiday Inn
at King Street, south side. There will be 1 room for Table Tennis
players, 1 room for Snooker players and 1 room for Ms. Pat Yager, who
will be sharing the room with a student from Toronto University (the
account for these rooms will be forwarded to Guelph).

Dinner on Saturday is arranged by Western. Other meals can be taken
in the cafeteria at Western during Tournament play. Please obtain
receipts for meals at Western for which you will be reimbursed.
Breakfast on Sunday can be at the Hotel.

Tournament play will commence at approximately 9:30 a.m. Saturday
morning.

Hope you enjoy your week-end.

See you at Western.

Wm. Goulden

WG/nd

*I was the University of Guelph Men's Snooker Champion, Doubles Champion,
Snooker League Champion and Inter-Varsity Champion in the early 1980's.
While I no longer frequented the downtown pool halls, I did play a little on
campus, in between acting classes and constructing theatre sets.*

WORKAHOLIC/ALCOHOLIC

*"Come to me,
all you who labor and are heavy laden,
and I will give you rest."*
–Matthew 11:28 (NKJV)

(Author's note: Out of respect for the privacy of my children and their mother, I have omitted much of the details of my life from the early 1980s through to the early 1990s. Therefore, we begin this chapter in 1993 when I am thirty-three years old.)

***

I stood, absolutely transfixed, unable to take my eyes off the poster taped to the door of the coffee shop. It just couldn't be. How? *Impossible.* When? I read and re-read what little text was on the poster, my mind going in a hundred different directions at once, trying to process, to make some sense of what I was reading. More to the point, I was trying to get my head around what I was seeing. *Unbelievable.*

The heading on the poster read, "Weekend of Compassion," under which were the photos of four individuals who would be speaking on the Saturday and Sunday of the advertised event. It was all happening at a church in the city of Kitchener, Ontario, the city in which I had been living for several years. Below each photo of the guest speakers was a brief biography followed by a description or title of their respective keynote messages they would give over the course of the weekend.

One photo in particular on the poster was the reason for my astonishment or, perhaps, disbelief. The photograph of the man I was staring at on the "Weekend of Compassion" poster was Serge Leclerc. The few words under the picture described Serge's miraculous conversion to Christianity. Serge Leclerc, the once-notorious drug lord and violent gang leader, the man whom I had shared a cell with in Toronto East and had done time with in Kingston and Collins Bay, was now a born-again Christian and would be speaking in a church just ten minutes from my house.

I was in my early thirties at the time, and hadn't attended a church service in over ten years. The last time would have been in the chapel in Collins Bay prior to my being paroled out to Calgary so many years ago. Since then, I hadn't given church, God, or Christianity much thought, if any at all, in the years that had followed my release from prison. Now, more than a decade later, who of all people would be the reason I would once again darken the doorway of a church? A man who had served some twenty-one years behind bars.

It wouldn't be Billy Graham, or his son Franklin, who had held a crusade in Kitchener back in the mid to late nineties, who would entice me back into a sanctuary. It wouldn't be some high-profile celebrity I admired or respected in some way and had seen on TV, talking about his or her conversion. Not someone I was very close to personally, someone I held in high esteem who also just happened to be a Christian. No. That would be too obvious, too easy perhaps. God's specialty, over and over again, throughout the entirety of the Bible and still today, is to use the unlikeliest individuals imaginable to accomplish His will. Such would be the case here. God would use a onetime multi-millionaire drug dealer/drug addict and former cellmate of mine to get my attention; to once again steer my thinking towards spiritual, eternal matters.

I was indeed staring at the picture of just such a man, an unlikely instrument of God's, on that poster taped to the door of the coffee shop that day. I knew I would have to go and hear Serge speak. I would have to see with my own eyes and hear with my own ears the details of Serge's almost mind-boggling transformation. The last time I had been together with Serge was in Collins Bay and he had just begun serving another long stretch inside.

Whatever the period of his incarceration was back then, suffice it to say that it would have been served with little to no chance of an early parole, if he would have been paroled at all. During his more than two decades in the penitentiary, he'd held just a grade four education and was considered "brain damaged" by at least one physician. Now, only ten years later, there he was, his picture on some church poster, a Christian with an honors degree in sociology from the University of Waterloo. A real, live, bonafide, staring-me-in-the-face miracle.

My immediate enthusiasm about re-connecting with Serge in church was due in part to the positive experience I'd had years earlier in the prison chapel. As I mentioned in the previous chapter, I did enjoy the services in Collins Bay and had experienced the forgiveness that can be found in Christ, although I did not walk it out at the time. Still, seeds had been sown and my heart had been prepared for what would be coming my way many years later. Had my brief encounter with church, church people, and the church service in general in prison been a negative one, I'm not so sure I would have been as enthusiastic to hear Serge speak, or anyone else for that matter, due to being turned off the whole church, religious, Christianity thing.

***

On a beautiful fall day in October, 1993, I drove onto the parking lot of KW Christian Fellowship, located at 1000 Bleams Road in Kitchener, Ontario. I parked my car, not entirely sure why I was there. I was beginning to have second thoughts about meeting Serge again and, as well, I was beginning to question my desire to spend a Saturday afternoon in church.

Sure, it would be interesting to hear Serge speak and perhaps have an opportunity to say hello to him and chat a little about the old days, but what of it? The old days we'd shared had not been great and I was not a Christian by any stretch of the imagination. I hadn't given God or spiritual matters in general a second thought since being released from Collins Bay some twelve years earlier when I had just been twenty-one.

I was now in my early thirties and if I could be described in a word or two it would certainly not be in the realm of Christianity. If anything at all, I had become a workaholic/alcoholic. I was working sixteen hours a day, five days a week, as well as half-days on Saturdays. I owned and operated a janitorial business, or rather it owned me. The money was good, very good, but it came with a hefty price. My life could almost have been described as one of "solitary confinement" on the outside.

I worked from two in the afternoon until six o'clock in the morning, day in, day out, for years, and was alone during those hours much of the time. This is not an exaggeration. My kids, grown up now, remember well the marathon-like hours I worked, as do others. I can only plead temporary insanity. Without realizing it, I had slowly been removing myself from the people around me until I had all but stopped interacting with anyone at all. My work schedule was absurd, to say the very least. It kept me from doing anything and everything except, well, work. My lifestyle epitomized a life out of balance.

I was married and had three children, but I saw very little of anyone. When I was home, it was for a brief sleep, a bite to eat, a quick hello and goodbye to whomever happened to be home and then back to work. Crazy. When I did have a day off, I'd do what I could around the house but I'd do it, typically, while drinking a beer or a whiskey, or both. I sipped a lot of beer and a lot of whiskey. I was probably a weekend alcoholic.

The over-the-top long work hours, lack of proper sleep and one too many hangovers had been catching up with me physically, mentally, and emotionally. I was burning out and was, to be blunt, just not much fun to be around. My moods were all over the place and I was becoming distrustful and resentful of everyone. Most of all, I was cultivating a very strong dislike for myself, of who I was, how I lived, how I behaved, how I treated those around me and, as well, I was experiencing a deepening sense of regret for the years I had wasted in my youth.

The truth is, I was damaged goods and had been for many, many years. On the outside I was a grown man in his early thirties with a nice home and family. Inside, however, I was still the same-old messed-up, anti-social, immature, misguided street kid fresh out of prison. I'd never really dealt with the damage I had done to myself and others during my years as a criminal. I didn't like what I saw when I looked back at who I used to be and I liked, even less, the reflection I saw in the mirror. I was an angry person in desperate need of a change, but to what and how? I simply didn't know.

Sitting in my car in the church parking lot, I felt at odds with the world at every turn. I'd been an outsider my whole life—largely self-imposed, but an outsider nonetheless. I thought back to the time many years ago when my friend had drawn those circles on a piece of paper, one circle representing the world and the other one representing me, living in my own world and conspicuously separated from everything and everyone. That illustration had been described to me by a fellow gambler and pool player perhaps fifteen years previously, but it was still relevant to my life a decade and a half later. How could that be? I hadn't played pool for years and robbing banks was a distant memory, but in some ways, now in my thirties, I was still the same misunderstood loner I always had been, and I was so sick of it.

It occurred to me that throughout much of my life I had been living in two distinctly different worlds at the same time. I loved the game of snooker and had always enjoyed watching the game being played beautifully by top amateurs and pros, and yet, for my part, I concentrated my efforts on smalltime, nickel-and-dime hustling rather than playing it straight and focusing on bringing my own game up to its maximum potential. The talent I had loved to see and admired in other players was the very thing I robbed myself of by playing and living like a two-bit bum.

I also enjoyed martial arts and weight training beginning in my late twenties. The discipline required to pursue both endeavors appealed to me tremendously, yet I always fell back on my old habits of partying at every opportunity. I would drink the weekend away and yet be back in the dojo first thing Monday morning for serious training in kenpo karate. I even attended seminars where I met and worked out with world champions on a couple of occasions. I admired their drive, passion, dedication, focus, and determination—all good, solid character qualities. For myself, however, as much as I loved to train, I kept just one foot in the gym while the other remained in the bar.

There had always existed, it seemed, an internal battle within me: right vs. wrong, good vs. bad, serving time yet going to church. The light of my conscience was turned completely off at times, while at other times I would find myself profoundly disturbed and haunted by my own actions. I could demonstrate discipline and dedication in the gym and dojo but a complete lack of discipline in so many other areas of my life. My struggle to find and hold on to self-respect was all-consuming, but at the end of the day, more often than not, I simply had no inner peace.

In my early thirties, I owned a successful business, a new car, a beautiful home (the bank owned it), had a family and yet there was a restlessness deep down in my soul that could not be appeased. I was so hard on myself and those around me. I couldn't or wouldn't give myself—or anyone else, for that matter—a break. It seemed I had been driven, insanely driven, for years, to try to convince myself and everyone else that I was a responsible, mature, decent guy and would prove it by working around the clock and providing for my family. In the end, I simply drove myself into the ground and drove those around me away.

My lifestyle was flawed and left wanting on every level. I wasn't mature; I was immature and misguided to think, for one minute, that I could erase my past and prove myself worthy by out-working everyone around me. I wasn't responsible, either. I was irresponsible with my time, energy, and money, which I spent as fast as it came in and justified doing so because I worked hard. Lastly, I was not, in many ways, a decent guy. Long work hours, little sleep, and too much booze often left me irritable and angry, if not outright impossible to be around.

And now, there I was, sitting in my car, alone of course, about to walk into a building where I had absolutely nothing in common with anyone, or so I thought, to hear a guy speak about life, prison, and God. A man I hadn't seen or spoken to for almost a dozen years. A man whose only words to me in three days of sharing a cell in Toronto East Detention had been, "Just keep your mouth shut and you'll be alright."

I mean, honestly, did I really want to meet this guy again? Well, I suppose, in a word, yes. In spite of my fears, quirks, phobias, and *enormous* self-esteem issues, yeah, I did want to meet Serge again. I very much wanted to listen to him share his story and possibly, I thought, be inspired in some way to put my own life in order. I mean, if he could do it, anyone could, right? What did I have to lose?

I had just stepped out of my car and was walking slowly to the entrance of the church when a car pulled into the lot and parked just a few cars away from mine. A lone male climbed out and, like me, began making his way towards the entrance of the church. The lone male was Serge Leclerc.

SAVED FROM MYSELF

"Therefore, if anyone is in Christ,
he is a new creation;
old things have passed away;
behold, all things have become new."
–2 Corinthians 5:17 (NKJV)

"There comes a special moment in everyone's life,
A moment for which that person was born…
When he seizes it,
It is his finest hour."
–Winston Churchill

(Author's note: again, out of respect for the privacy of my children and their mother, I have "fast forwarded" several years. We begin this chapter in 1997. I am now thirty-seven.)

***

Pride—silly, stubborn pride—is a monster. It will wrestle with our conscience, with our sense of right and wrong, with what we know to be morally and ethically good or bad behavior, to the absolute ends of the earth. My pride, my reliance on self-sufficiency, my stubbornness to hold on to me, to what and who I was, like that was a great package, knew no limits. I was determined to hold on to my old-school thinking and way of life, as destructive as it was, rather than yield to the promptings of my heart, my soul, my conscience, and my common sense to the absolute bitter end.

How foolish. Pride has destroyed marriages, put wedges between otherwise healthy friendships and relationships, personal or business, and caused complete breakdowns in communication between scores of parents and their children. It's very sad. We can be so stubborn, so full of pride at times, that it can blind us to common sense and reason.

Pride has been the undoing of many of us, keeping us from taking responsibility or ownership of our failings and shortcomings, often resulting in fractured relationships with others that were once healthy and whole. This can also result in a deteriorated sense of confidence, self-respect, and self-worth. In short, pride keeps us from doing the right thing and from saying the right thing, at the right time.

Pride prevents us from saying, "I'm sorry." Just two little words that hold all the power of reconciliation and forgiveness if used with sincerity and yet can be so elusive to our use in our day-to-day vocabulary. Being right all the time or having the final word in a matter can become "off the charts" important to us, paramount to our psychological makeup. How terrible! Such thinking is immature, selfish, and counterproductive. Oh, may we guard our hearts and minds against prideful, stubborn thinking.

Little wonder that the Bible has so much to say about a prideful spirit and the folly of harboring one. In Proverbs 6:17–19, a proud demeanor or countenance is listed among other less appealing or destructive attributes to one's character, including lying, physical violence, a heart bent towards wickedness, a willingness to embrace evil, a false witness or unreliability, and someone who continually stirs up strife among others.

All of these the Lord considers "abominations" in one's character, and pride is right up there at the top of the list! As if that were not enough, the Bible goes on to warn us in Proverbs 16:18 that *"Pride goes before destruction, and a haughty spirit before a fall"* (ESV). I know with certainty that not far behind every destructive, anti-social, ill-fated decision I made over the years—of which there were dozens, perhaps hundreds—a spirit of pride, in some way, at some level, was lurking. My hand goes up, sky high, with a declaration of, "Yup, that's me, here I am," as I acknowledge without hesitation that I was guilty, guilty, and *guilty* again of extremely prideful behavior. I know what you're thinking: "*Whew*, I'm glad I'm not like that." Oh, really? Never?

I've often known or felt, sensed perhaps, at least in some way, the presence of God in my life, even in my darkest days, yet I simply would not yield, give, bend a little, open up, give up, or give in. I knew that God had come calling several times over the past ten or fifteen years, but pride kept me from giving Him my undivided attention. I also knew what God was capable of, in terms of transforming one's life 180 degrees should one so desire it, and yet I held my ground with a prideful and at times arrogant attitude.

I had seen the transformation in others several times while attending the chapel services in Collins Bay. Inmates shared their stories of God delivering them from every conceivable vice, addiction, and other deviant, destructive behavior patterns. They shared how God had given them a new heart with new desires, new hope and a new beginning for their lives, even though they were still incarcerated. One could see the joy and sincerity in their eyes, in their enthusiasm for life. It was real. I believed it yet still held back. Pride, pride, pride.

More recently of course, I had once again met Serge Leclerc and had witnessed, personally, the miraculous change/conversion in his life, all due to his asking and receiving Jesus Christ as his personal savior. If Serge could do it, why couldn't I? Why was I so hesitant to just take that step? I thought often about that day with Serge. The day we met in the parking lot of the church, our conversation, listening to him speak and saying goodbye.

He had changed so much, from the inside out. No longer was he a hardened, cold, ice-in-his-veins criminal. The Serge I met that day at church was a warm, genuine, sincere man of God with a new heart, who was living out a new life, productively, rather than destructively. Serge had moved on, closed the door shut on the old days, but I had not, at least not emotionally, mentally, or psychologically. Serge had found peace. I had not.

***

On the evening of October 14, 1997 (I recorded the date in a Bible my grandmother gave me when I was eight years old), approximately four years after re-connecting with Serge at KW Christian Fellowship, unable to endure another moment of the conflict, unrest, and turmoil that had been boiling up inside of me for years, I sank to my knees, alone, in a medical building I was cleaning in Cambridge, Ontario, and surrendered my life to Jesus Christ.

I did so while listening to *Focus on the Family* on the radio, one of the Christian programs I listened to nightly at work. The program that night centered on a Thanksgiving theme. Wives and children were calling in and sharing with the listening audience why they were so thankful for their husbands and fathers and how much they loved and appreciated them. I never felt so alone in my entire life, not even when I was in prison.

The children on the radio were going on at length about all the reasons why their daddies were so great, and the wives were sharing heartwarming stories about the tremendous sacrifices their husbands made for the family and how blessed they all were because of the dad's presence in their lives. It was killing me. I was not the kind of guy being described on the radio that night. I'm still not, but I've come a long way. I was completely undone inside, coming apart at the seams, and could take it no longer.

I wanted what I was hearing on the radio that night. I had wanted it for some time, but I just didn't know how to begin walking it out. I was also very afraid of the cost. What would people think? If I became a Christian, I mean if it was the real thing, all the way, no holding back, would my kids even want anything to do with me or would they be embarrassed by me because I had become some sort of "religious nut"? I was very concerned, because I knew if I asked Christ to be the Lord and Savior of my life, that my life would change—radically, drastically change—and it terrified me.

I had been wrestling with the whole notion of change for several years, and it had kept me from making the big, once-and-for-all decision to become a Christian. Four years had passed since I'd heard Serge speak at church. It had been a wonderful day and one that had caused me to look closely at my own life, to re-examine myself in light of what God wanted for my life, but I had still not made a commitment to the Lord. Like I've said, seeds were planted on that day, no question about it, but I was just not ready back then to take the next step.

As the weeks, months, and years had passed following that day with Serge, I became something of a seeking/secret/sort-of/once-in-a-while kind of Christian, if there is such a thing. I would go to church occasionally, sporadically, sometimes enjoying the service, sometimes not, but the biggest influence in my life was Christian radio. Every evening from Monday to Friday at that time, approximately 1995 to 1997 or so, I would listen regularly to a great line-up of Christian broadcasting with speakers such as Charles Stanley, Chuck Swindoll, and others.

I was being fed a fairly steady diet of Christian teaching on the radio four or five nights a week as well as on Sunday mornings. Sunday was always a work day for me back then and I was typically out on the job by six or seven in the morning. On occasion I was still hung over and very tired from the night before. Once or twice I was still half in the bag from the previous evening's suds, but I always tuned in to a Christian radio show called *Joyful Country*, which aired early Sunday morning, just about the time I started work.

The host, Pat Murphy, played some terrific country gospel music, mixed with scripture readings that I found very soothing and comforting to my more often than not worn-out state of mind. Again, I believed everything I heard, I knew I was listening to the truth, I just didn't know how to make it a reality in my life. Still, with all of the Christian programming I was listening to, as well as reading some literature here and there, I was inching closer and closer, slowly, towards a profound belief in and acceptance of God and his Son and our Savior, Jesus Christ.

I received counsel and guidance periodically from a few people I knew to be individuals of faith. One such gentleman was my martial arts instructor. I believe I have the distinction of being his only student to twice achieve red belt without going further. Next would be brown, and then black. I would stop by his school occasionally just to chat about God, church, and life in general. One evening after he had taught his last class, we went for a long walk. I asked a lot of questions about Christianity and listened carefully to his answers. Again, I believed, but once again I would not commit.

Always, throughout the process, I would consider the cost. What would it mean to become a Christian? What did it matter? I had no life. I had distanced myself from everything and everyone. Whatever was left of my home life by the mid to late 1990s was all but over, largely due to my never being there and when I was, I was no fun to be around anyway. I would often, in those days, threaten my now ex-wife with divorce, for anything and everything, just because I didn't have a grip on life. It was abusive behavior and I regret it deeply. If you, dear reader, are caught in this cycle, either as the victim or the abuser, get some form of help or counseling immediately.

On an almost daily and most certainly weekly basis I fought, wrestled, argued, and agonized with one demon after another, one regret after another, one "if only I'd..." after another, a world of disharmony and turmoil inside that was driving me absolutely mad and then...*Focus on The Family*: a radio broadcast showcasing the family man I wasn't and never had been. Children praising their fathers, wives grateful for their loving husbands, and there I was: a walking disaster area.

***

I was on my knees that evening for some time. It was not a quick "sinner's prayer" type of thing that I muttered in a half-hearted, hurried fashion and then back on my feet with a "well, that's that, where was I?" kind of afterthought. No, not hardly. I was undone, at the end of myself, and was not, would not, be back on my feet to continue on with my evening's work until I had finished my business with God, once and for all.

I would like to give you, dear reader, an opportunity to "listen in," if you will, to my prayers that night on October 14, 1997, at about 7:30 p.m. On my knees I asked, begged, implored, questioned, and doubted

God's ability to take away my sins, to forgive me, truly forgive me, to perform emergency surgery on my heart, to be my friend. I was never more ready to ask Jesus Christ to be my Lord and Savior, and I was never more frightened in my life.

I had robbed banks, hustled pool without a dime in my pocket, conned, lied, and ripped people off from Ontario to British Columbia and back, stared down cops with loaded guns aimed at my chest without batting an eye, and done time with some of the hardest criminals in a couple of the toughest prisons in Canada, all with more composure than I was demonstrating that evening on my knees before God.

Understand that what you are about to read in no way describes an audible conversation I had with God. I was not literally speaking out loud to God, with God in turn answering me in some heavenly, majestic voice, which anyone could have heard had they happened upon me while I was on my knees in prayer. It was not an animated, vocalized discussion between God and me, but an internal time of mostly silent prayer, which I uttered in a somewhat awkward and hesitant fashion, alone, in the empty waiting room of a doctor's office.

While I did, at times, pray out loud as many of us do, the bulk of what you are about to read articulates, in the written word, what I was struggling with silently while on my knees, and what I was sensing, not hearing, but sensing how God may have responded to my prayers, concerns, and questions that evening. Come with me, back to the fall of 1997, and join me as I fall to my knees, at last, before God. I'm about to come face to face with my fears, doubts, concerns, and—finally—my Creator.

"God, I've never been more afraid in my life. I know I don't deserve forgiveness. I know I have failed so many times. I don't feel worthy to even ask you for forgiveness, but...

Ted, stop, you are forgiven.

"I'm not sure that I can be, I've hurt a lot of people over the years and I've..."

You're forgiven.

"Yeah, but, even if I am, how will I ever...?"

You are. It's not "if" you are forgiven; you are forgiven, period. Accept it.

"How can I, just like that?"

I would never lie to you, Ted. I would never hurt you. I love you.

"I believe you, God. It's just hard for me to understand."

I know it is. I know what you are going through, but I also know that you're ready for this.

"What will everyone think? How am I going to explain this to…?"

One step at a time, and I'll be with you every step of the way. You'll be alright.

"I'm not so sure."

I am.

"How?"

Ted, I've been waiting for you for a long time. You are exactly what I've been looking for. You're perfect for what I have in mind. In fact, I have work for you, if you want it. I forgive you, I love you, and I want you with me, now, tonight. Trust me. It'll be okay.

"There is so much I don't know; so much more that I would like to know, but God, I do know your Son died on the cross for me. I don't understand it all. There is so much I don't understand, but I do believe that Christ died on the cross for my sins. Tonight, I'm putting my faith and trust in Jesus Christ to be my Lord and Savior. God, please forgive me. I want to live for you. Please, come into my heart, come into my life. Show me what to do. I don't want to live like this anymore."

I've been waiting to hear those words from you for a long time, Ted.

"I know. I said them before, or something like it one time in prison, but I didn't really follow through with anything. I meant it at the time, or at least I thought I did, but I wasn't as serious about it all back then, I guess."

That's okay. You are serious about it tonight and I'm here with you.

"I know you are. I've always known you were right there. I just wouldn't reach out; I wouldn't ask…oh man, I've blown it so many times. I'm so stupid."

You didn't blow it tonight, and you're not stupid.

"I've always thought that something was wrong with me, always, even when I was a kid."

I know. Ted, there is nothing wrong with you. Nothing. I created you, for me, for my purposes, and I don't make mistakes.

"What do I do now? Now what?"

Get back on your feet. Go back to work. I'll let you know what to do and how to do it as we go along and you get to know me a little better. You'll see. Just know that you're not alone. You'll never be alone again, Ted.

"I want that to be true. I want to believe that."

It is true.

"It might take me a while to accept that. I mean, to really believe it. To believe that you, God, will always be with me, no matter what. I know you mean it…it's just a little overwhelming."

It takes time. But we have all the time in the world. You can talk to me whenever you like. I'm always here for you. Always.

"Yeah, I know. I have a lot to talk to you about. I can't believe that I actually did this. Finally!"

It took a while.

"God, thank you for forgiving my sins. I know I have failed and fallen so short so many times. I believe Christ died on the cross for my sins. There's so much I just don't get, but I'm coming to you by faith. I know you've heard and answered my prayers tonight. I repent and want to live a new life for you, God. Tonight, I'm inviting your Son, Jesus Christ, to come into my life, into my heart, to be my Lord and Savior. Amen."

I got to my feet, slowly, not quite sure how long I had been on my knees. It may have been seconds, minutes, I really had no idea. The waiting room I'd been cleaning was still empty. No one. Just me and… good thing no one came by. I was a mess. I'd been crying and perspiring at the same time—actually, hyperventilating may be closer to the truth. Whatever it was, whatever had happened that evening, I know with certainty that the man who got back to his feet that night was not the same man who fell to his knees just moments earlier.

I felt a deep sense of calm and tranquility inside that I had never felt before in my life, ever, like the weight of the world had been taken off my shoulders. The rest of the night was something of a blur. My mind was racing in a hundred different directions at once, trying to process what had happened, what I had experienced. It had been real but dreamlike all at the same time. I went home about eight hours later and slept like a baby.

Monday, June 12th, 2000

Dear Ted:

This is a small baptismal gift from Dad and I along with a few words to let you know that Sunday was one of the happiest and proudest days of our lives.

It took courage to do what you did Ted, and we thank God for your new-found peace and happiness.

Your journey has just begun.

Love for always and forever

Mom and Dad

A card I received from my parents, the day after I was baptized.

WHAT ABOUT YOU?

"And we know that for those who love God all things
work together for good, for those who are called
according to his purpose."
–Romans 8:28 (ESV)

Well, here we are. We have come to the end of the journey, although for me, the evening of October 14, 1997, as described in the previous chapter, marked just the beginning, literally, of a new journey, a new life. A new life born out of the forgiveness and redemption I found that night when I asked Jesus Christ to come into my life and accepted Him as my Lord and Savior. I had indeed kept Him waiting a long time.

On Sunday, June 11, 2000, almost three years later, I was baptized at KW Christian Fellowship. It was the same church I had heard Serge speak in seven years previously. I'm not entirely certain why I waited so long to be baptized, but I do remember the day as being very special. It was every bit as significant for me as the evening when I had prayed for Christ to come into my life.

Perhaps the wait was due in part to my personal life undergoing a great deal of transition. I went through a divorce during that time, and moved into an apartment not far from my kids' home. I continued to listen to Christian radio every evening at work, and read through the entirety of the Bible, cover to cover, which took about a year and a half the first time.

I also began reading other Christian books from well-known speakers and authors, and began spending a little time in prayer every day. I had not yet begun to attend church regularly, however. My work schedule was still off the charts at that time, with Sunday being my busiest day of the week. If I did go to church in the morning, it meant working well past midnight into the wee hours of Monday morning. I did go to church occasionally, but the thought of a twenty-four-hour shift because of it was often less than appealing.

Let me make it clear that my life did not suddenly become easy in some way, or in any way, because I had become a Christian. With poor choices come consequences, and I had made a lot of poor choices over many years. Christians are no more exempt from having to take responsibility for their actions than anyone else. God didn't wave a magic wand over me when I asked Him to come into my life and suddenly, poof, just like that, my life was all rainbows and sunshine.

People who decide to give God a whirl just to see if it steers them towards Easy Street are misguided at best and delusional at worst. Life just doesn't work that way for anyone, Christians included. God is not some warm, fuzzy Santa Claus just hanging out in heaven waiting to shower gifts and blessings on anyone who calls out to Him. My life was very much out of balance when I became a Christian, and it would take several years to get things adjusted so I was able to live a life that allowed time for work, family, and church. It was not easy and still isn't. It takes work. Sometimes I get it right and sometimes I don't.

I have been sober now for over fourteen years. I continued to have a few drinks here and there for about a year after my decision to accept Christ, but drinking simply didn't do it for me anymore. When I did throw back a few, it was with some measure of reluctance and was inevitably followed by a world of guilt. I would walk around in a tortured state of mind for days, knowing full well it was not what God wanted for me.

When I did make the decision to pack drinking in once and for all, I did so with complete resolve and determination that I would never look back and, almost a decade and a half later, praise God, I never have. I've never so much as had a craving for a drink, not once, even for a second, since I decided to quit. I give all the credit to Jesus Christ. My love for Him and desire to please Him made the decision an easy one. He willingly sacrificed Himself on a cross for me. The least I could do was quit drinking for Him.

As I continued to study the Bible, listen to Christian teaching on the radio, and attend church when I could, change came, slowly. Change mentally, emotionally, and most of all, spiritually. My outlook towards life in general was far more optimistic. I began cultivating a strong sense of self-respect and, in turn, a strong sense of respect, appreciation, and love for others that I had never really known before. I began to appreciate people and enjoyed the friendships and relationships I had with others.

That old piece of paper with those circles drawn on it representing me and my relationship to the world had completely lost its significance. In fact, for the first time since the illustration had been shown to me, it had become nothing more than a distant and faded memory. And as for that lifelong, nagging, if not haunting question, "What's wrong with me?" That one I'd been asking myself forever? Well, that one was answered by my heavenly Father while on my knees in an empty waiting room, and I had no reason to doubt Him, nor have I.

I met a wonderful woman, again at KW Christian Fellowship, shortly after I was baptized. We were married on April 27, 2001. Janet has been a blessing to me in more ways than I could ever have fathomed possible. Her quiet, gentle demeanor has been like a steadying hand about my arm for the past twelve years. She has loved, encouraged, and supported me without question or reservation from the moment we met. My love and appreciation for her runs very deep. I am, indeed, a most fortunate man.

Though I no longer attend KW Christian Fellowship, it will always have a very special place in my heart. It was on this property that I was reunited, remarkably, with Serge Leclerc. It was also where I was baptized and met my wife, Janet. I thank The Lord for leading me to KW all those years ago and for the many wonderful people I met, worked with and fellowshipped with while I was there.

I was deeply touched when my wife's niece asked me to perform the ceremony at her wedding in the summer of 2012.

***

Life is not easy. It can, at times, stretch us to the absolute limit of what we are able to endure. When the day is over and you find yourself alone with your thoughts before sleep overtakes you, do your thoughts, dear reader, ever dwell on the eternal? Do thoughts about life and death, heaven and hell, God or no God, ever concern you? They should, because where death is concerned, ten out of ten people die. Death really is the ultimate statistic, isn't it?

It would be so easy and understandable to consider a life such as mine and regard my decision to become a Christian almost as a necessary means of survival. That is, to think that someone as lost and, quite frankly, as desperate as I was needed forgiveness from God more than someone who has lived a generally rewarding, happy, prosperous, and decent life. Such thinking is entirely natural and, it would seem, obvious to many.

Getting on the right side of God, however, has nothing to do with happiness but instead has everything to do with righteousness. Happiness, money, a good career, beautiful children, a nice home, a university education, vacations, and good deeds will not bring an individual any closer to heaven than I was when I was robbing banks or hustling pool. This may seem a little offensive to some, but remains, nonetheless, true.

Being a "good person" is simply not enough to merit brownie points with God, whose standard of good is considerably higher than ours. God's standard of good, which is moral perfection in thought, word, and deed, can be seen in the Ten Commandments as well as the teachings of Jesus Christ. If you believe you're a good person, generally, and most people do, certainly nothing like I was in my younger days, try measuring yourself up against God's standard and see how well you do. I assure you it will be a most sobering and humbling experience.

Answer these few simple questions honestly: have you ever told a lie, even just one in your entire life? Who among us hasn't? What do you call someone who tells lies? Have you ever stolen anything, big or small, at any time, past or present? What do you call someone who steals or takes things? What about using the Lord's name in vain? Instead of using a four-letter word to express disgust, maybe you used the name of Jesus Christ. Using the name of our Lord and Savior rather than uttering an obscenity is very serious indeed. It's called blasphemy. Let's try one more. Have you ever looked at someone with lust? That is, have you ever checked someone out sexually? Jesus said that if we even look at someone with lust, we have committed adultery already in our heart (Matthew 5:27–28).

The above questions relate to just four of the Ten Commandments. How have you done, answering honestly, before God? If you responded yes to all of the questions, do you realize that by your own admission you are a lying thief as well as a blasphemous adulterer at heart? Don't try to intellectualize or justify your way around the matter, but instead let your conscience, which is God-given, speak for you.

If God used this standard, which is His standard to judge you on Judgment Day, would you be innocent or guilty? When you are found to be guilty, and you will be (we all are), will you go to heaven or hell? Many people, though they are absolutely guilty, will respond to this last question with heaven. They do so with the belief that God is all good and forgiving and therefore would never send anyone to hell. They reason that a good God would never do that, but this common response comes from a wrong or misguided understanding of what it means to be good.

The truth the guilty person is counting on in order to escape punishment is the very thing that will condemn them. Imagine that a criminal is standing in front of a judge in court and is guilty of all charges. In fact, the criminal has entered a plea of guilty to everything that is before him. The judge asks the condemned criminal if he'd like to say anything before a sentence is handed down. The criminal looks at the judge and, after saying he's sorry for what he's done, goes on to suggest that because he knows the judge is a good man, perhaps he'll forgive him and let him go free just this one time.

Such a thought would be preposterous. The judge would probably say something like, "You should be sorry. You've broken the law, and you are right about one thing: I am a good man, and because I am I will do my job properly and see that justice is served. You're going away to prison for a long time," and the gavel would come down. If the judge is a good, fair, and decent man, then he must see that justice is served. A decent, good judge would never, ever, under any circumstances, look the other way and let convicted, guilty criminals walk free and neither would a fair, decent, good God.

Don't you see? We are all guilty before God. We are all condemned and deserving of punishment before an all-knowing (God knows our thought life), perfect, holy God whom we will stand in front of one day to give an account of ourselves, our conduct, and our lives. What will you have to say for yourself on that day? You may be thinking that it doesn't matter because you don't believe in God or heaven and hell but that, my friend, doesn't matter either. All that matters is the truth. The truth stands on its own merit and what we believe or do not believe, personally, does not change a thing.

The bad news is that all of us are guilty of breaking God's law, and all stand condemned and helpless before God. We are all in need of a savior. The good news is that we have one. God gave us a savior when He sent His Son, Jesus Christ, who was perfect in thought, word, and deed, to die on the cross for our sins. Jesus Christ took our place.

Look at it this way. You are standing in front of a judge and have a very large fine to pay but don't have a dime to your name. The judge tells you that because you can't pay your fine, you will have to go away to jail for a long time. You are ordered out of the courtroom to begin serving your sentence when, at the last moment, a stranger stands up and informs the judge that he'd like to pay your fine for you. He approaches the bench and places the cash in front of the judge.

The judge looks at you and tells you that you are a very fortunate man. The fine has now been paid, justice has been served, and you are free to go. Imagine how you would feel towards the stranger, someone you had never met, the man responsible for your freedom. You would look upon him with incredible gratitude! That is exactly what Jesus Christ did for you, for all of us, when He went to the cross. We broke the law, God's law, but Christ paid our fine.

Because Christ paid our debt, we are now free to go. The charges against us have been thrown out. We who are guilty, guilty, and guilty again, over and over throughout our lives, do indeed have a savior in the name of Jesus Christ. If you will repent of your sins, your transgressions before God, believe what Christ has done for you on the cross, and trust in the name of Jesus Christ for your salvation, then all charges against you will be dropped. Case dismissed! You who are guilty will be declared innocent on that great and awful day, Judgment Day, and you will be in heaven for eternity. (For more information on this teaching, go to www. livingwaters.com.)

Please give this matter some serious thought. Look into it more deeply for yourself. Don't simply take my word for it, but research it for yourself with a mind and heart that is open to common sense, reason, and logic. You have absolutely nothing to lose and everything to gain. I'm not talking about joining a church, wearing nice clothes on Sundays, or throwing a little money into the offering.

I'm talking about a relationship, not religion. There is a *huge* difference between the two. I'm talking about having a relationship with God through His Son, Jesus Christ. I'm not merely suggesting, but am imploring you, dear reader, to get on the right side of God. What's stopping you from doing so today? Please don't put it off until tomorrow. All we have is this moment. We don't know what awaits us an hour from now, much less tomorrow. Don't place your eternal destiny on hold for one more second.

***

Our time together is finished, at least for now. Perhaps, throughout the pages of this book, you found cause to reflect upon your own life, your own journey, your own challenges, defeats and triumphs. Perhaps, by chancing a look at my own failures and struggles, you saw something of yourself, to a greater or lesser degree, or of someone you know. Perhaps you found some comfort, some solace, in the realization that you are not alone in your fears, your anxieties and doubts, your struggle with your own identity, your self-worth, your self-esteem, your place in this world.

Perhaps you have never dealt with any of these all too common challenges, but the pages of this book have only reminded you again, or for the first time, how fortunate you are to have lived a life free of the many challenges and trials that I've had in my life. That's wonderful as well! We are indeed, each of us, on our own path, at our pace, on our own journey, making our own way through life as best as we can.

I hope we have a chance to meet one day. I hope we can have a moment sometime, you and I, for a handshake, a hug, a quick hello, or to share a word or two of comfort to each other. I'd love to hear from you. (Especially if you have kind things to say about the book.) Seriously, though, I would enjoy hearing from you. Don't hesitate to email me and share your thoughts about the book, be they positive or negative, or about life in general, where you're at with God, or whatever faith you follow, or to just say hi.

You do matter. You do count. You are important. You are needed. You are necessary. You are loved.

Best wishes and blessings,
Ted

With open air preacher, speaker and author Ray Comfort and actor Kirk Cameron (seated) on the streets of Ottawa, On. Ray's ministry, Living Waters, has had a profound impact on me since my earliest days as a Christian.

Standing in front of the "Storehouse Christian Bookshoppe" in Guelph, On. with owner and manager Glenn Pioveson. Thirty-five years ago it was called "The Good Book Bible Store" and was the bible store that I robbed when in my teens. The owners at that time, friends of Glenn Pioveson, told the police that I was a "good boy" and hadn't meant any harm.

EPILOGUE

On February 18, 2011, my wife Janet and I were back in my home town and we visited The Storehouse Christian Bookshoppe, formerly known as The Good Book Bible Store. It was this very store, which was at one time located in the heart of the downtown district, directly across the street from the pool hall where I had learned to play snooker, that I had robbed thirty-five years ago, when I was sixteen.

I wasn't in the Christian store on this day in February to shop. I was there to once and for all deal with a part of my past that had haunted me for thirty-five years. I met the owner at the back of his store and, after introducing myself, I apologized for what I had done all those years ago. I told him how sorry I was for the robbery and how terrible I had felt regarding the older woman who owned the store at that time, and explained how she had been pushed aside during the robbery.

I was very uncomfortable as I shared my story, and struggled with my emotions as I asked him if he could forgive me for what I had done. I told him that I was now a Christian and that I had never forgotten the older woman's kindness in not wanting to press charges that day after the police had caught us. The owner listened quietly as I spoke, not saying a word until I had finished speaking. When he did respond, his speech and manner were as gentle and forgiving as the woman's had been thirty-five years earlier.

He explained that the people I had attempted to rob had sold the store to him about a year after the robbery. They had then retired and, I believe, moved out to British Columbia. They were friends of his and in their name, on their behalf, without hesitation, he forgave me. Those three words, "you are forgiven," were the sweetest words I had heard since giving my life to Christ and being forgiven by God that night in the waiting room of the doctor's office.

The owner remarked that it was God's story, and that my being there that day was for His glory, to which I wholeheartedly agreed. He then placed his hands on both Janet's and my shoulder and prayed for both of us before we left his store. As I sat in the car afterward before driving away, I felt a sense of release, a sense of being cleansed, of being free from my past once and for all, that words simply cannot describe. I had closure.

I have found forgiveness and freedom in Jesus Christ. I have found peace.

For more information about Ted Nellis,
including contact information,
go to
www.tednellisredemption.com